Lincoln E. Flake

DEFENDING THE FAITH

The Russian Orthodox Church and
the Demise of Religious Pluralism

With a foreword by Peter Martland

Bibliografische Information der Deutschen Nationalbibliothek
Die Deutsche Nationalbibliothek verzeichnet diese Publikation in der Deutschen Nationalbibliografie; detaillierte bibliografische Daten sind im Internet über http://dnb.d-nb.de abrufbar.

Bibliographic information published by the Deutsche Nationalbibliothek
Die Deutsche Nationalbibliothek lists this publication in the Deutsche Nationalbibliografie; detailed bibliographic data are available in the Internet at http://dnb.d-nb.de.

Cover image: Maria Moskvitsova / Shutterstock.com.

ISBN-13: 978-3-8382-1378-1
© *ibidem*-Verlag, Stuttgart 2021
Alle Rechte vorbehalten

Das Werk einschließlich aller seiner Teile ist urheberrechtlich geschützt. Jede Verwertung außerhalb der engen Grenzen des Urheberrechtsgesetzes ist ohne Zustimmung des Verlages unzulässig und strafbar. Dies gilt insbesondere für Vervielfältigungen, Übersetzungen, Mikroverfilmungen und elektronische Speicherformen sowie die Einspeicherung und Verarbeitung in elektronischen Systemen.

All rights reserved. No part of this publication may be reproduced, stored in or introduced into a retrieval system, or transmitted, in any form, or by any means (electronic, mechanical, photocopying, recording or otherwise) without the prior written permission of the publisher. Any person who does any unauthorized act in relation to this publication may be liable to criminal prosecution and civil claims for damages.

Printed in the EU

Soviet and Post-Soviet Politics and Society (SPPS) Vol. 232
ISSN 1614-3515

General Editor: Andreas Umland,
Swedish Institute of International Affairs, umland@stanfordalumni.org

Commissioning Editor: Max Jakob Horstmann,
London, mjh@ibidem.eu

EDITORIAL COMMITTEE*

DOMESTIC & COMPARATIVE POLITICS
Prof. **Ellen Bos**, *Andrássy University of Budapest*
Dr. **Gergana Dimova**, *University of Winchester*
Dr. **Andrey Kazantsev**, *MGIMO (U) MID RF, Moscow*
Prof. **Heiko Pleines**, *University of Bremen*
Prof. **Richard Sakwa**, *University of Kent at Canterbury*
Dr. **Sarah Whitmore**, *Oxford Brookes University*
Dr. **Harald Wydra**, *University of Cambridge*

SOCIETY, CLASS & ETHNICITY
Col. **David Glantz**, *"Journal of Slavic Military Studies"*
Dr. **Marlène Laruelle**, *George Washington University*
Dr. **Stephen Shulman**, *Southern Illinois University*
Prof. **Stefan Troebst**, *University of Leipzig*

POLITICAL ECONOMY & PUBLIC POLICY
Dr. **Andreas Goldthau**, *Central European University*
Dr. **Robert Kravchuk**, *University of North Carolina*
Dr. **David Lane**, *University of Cambridge*
Dr. **Carol Leonard**, *Higher School of Economics, Moscow*
Dr. **Maria Popova**, *McGill University, Montreal*

FOREIGN POLICY & INTERNATIONAL AFFAIRS
Dr. **Peter Duncan**, *University College London*
Prof. **Andreas Heinemann-Grüder**, *University of Bonn*
Prof. **Gerhard Mangott**, *University of Innsbruck*
Dr. **Diana Schmidt-Pfister**, *University of Konstanz*
Dr. **Lisbeth Tarlow**, *Harvard University, Cambridge*
Dr. **Christian Wipperfürth**, *N-Ost Network, Berlin*
Dr. **William Zimmerman**, *University of Michigan*

HISTORY, CULTURE & THOUGHT
Dr. **Catherine Andreyev**, *University of Oxford*
Prof. **Mark Bassin**, *Södertörn University*
Prof. **Karsten Brüggemann**, *Tallinn University*
Dr. **Alexander Etkind**, *University of Cambridge*
Dr. **Gasan Gusejnov**, *Moscow State University*
Prof. **Leonid Luks**, *Catholic University of Eichstaett*
Dr. **Olga Malinova**, *Russian Academy of Sciences*
Dr. **Richard Mole**, *University College London*
Prof. **Andrei Rogatchevski**, *University of Tromsø*
Dr. **Mark Tauger**, *West Virginia University*

ADVISORY BOARD*

Prof. **Dominique Arel**, *University of Ottawa*
Prof. **Jörg Baberowski**, *Humboldt University of Berlin*
Prof. **Margarita Balmaceda**, *Seton Hall University*
Dr. **John Barber**, *University of Cambridge*
Prof. **Timm Beichelt**, *European University Viadrina*
Dr. **Katrin Boeckh**, *University of Munich*
Prof. em. **Archie Brown**, *University of Oxford*
Dr. **Vyacheslav Bryukhovetsky**, *Kyiv-Mohyla Academy*
Prof. **Timothy Colton**, *Harvard University, Cambridge*
Prof. **Paul D'Anieri**, *University of Florida*
Dr. **Heike Dörrenbächer**, *Friedrich Naumann Foundation*
Dr. **John Dunlop**, *Hoover Institution, Stanford, California*
Dr. **Sabine Fischer**, *SWP, Berlin*
Dr. **Geir Flikke**, *NUPI, Oslo*
Prof. **David Galbreath**, *University of Aberdeen*
Prof. **Alexander Galkin**, *Russian Academy of Sciences*
Prof. **Frank Golczewski**, *University of Hamburg*
Dr. **Nikolas Gvosdev**, *Naval War College, Newport, RI*
Dr. **Guido Hausmann**, *University of Munich*
Prof. **Dale Herspring**, *Kansas State University*
Dr. **Stefani Hoffman**, *Hebrew University of Jerusalem*
Prof. **Mikhail Ilyin**, *MGIMO (U) MID RF, Moscow*
Prof. **Vladimir Kantor**, *Higher School of Economics*
Prof. em. **Andrzej Korbonski**, *University of California*
Dr. **Iris Kempe**, *"Caucasus Analytical Digest"*
Prof. **Herbert Küpper**, *Institut für Ostrecht Regensburg*
Dr. **Rainer Lindner**, *CEEER, Berlin*
Dr. **Vladimir Malakhov**, *Russian Academy of Sciences*
Dr. **Luke March**, *University of Edinburgh*

Prof. **Michael McFaul**, *Stanford University, Palo Alto*
Prof. **Birgit Menzel**, *University of Mainz-Germersheim*
Prof. **Valery Mikhailenko**, *The Urals State University*
Prof. **Emil Pain**, *Higher School of Economics, Moscow*
Dr. **Oleg Podvintsev**, *Russian Academy of Sciences*
Prof. **Olga Popova**, *St. Petersburg State University*
Dr. **Alex Pravda**, *University of Oxford*
Dr. **Erik van Ree**, *University of Amsterdam*
Dr. **Joachim Rogall**, *Robert Bosch Foundation Stuttgart*
Prof. **Peter Rutland**, *Wesleyan University, Middletown*
Prof. **Marat Salikov**, *The Urals State Law Academy*
Dr. **Gwendolyn Sasse**, *University of Oxford*
Prof. **Jutta Scherrer**, *EHESS, Paris*
Prof. **Robert Service**, *University of Oxford*
Mr. **James Sherr**, *RIIA Chatham House London*
Dr. **Oxana Shevel**, *Tufts University, Medford*
Prof. **Eberhard Schneider**, *University of Siegen*
Prof. **Olexander Shnyrkov**, *Shevchenko University, Kyiv*
Prof. **Hans-Henning Schröder**, *SWP, Berlin*
Prof. **Yuri Shapoval**, *Ukrainian Academy of Sciences*
Prof. **Viktor Shnirelman**, *Russian Academy of Sciences*
Dr. **Lisa Sundstrom**, *University of British Columbia*
Dr. **Philip Walters**, *"Religion, State and Society", Oxford*
Prof. **Zenon Wasyliw**, *Ithaca College, New York State*
Dr. **Lucan Way**, *University of Toronto*
Dr. **Markus Wehner**, *"Frankfurter Allgemeine Zeitung"*
Dr. **Andrew Wilson**, *University College London*
Prof. **Jan Zielonka**, *University of Oxford*
Prof. **Andrei Zorin**, *University of Oxford*

* While the Editorial Committee and Advisory Board support the General Editor in the choice and improvement of manuscripts for publication, responsibility for remaining errors and misinterpretations in the series' volumes lies with the books' authors.

Soviet and Post-Soviet Politics and Society (SPPS)
ISSN 1614-3515

Founded in 2004 and refereed since 2007, SPPS makes available affordable English-, German-, and Russian-language studies on the history of the countries of the former Soviet bloc from the late Tsarist period to today. It publishes between 5 and 20 volumes per year and focuses on issues in transitions to and from democracy such as economic crisis, identity formation, civil society development, and constitutional reform in CEE and the NIS. SPPS also aims to highlight so far understudied themes in East European studies such as right-wing radicalism, religious life, higher education, or human rights protection. The authors and titles of all previously published volumes are listed at the end of this book. For a full description of the series and reviews of its books, see www.ibidem-verlag.de/red/spps.

Editorial correspondence & manuscripts should be sent to: Dr. Andreas Umland, Kyiv-Mohyla Academy, Department of Political Science, vul. Voloska 8/5, korp. 4, UA-04070 Kyiv, UKRAINE

Business correspondence & review copy requests should be sent to: *ibidem* Press, Leuschnerstr. 40, 30457 Hannover, Germany; tel.: +49 511 2622200; fax: +49 511 2622201; spps@ibidem.eu.

Authors, reviewers, referees, and editors for (as well as all other persons sympathetic to) SPPS are invited to join its networks at www.facebook.com/group.php?gid=52638198614
www.linkedin.com/groups?about=&gid=103012
www.xing.com/net/spps-ibidem-verlag/

Recent Volumes

223   *Daria Buteiko*
Erinnerungsort: Ort des Gedenkens, der Erholung oder der Einkehr?
Kommunismus-Erinnerung an einem historischen Ort am Beispiel der Gedenkstätte Berliner Mauer sowie des Soloveckij-Klosters und -Museumsparks
Mit einem Vorwort von Sigrit Jacobeit
ISBN 978-3-8382-1367-5

224   *Olga Bertelsen (Ed.)*
Russian Active Measures
Yesterday, Today, Tomorrow
With a foreword by Jan Goldman
ISBN 978-3-8382-1529-7

225   *David Mandel*
"Optimizing" Higher Education in Russia
University Teachers and Their Union "Universitetskaya solidarnost'"
ISBN 978-3-8382-1519-8

226   *Daria Isachenko, Mykhailo Minakov, Gwendolyn Sasse (Eds.)*
Post-Soviet Secessionism
Nation-Building and State-Failure after Communism
ISBN 978-3-8382-1538-9

227   *Jakob Hauter (Ed.)*
Civil War? Interstate War? Hybrid War?
Dimensions and Interpretations of the Donbas Conflict in 2014–2020
ISBN 978-3-8382-1383-5

228   *Tima T. Moldogaziev, Gene A. Brewer, J. Edward Kellough (Eds.)*
Public Policy and Politics in Georgia
Lessons from Post-Soviet Transition
ISBN 978-3-8382-1535-8

229   *Oxana Schmies (Ed.)*
NATO's Enlargement and Russia
A Strategic Challenge in the Past and Future
With a foreword by Vladimir Kara-Murza
ISBN 978-3-8382-1478-8

230   *Christopher Ford*
UKAPISME - Une Gauche perdue
Le marxisme anti-colonial dans la révolution ukrainienne 1917 - 1925
Avec une préface de Vincent Présumey
ISBN 978-3-8382-0899-2

231   *Anna Kutkina*
Between Lenin and Bandera
Decommunization and Multivocality in Post-Euromaidan Ukraine
With a foreword by Juri Mykkänen
ISBN 978-3-8382-1506-7

Disclaimer

The opinions expressed in this book are the author's own and do not represent those of the Department of Defense (DoD), or the United States government.

Contents

Foreword by *Peter Martland*   ix

Acknowledgments   xi

1. The Path of Protectionism: Church, State, and an Oppressive Institutional Design for Religion   1
2. Legacies of Sovietism: Structural-Historical Constraints   25
3. Post-Soviet Market Features: The Immediate-Strategic Context   61
4. The Georgian Orthodox Church: A Case Study in Authoritarianism   89
5. The Lithuanian Catholic Church: A Case Study in Indifference   115
6. The Russian Orthodox Church: Finding Its Voice at the Expense of Others   145
7. Regional Findings and Methodological Implications   191
8. Collusion That Matters: Church-State Symbiosis After Crimea   209

Bibliography   233

Appendix: Interview/Questionnaire Questions   255

Foreword

In the aftermath of the 16th century English Protestant reformation, the Church fragmented and the Stuart kings, who saw "Crown and Altar" as indivisible, reacted badly. They tried enforcing conformity with coercion, including fines, imprisonment and even the execution of unlicensed preachers and their dissenting adherents. It did not work; dissent persisted and became bolder with the building of unlicensed dissenting meeting houses and chapels. Some nonconformist communities went into exile and events led, eventually, to the bloody English Civil War which culminated in 1649 with the execution of the King. It was not the best model for dealing with the reality of religious plurality and in 1688 despite all the previous excesses, hatreds and bloodshed, the English Parliament passed the Act of Toleration permitting dissenters to worship in their own way. This may seem a long way from the remarkable narrative Lincoln Flake has created. However, scratch it a bit and many familiar features emerge; not least the inability of strong national governments to impose a single religious belief system on the populations they are trying to control.

Any book trying to understand Russia and its workings, both internally and externally is going to run into difficulty; Russia was famously described by Winston Churchill as "a riddle wrapped in a mystery inside an enigma." Less famously, he added "... but perhaps there is a key (to that enigma). That key is Russian national interest." In this book, despite all the problems of understanding Russia, Lincoln Flake, comes close to turning that key. The case studies examined in this work include both Russia—pre- and post-Soviet era—and its peripheral or satellite territories. It shows how the atheistic Soviet Union brutally suppressed all pre-Soviet institutions of the state, especially religious. It also shows how the Russian Orthodox church tried to make peace with the new state, became corrupted and failed to either spot or come to terms with the post-Soviet settlement.

Lincoln Flake also shows how the Putinite state successfully harnessed the Russian Orthodox Church to its quest of building a new Russia, by combining an authoritarian religious structure with a traditional nationalism—like the Stuart kings, it was a "Crown and Altar" attempt to create a truly national religion and state. Of course, in the freedom of the immediate post-Soviet era, the emerging Free Trade in religion saw the import of many foreign brands. Several found in Russia fertile ground for proselytizing; the Orthodox Church in turn saw these foreign incomers as a threat to its power and dominance and the State saw them as an enemy within; enemies it could attack and use to strengthen its own position.

Interestingly, the case studies of the Russian peripheries and satellites show how national identities and the varied experiences and reactions of national churches to Soviet rule determined how and if they survived to the 1990s breakup of the Empire. The contrast between the former Soviet republics and Poland for example is instructive, with the Roman Catholic church in Poland forming a powerful national identifier among the devout (in the same way the Catholic church in Ireland did during the centuries of British occupation).

All in all, this book breaks new and important ground in our understanding both the religious and secular interactions of the Soviet and post-Soviet state of Russia, its peripheral republics and satellites. It is not just a work to give meaning to those religious groups in the West who saw the Post-Soviet world as a perfect opportunity for proselytizing but also provides important insights into the mindset of the sinister penumbra of Putin's Russia.

Dr. Peter Martland

Emeritus Member of the Faculty of History, Cambridge University

Acknowledgments

This book would not have been possible without the generosity of numerous institutions and individuals. First the institutions. Much of the early research was performed during my doctoral endeavors at St. Andrews University. That school provided invaluable financial scholarships, which combined with an Overseas Research Scholarship gifted by the United Kingdom, allowed for two full years of research in Russia, Lithuania, Georgia, and Ukraine. More recently, Cambridge University, and particularly Wolfson College, have been gracious in offering the use of their unrivalled libraries. In terms of individuals, the list of supporters and academic advisors is long. But the short list includes Professor Sally Cumming, who at the start of it all encouraged me to hike the Highlands until I discovered a topic I felt passionate about. Near the end of it all, Dr Peter Martland inspired me to return to academic inquiry after so many years in public service. I am indebted to both of these remarkable individuals for their patience and guidance. I also thank my mother, Jana, for her assistance. It helps to have one of the smartest people you know reviewing your work. My wife and five children have never wavered in their support. I love and thank them for providing a harmonious space for me to write this book. Last and perhaps most significantly, I am grateful for the hundreds of individuals who took the time to discuss their religious experiences with me. A person's spiritual journey is often the most private aspect of life. Yet, many at some personal risk, shared with me their hopes, fears, misgivings, and conversion stories. These included those in and outside of the Russian Orthodox Church. This book is dedicated to these inspiring individuals who retain the courage of their conviction even in the face of growing religious intolerance.

To Siobhán, Eileen, Sinéad, and Jana

1. The Path of Protectionism
Church, State, and an Oppressive Institutional Design for Religion

Religious tolerance is abating quickly in Russia with little notice in the West. Anti-extremist amendments which were approved in the summer of 2016 have effectively made the country a non-permissive environment for those religious groups unlucky enough to be deemed non-traditional. Spiritual life in Russia has not seen such dark days since Soviet rule. Yet this relapse was never a foregone conclusion. For a quarter-century, from the disintegration of the Soviet Union to the passing of the restrictive measures, there were many threatening moments and ominous legislative machinations. But religious pluralism always endured, albeit tenuously, as authorities remained more or less indifferent to the religious sphere. Indeed, even in the early Putin era, the religious institutional design in Russia proved a surprising exception to the rule. While every other element of civil society trended authoritarian after 2000, religious groups of nearly every stripe continued to operate relatively unfettered. Religious freedoms faired no worse during the first decade or so of Putin's reign than they did during Yeltsin's presidency.

Five years on from the restrictive measures, labelled the Yarovaya laws, it is clear that the Kremlin is no longer indifferent to religious life. Raids and arrests are now commonplace as authorities have all but declared open season on those groups, such as the Jehovah's Witnesses, that do not meticulously adhere to the draconian restrictions. Examples of repression are myriad. The Supreme Court's 2017 ban on Jehovah's Witness activity and its later decision to declare the group's headquarters and all 395 local communities "extremist organizations" is but one early instance of repression (Arnold 2019). 2018 saw at least 159 prosecutions from all religious groups for violating just the anti-missionary provisions of the law, with those cases achieving a 90 percent conviction rate (Arnold 2019a). In the first half of 2020, at least 42 prosecutions of "missionary activity" in violation of the 2016 measures occurred, with a 92 percent conviction rate (Arnold, 2020). Among those convicted was old a 61-year-old Jehovah's Witness member who received a six-and-a-half-year jail term in a Pskov court simply for organizing a religious meeting. (Arnold, 2020a). The number of convictions continued throughout 2020 including against Nikita Glazunov, fined by a court in Kazan for organizing a Catholic Mass in a hotel conference hall (Del Turco, 2020).

For those churches that decide to obey the letter of the law, such as The Church of Jesus Christ of Latter-day Saints, the rules make operating almost impractical. All proselytization efforts, the life blood of most small or new entrant churches, are effectively outlawed. The measures have stifled religious activities for most denominations with tight controls on religious education, the right to print literature, registration and visas requirements, access to worship premises, and the right to assembly. In just the educational realm, the Pentecostal Union's Eurasian Theological Seminary's license was annulled in October 2018, while the Baptist Union's Moscow Theological Seminary was forbidden to add new students in January 2019 (Arnold 2019b). The assault has not been limited to Christian churches, as Islamic groups have also suffered (Arnold 2018).

The dramatic rollback of rights is palpable across the entire religious domain. When judged across eight religious freedom criteria by the Pew Research Center, Russia declined in all categories from 2007 to 2017—undoubtedly with the most negative change after the passing of the Yarovaya law. With the scores ranging from least restrictive at 1 to most restrictive at 10, Russia deteriorated from a 4.5 score to 8.2 in the category of state favoritism for select religious groups. Russia also went in the wrong direction in the category of laws and policies impacting religious freedom. The negative trends in other criteria are just as disconcerting and align with conditions articulated by clergy and members of non-traditional churches throughout Russia. In terms of harassment of religious groups, Russia declined from 7.7 to 9.4, on limits of religious activity 4.5 to 7.9, interreligious tension and violence 5.6 to 6.7, individual/social group harassment 3.3 to 5.8, religious violence by organized groups 3.1 to 3.6, and hostilities related to religious norms 3.0 to 8.0 (Pew 2019). These ratings have almost certainly held steady or worsened from 2017 to the present day.

It is noteworthy, and somewhat unexpected, that Russia is one of the last in the region to abandon a western-inspired institutional blueprint for the religious sphere. Of the twelve non-EU former Soviet republics,

Ukraine is now the sole nation that allows foreign ecclesiastical missionaries to operate more or less unfettered. A type of counter-reformation against the liberal design for the religious sphere of the 1990s has taken root. And yet, apart from the obligatory section in an annual report, there is nothing but deafening silence from Capitol Hill or Brussels on the region's oppressive operating environment for most churches. The Trump Administration, particularly former Vice President Mike Pence, made religious freedom a frequent talking point. But his rhetoric was almost exclusively directed at the domestic cultural wars in the United States. His primary aim was to allay the fears of Christians with regard to liberal attacks on freedom of operations and rights to exclusivity. Attention to foreign government restrictions, such as Russia's 2016 about-face on religious diversity or Chinese oppression of religious monitories was infrequent and weak compared to the 1980s and 1990s. While President Biden is likely enacting the greatest broad-spectrum policy reversal of a presidential predecessor in the history of the United States, there is much to suggest that on the specific policy of shining light on foreign religious repression, inattention may continue. For one thing, his party in 2019 praised "religiously unaffiliated" Americans as the "largest religious group within the party" (DNC 2019)—a declaration that hardly bodes well for a vigorous defense of persecuted religious minorities across the globe.

    The media, and even academia to some extent, have also largely ignored the disturbing developments. The disinterest may stem from a sense of the inevitability that religious freedoms would eventually go the way of all other civil institutions in Russia. The issue may also be deemed too trivial when viewed against the avalanche of bad news coming from Russia following the annexation of Crimea in 2014 through to the interference in the 2016 U.S. presidential elections to present-day military bluster. Alternatively, the omission could be due to secularization trends in Western society, and particularly the post-modernist interpretations in media and academia that creates a disdain for expending effort supporting antiquated church structures.

    Whatever the reasons, the destruction of another pillar of a free society in Russia is no trifling matter, if for no other reason than it makes any eventual reversal of authoritarianism in Russia all the more improbable. Western policy makers that think the present threat from Russia is momentary, Putin-centric, or easily reversable, should understand that when the roots of totalitarianism run deep into the soil of social institutions—altering the very design of those structures—they become hard to uproot. Institutional design ossifies to a point that a simple change in leadership fails to course correct. Structure begins to trump agency. This is all the more disconcerting as religious freedoms are not simply another civil society domino to fall. Religion is so integral to Russian society—ingrained in politics, education, and national identity—that a steep descent into a despotic institutional design carries ramification beyond the immediate or the apparent.

So why the shift in policy in 2016 after so many years of allowing, even if begrudgingly, religious freedoms and pluralism? The factors are myriad, and undoubtedly explained, in part, by inclinations and proclivities of Putin and the culture that surrounds him. But three major converging factors seem to have explanatory value.

First is Putin's rejection of Western norms. For all intent and purposes, the charade ended after Crimea. The Kremlin no longer sees value in giving deference to Western values in aggregate, and to progressive notions of religious freedoms, in particular. In the current climate, the definition of religious liberties espoused by the U.S. Congress has become less than irrelevant in the corridors of the Kremlin. In fact, it is a standard to openly deride. In the 1990s, Yeltsin may have been genuinely open to a vibrant and free civil society, but conditions for Western aid certainly helped the cause. Backsliding across the civil society spectrum began almost from day one with Vladimir Putin as Western condition-based cooperation gradually receded. Even so, the Kremlin continued to pay lip service to individual freedoms and maintained the pretense of democracy. No matter how disingenuous, Russia saw value in portraying to foreign audiences a religiously tolerant and pluralistic society. Deterioration in relations post Crimea altered drastically Kremlin's decision calculus. The timing of the 2016 restrictive measures following the Ukraine crisis and subsequent Western sanctions is surely not coincidental. There were, and continue to be, essentially no external restraints placed on the Kremlin, particularly as it relates to decision-making on regulating the religious sphere.

Second is the encouragement of the Russian Orthodox Church. The state may have lost its inhibition, but it still needed nudging. Harassing Latter-day Saint missionaries or blocking Pentecostal education were likely never a high priority for Putin's inner circle, even after Crimea. Senior Kremlin officials were not waiting with bated breath for a dip in relations with the West to justify abuse of Baptist congregations. They were encouraged in that direction from many quarters, but primarily from the leadership of the Russian Orthodox Church. The church objected to the flood of foreign religious entities streaming into Russia post 1991 and pleaded with the state for action. In 1992, the patriarch called them zealots who were uprooting people from their millennial Orthodox traditions (Volf 1996, 26), while an Orthodox-nationalist politician labelled them as "filth and scum" (Ogden 1996). Notwithstanding this rhetoric, for most of the post-Soviet period the patriarchate did not have enough to offer the Kremlin to convince authorities to take action against undesirable religious entities.

Third is the advent of Russia's whole-of-society approach to modern warfare and the church's relatively seamless integration into that effort. Church-state cooperation or 'symphonia' in Russia is a matter of historical record dating back to tsarist times. The level of cooperation ebbed and flowed over the centuries, and was at all times unequal in favor of the state. That dynamic continued under Yeltsin and Putin who were all too happy to take advantage of church symbols for political gain. In return for this cloak of Orthodox legitimacy, the church received political access, property, and tax privileges. Yet, it was not until the war in Ukraine and subsequent events that interaction moved to unprecedented levels. The key new ingredient was Moscow's renewed interests in employing a range of non-traditional entities in statecraft. The state finally needed the church in a more meaningful way as one of many social levers of influence in its multi-domain (political, economic, military, information, social) effort to affect change at home, in the Near Abroad, and globally. It was no longer enough to offer notional backing for the state; the church was called on to be fully assimilated into the system for the sake of regime and national interests. As a more active participant, the patriarchate finally had leverage to demand more significant returns.

These three factors have converged to the detriment of religious pluralism in Russia today. The first proposition of Putin's rejection of Western norms is so self-evident it needs no elaboration here. President Putin said as much in a June 2019 interview with the Financial Times when he declared western liberalism obsolete (Barber 2019). Volumes exist delineating Russia's wholesale rejection of Western norms. The second two phenomena require a little more explanation and scholarship. The Russian Orthodox Church's role in shaping the institutional design of the religious sphere is too often overlooked in the discourse on religious rights in Russia. This omission is particularly egregious in light of post-Crimea church-state collusion and the far-reaching consequences of the Yarovaya law. This book endeavors to fill that void by contextualizing the role of the Russian Orthodox Church in the demise of Religious Pluralism. It does this by first examining the history and motivation behind Factor Two (church opposition to religious pluralism) and then elaborating how Factor Three (church assimilation into Kremlin's whole-of-government approach) occasioned the Yarovaya law and its calamitous impact on present-day religious freedoms. The patriarchate is no mere bystander in institutional formation of religious life; nor is it any longer just an occasional participant in domestic and foreign influence schemes by the Kremlin. Church posture and the factors affecting clergy decision-making is, therefore, highly germane to any discussion on religious freedoms in Russia today and on regime efforts to attract, influence, or coerce target audiences.

Post-Soviet Upheaval

Regrettably, the retreat of religious tolerance in Russia after 2016 mirrors a wider global tendency toward government-imposed restrictions. The Pew Research Center found that nations with high/very high restrictions rose from 40 in 2007 to 52 in 2017. Eight of the 15 post-Soviet nations were among the 52 (Pew 2019). One reason for the latter trend was the similar path many ex-Soviet republics travelled after the fall of the Soviet Union. It's hard to overstate the upheaval following Mikhail Gorbachev's 25 December 1991 resignation. Almost overnight, businesses, institutions, politicians, and the general public found the circumstances in which they operated altered dramatically from one of censorship, restriction, repression, and indoctrination to one of uncertainty, yet lined with promises of democracy, liberalization, and prosperity. Both optimistic and pessimistic predictions for the future of the region were expressed, yet most were in agreement that in order to reap the rewards of democracy and capitalism, the Soviet institutions—from industry to the political party system—had to be significantly transformed. State-owned corporations had to be privatized, restructured and made competitive; laws and constitutions required rewriting so as to grant long-deprived freedoms to the public. Electoral systems needed to be reworked to provide for democracy, and independence had to be granted to judiciaries. Three decades after the collapse of communism, the success of such institutional change and follow-on economic prosperity and democratic vitality has been piecemeal at best across the post-Soviet space.

As a concomitant to post-communist democratization, the institutional arrangements within the religious environment were also predicted to benefit greatly and transform considerably after the fall of communism. The central tenet of Marxist-Leninism, that religion was an obstacle to progress and needed to be eradicated from society, was vigorously implemented through Soviet religious policy. Alexander Solzhenitsyn wrote, "Within the philosophical system of Marx and Lenin, and at the heart of their psychology, hatred of God is the principal driving force, more fundamental than their political and economic pretensions" (1983). The sudden cessation of seventy years of atheistic propaganda, anti-religious campaigns, and church oppression was expected to usher in an era of religious freedom and religious pluralism comparable to that of the West. And to be fair, weighed against other promises made and institutional liberalization forecasted in the immediate demise of the USSR, the expansion of religious freedoms both on the individual and organizational level appeared, at first glance, to be an unqualified success. In the early 1990s, foreign missionaries began pouring into most nations; churches and monasteries were re-opened and new ones built; religious literature became abundant; spiritual symbols were commonplace; and both old and new religious organizations were generally tolerated by authorities. This movement towards religious liberalization and what Francoise Champion defined as "pluralism-emancipation" (1999, 42) was codified in new constitutions throughout the former Soviet Union. Although progress varied from nation to nation, trends in the region suggested that genuine liberal-democratic religious freedoms were beginning to take root.

The events of recent years have exposed such a promising appraisal as naive. Across the region, the initial acceptance of a religious free market that loosely characterized the early 1990s has been questioned, and in the case of Russia, abruptly reversed. Movement toward curtailing or even reversing the development of a religiously liberated society commenced in the middle of the 1990s. The anti-pluralistic push was led by many traditional dominant churches, the Russian Orthodox Church included, which were never entirely onboard with such a *laissez-faire* institutional design. Concerns over social stability, unbalanced competition, and the deterioration of national identity were used as justification for regulatory restrictions on religious activity (Anderson 2003,1). Toward the end of the decade, legislatures began distinguishing between tolerated and disagreeable religious bodies, endeavored to place restrictions on certain churches, and promoted one religion at the expense of others. In addition to the controversial Russian religious law of 1997, some country-specific examples of this trend include the 2002 restrictive legislation in Belarus and Bulgaria, and the 2005 national security amendments in Kazakhstan.

Even so, most countries did not experience as severe a repudiation of a liberal design for religious life as was seen in Russia in 2016. The suddenness was partly owing to religious pluralism surviving for so long as a type of anachronism in an increasingly insular, nationalist, and intolerant society. The 1997 law and even Putin's ascension did not present a serious threat to religious pluralism (See Rousselet 2000, Anderson 2002, March and Mark 2004). Irina Papkova noted in 2011 that following the 1997 Law of Freedom of Conscience and Religious Organization, "the ROC leadership failed to translate any of its substantive political preferences into actual federal policy" (2011, 93). From 2011 to 2016, the Russian Orthodox Church achieved tangible progress in the restoration of property, introduction of military chaplains, integrating Orthodox culture courses into public schools, and reincorporation of splinter groups. Furthermore, seemingly innocuous legislative acts on land use (2001), NGOs (2006), terrorism (2006), foreign finance (2012) and education (2012) made for unequal treatment and cumbersome regulations for non-traditional churches (Clay 1997, 198). But on the issue of restricting religious pluralism, Papkova's characterization remained valid until the Yarovaya measures in 2016. The number of protestant church organizations doubled from 1996 to 2014, despite such pre-Yarovaya legislations (ibid., 199). State favoritism for Orthodoxy drastically increased, but pluralism and religious liberties survived until the advent of the Yarovaya law— named after its chief proponent and Deputy Chairman of the State Duma, Irina Yarovaya.

The post-Soviet histories of former Soviet republics illustrate that societies do not automatically default to a religious system that is pluralistic and liberal once an authoritarian and atheistic regime is removed. Rather, religious democracy is a product of a lengthy process of constructing democratic institutions and a civil society supportive of a free-hand religious market. A successful transition involves "the replacement of one set of authoritarian institutions with another set of democratic institutions" (McFaul 1999, 105). Some societies fared well in transitioning from a closed and authoritarian religious design, as many post-communist Central European nations typify. Others, most notably Russia, failed. While the explanation for the variance is undoubtedly multifaceted, the role of non-governmental actors on institutional design is undoubtedly significant. Examining that role can assist in understanding the de-democratization trend occurring, not just in Russia, but in many post-Soviet religious markets.

The Church as a Principal Actor in Institutional Design

It comes as no surprise that in nations with a well-established dominant religion, the clergy of such organizations has far-reaching influence over religious marketplace structure. Anthony Gill astutely notes that "variations in religious liberty can best be explained by examining the political opportunity costs of the principal actors involved in defining church-state relations, that is, political and religious leaders" (2005, 2). This is certainly the case in Russia. With three-fourths of Russians claiming an affiliation with Russian Orthodoxy, the Moscow Patriarchate qualifies as a principal actor. Indeed, the historical linkage between Orthodoxy and nationalism, and the church's significance in the cultural fiber of society has allowed its voice to resonate loudly in the debate over the regulatory framework for religious activity.

The views and machinations of traditional dominant churches are significant factors that have influenced the present-day retreat of religious tolerance in the region. The religious institutional designs in a particular country appear to be heavily dependent on the views of senior clergy from the largest church in the respective nation. Indeed, the retreat of religious freedoms within many nations of the region has corresponded with a more activist and interventionist stance by traditional churches. Many of the historically dominant churches, which previously operated in the Soviet Union have, to varying degrees, promoted and supported restrictions on religious freedoms. Fearful of evangelical poaching of their constituents, many of these churches have resorted to various negative means, including using the media to condemn the proliferation of 'totalitarian cults'. They have relied upon arguments ranging from the necessity of social stability in uncertain times to nationalistic solidarity against encroaching Westernization. The degree to which their pleas and petitions have been embraced depends upon the myriad international and domestic pressures bearing down on the government. However, the roll back of religious freedoms in the region is undoubtedly influenced, in part, by the encouragement of some of these churches.

The posture of dominant churches towards a plural-religious society is typically addressed in academia as an appendage to the overall study of religious affairs. The cursory treatment of dominant churches often frames them within the 'Clashes of Civilization' debate where the churches' motives are described purely in terms of resisting western modernity and defending ethnic identity. Quite frequently, Eastern Orthodoxy appears in such generalizations as inherently totalitarian. Yet this broadbrush approach misses the intricacies of church hierarchical decision-making on religious liberties. This is particularly true in Russia where research for this book exposes internal church division that, among other things, likely explains the delay in repressing religious freedoms until 2016. Friction between conservative and moderate elements likely hindered consensus on pursuing anti-democratic measures. Such nuances are prerequisites to understanding why some traditionally dominant churches have focused on promoting religious protectionism while others are more religiously tolerant. By religious protectionism, I imply a church's attempt to use all means at its disposal, both political and social, to influence the state in limiting the religious activities of other organizations. By so doing, church leaders seek protection from the competitive forces of the market. They seek government interference in the religious economy in order to gain an advantageous environment in which to operate.

Not all traditional churches in the region, however, have shown such hostility to democratic institutions or enmity towards non-traditional religious groups. Several traditional churches have shown a progressive attitude toward religious institutional design and the establishment of a multi-religious society. Even among Orthodox national churches in the region, discernible variations in attitude and agenda on religious diversity exist. Though not widely acknowledged, the Russian Orthodox Church has historically contained diverse ideological views. The church has only relatively recently succumbed to its more illiberal urges. This book builds a conceptual model of church hierarchical behavior to not only explain Russian Orthodox decision-making on religious pluralism, but also why other churches have pursued courses that have impeded the liberal religious design that many had hoped the events of 1991 would guarantee.

To properly grasp the Russian Orthodox Church's role in the demise of religious pluralism in Russia, it is essential to first recognize that religious bodies formulate agendas that affect the institutional design process. Factors influencing those agendas need to be isolated and scrutinized in order to understand motive and predict future action. Considering the plethora of factors in play, the process of contextualizing the church's role in institution building is no easy task. For one thing, such contextualization certainly cannot be accomplished in a vacuum or be the prisoner of a particular moment in time. The decisions of ecclesiastical institutions are undoubtedly influenced by past and present experiences. For bodies that endured Soviet religious policies, such as the Orthodox Synod and Moscow Patriarchate, the 70-year Soviet captivity holds great sway. But so too do the market disruption of the post-Soviet era. The constraints and opportunities of these past and present contexts are germane to this scholarly inquiry. In her methodologically insightful work on institutional change in post-Soviet Central Asia, Pauline Jones Luong stresses the necessity of utilizing both historical and immediate factors in understanding institutional formation:

> "The underlying sources of institutional continuity and change can be found in the structural-historical context and the immediate strategic (or transitional) context, respectively. While the former generates the political identities through which established elites transfer legacies from the past onto new institutions, the latter provides the exogenous shock that can sever elites long-standing attachments to these political identities. The key to predicating the extent of institutional change versus continuity, then, is the perceived effect of this shock on pre-existing power relations" (Luong 2002, 254).

Luong's advice is certainly sound for the examination of any post-Soviet institution. One must look at both the Soviet legacy and the post-Soviet exogenous shocks to properly account for change or continuity in institutional design. For the present endeavor, both contexts have to be accounted for to properly contextualize Russian Orthodox support for the 2016 measures. The present work builds upon the Luong's methodological scaffolding by employing a slightly modified version of her framework to explain the path that led the Russian Orthodox Church to support the Yarovaya law. My research has been sub-divided into two spheres: (1) the conceptualization of the Soviet experiences that produces Soviet residues on present-day behavior; and (2) the contextualization of church activities within the changing dynamics of the post-Soviet marketplace.

The Long Shadow of Sovietism and Free Market Hazards

The two research orientations are essential to accurately understand outcome of design in any post-Soviet institutions. For instance, to properly grasp the behavior of former state-owned industries, both past and present factors need to be considered. One would need to examine structural business inefficiencies, such as poor consumer service, supply-chain weakness, and resource waste in production, that were inherited from the previous command economy. But of equal significance would be the constraints facing industries in the post-Soviet marketplace. These would include but not be limited to new regulations, the emergence of specialized competitors, and consumer demand shifts. Indeed, in the 1990s, abundant scholarship utilized both contexts to better understand industry transition from Soviet to post-Soviet economic systems. Scholars of such works intuitively understood that to properly appreciate institutional behavior, motives, and procedures, it is imperative to look at both institutional origin and change in a historical and transitional context.

The churches of the former Soviet Union are no exception to this rule. The process by which some historically dominant churches in the region have sought privileges and recognition over other religious groups is highly reminiscent of Soviet-type bargaining. Apart from political positioning on the part of the churches, other manifestations of continuity suggest the durability of Soviet legacy on church behavior. Yet, the behavior and successes of institutions endeavoring to survive in a post-communist environment are not simply determined by Soviet-era encounters or the degree of Sovietization experienced, but also by the changing contours of post-Soviet market features. Those features—which in the 1990s were largely characterized by a liberal, vibrant, and hyper-competitive market—were unlike anything many of these churches had faced in their histories. It is not hyperbolic to posit that churches, and particularly the Russian Orthodox Church, had more historical points of reference for Soviet-era institutional arrangements than they did for post-Soviet circumstances. After all, as Sabrina Ramet notes, "The Russian Orthodox Church, which from 1721 to 1917 had been the handmaid of the tsars, had proven capable of adapting to the service of atheist, even atheizing, masters" (1998, 22). The 1990s' marketplace was a larger departure from the norm than was the Soviet era.

Academia as a whole has taken for granted the way the Soviet experience changed churches—both in the operational terms of delivering a credible, competitive religious commodity to the citizenry, and in terms of altering the world view and political culture of persecuted churches. The Soviet experience was so all-encompassing and defining for persecuted churches, that its impact on present-day decision-making, particularly as it relates to religious pluralism, cannot be ignored. At the same time, the period after 1991, when churches endured the 'shock therapy' of an explosion of religious groups after 70 years of inactivity, presented its own set of challenges. The reason both contexts are so highly relevant is because institutions and entities appraise the degree and direction of changes in their relative power against the backdrop of both the structural-historical context (communist-era setting) and the immediate-strategic context (post-Soviet circumstances) (Luong 2002, 254). And only after such an assessment, they "develop strategies of action based on what they expect their influence over the outcome to be vis-à-vis other actors" (ibid., 14). A church's posture on issues of religious pluralism is one such strategy developed in this past-present, relative power decision space.

Against the backdrop of this historical-contemporary framework, research over several years has revealed a step-wise correlation between the level of subservience by traditional churches to the Soviet regime and the degree to which churches seek a restricted religious playing field in the post-Soviet era. Put more practically, those churches, the Russian Orthodox Church paramount among them, that cooperated extensively with Soviet authorities are those same churches that are most vocal in advocating restrictions on the religious activity of non-traditional churches. On the other hand, traditional churches which resisted Soviet encroachment have shown less interest in inhibiting religious activity. The central component of this hypothesis is that church hierarchies perceive shifts in their relative power differently according to the nature of their Soviet and post-Soviet experiences. The behavior of these churches' leaders, and specifically of their market strategy, is based on and vary according to these perceptions. Therefore, both the Soviet institutional legacy and transitional dynamics determine present-day church agenda. Put another way, a church's tendency toward protectionism is shaped by their wish to "acquire or retain as much power as possible given their perceptions of how present changing circumstances are affecting their previous ability to influence the distribution of goods and/or benefits" (ibid., 3).

This distributional and rationalist approach to religious supply-side behavior relies upon modelling which is highly sequential. It begins with a church's course of either compromising with or resisting Soviet encroachment and continues with the reinforcing mechanisms produced by that decision, which in turn both shape constraints and limit future opportunities. For instance, a church that compromised heavily with the state, experienced an intense Sovietization and politicization of its leadership, organizational paralysis and, after 1991, a legitimacy crisis. These consequences of compromise have, in the more free-market environment of the post-Soviet era, acted as fetters on the organization's ability to compete. After the fall of communism, these non-competitive churches found themselves in a vibrant religious marketplace without historical precedent. The market was characterized by intense demand-side mobility, fierce proselytization, supply-side specialization, and increased consumer preference. These features and institutional arrangements in the transition were as foreign as they were damaging to non-competitive traditional churches. Hierarchs perceived their relative influence to be waning. As a rational response to these and other constraints confronted during the transition, leaders of monopolistic-style, former Soviet co-opted churches, turned to old tendencies of political bargaining to promote religious protectionism against groups referred to as "agents of imperialism and as the destroyers of national unity" (Rousselet 2000, 66). Attempts at regulatory restrictions were not only intended to check the spread of Western evangelical groups, but also, centered on centuries-old competitors. However, where Sovietization and political compromise did not occur, transitional constraints on a church's competitiveness were less pervasive and opposition to religious pluralism less prevalent. The primary hypothesis, therefore, argues that the extent to which a church seeks protection from religious competitors corresponds with the degree to which church leaders conformed to Soviet political culture.

The theoretical and methodological underpinnings of this book are greatly influenced by Pauline Jones Luong's excellent work in 2003 in which she examined the institutional developments of electoral systems in three Central Asian nations. In adapting Luong's approach to post-Soviet churches, I also confirm and build upon the work of Sabrina Ramet. She contrasted Bulgaria's post-Stalinist Orthodox Church and the Polish Catholic Church and she asserts that "patterns set under one system may carry over or exert influence into the next" (1998, 307). She examines the Bulgarian Orthodox Church, which was a "Stalinist church that had lost all decision-making autonomy and had been reduced to a mere agency of the state" (ibid., 307). As a result, upon independence the church found "its credibility and strength steadily ebbed, leaving the church divided, vulnerable, fearful of proselytization by foreign-based missionaries, and forced to the defensive" (ibid.). The Polish Catholic Church, on the other hand, with its history of anti-communist resistance entered the transitional era "with enormous credibility, an aura of legitimacy, a united hierarchy, and an offensive posture" (ibid.). Polish Catholicism became a "symbol of a solid nation against an atheistic communist regime" (Osa 1997, 339). The two divergent post-Soviet paths were largely determined by the Cold War-era choices of the Bulgarian and Polish churches.

The same pattern is found in the churches of the former Soviet Union and serves as an explanatory backstory to the Yarovaya law and other restrictive measures. For example, the path of the Belarusian Orthodox Church is not so dissimilar from that travelled by the Bulgarian Orthodox Church. The Belarusian church's collaboration with Soviet authorities resulted in a plethora of post-Soviet constraints that would make operating in a free-market difficult. Such churches have been called Sergianist—a term referring to churches that compromised heavily with the Soviet state and is derived from an early Soviet-era Russian Orthodox patriarch, whose policies brought the church into close collaboration with the state. In general, such religious entities were not well suited for circumstances that greeted them after independence; and, as a result, many turned to a policy of religious protectionism. By contrast, the Lithuanian Catholic Church path parallels that walked by the Polish Catholic Church and resulted in both being less inclined towards using the political arena to advocate restrictions on other religious organizations. Remarkably, the diversity of experience and outcome in the region among churches on religious pluralism does not hold to a Catholic-Orthodox confessional variable, but to the pivot point of the Soviet-era choice between submission or resistance.

Methodological Considerations

To make sense of the many disparate factors at play on church decision-making, this book uses a mixed theoretical approach that combines insights from both rational choice theory and historical institutionalism. This is done to account for the institutional and political legacies of the Russian Orthodox Church inherited from the Soviet Union as well as the shifting features of the present-day religious environment, including the constraints and opportunities that occurred following the demise of communism. I will roughly follow Luong's process-tracing approach in explaining institutional design in transitional states by combining the structural and agency-based approaches. Although she used her approach to explain variations in electoral systems in Central Asia, I adapt it to account for variations in religious tolerance in the former Soviet republics.

Luong's belief that rational choice and historical institutionalism individually are inadequate to explain such a complex situation, and that an intermixture of the two is required, applies equally to the subject at hand. These contexts are not independent of each other and are in fact, highly interactive. The structural-historical context sets up the original parameters within which strategy formulation occurs. However, those parameters are not rigid. Luong asserts that "rather, the immediate-strategic context indicates the degree to and direction in which these initial parameters shift or change, as well as which indicators are more relevant for determining the nature and extent of these changes, throughout the institutional design process" (2002, 14).

Soviet Institutionalism

The overriding tenant of historical institutionalism is that constraints on an institution's behavior "characteristically have historical roots, as artefactual residuals of past actions and choices" (Goodin 1996, 20). This analysis rests upon a path-dependent model where organizational development is punctuated by critical events or junctures that shape the basic contours of future behavior (Pierson 2000, 251). Applying this logic to the communist-era policy choices of churches, we would expect to see legacy constraints "restrict[ing] subsequent evolution so that a kind of path-dependency influences" (Bulmer, 1997) church policies to this day. Manifestations of structural constraints inherited from Soviet rule include:

(1) The *transformation* of church elites' points of reference from the public to the political sphere as a result of Soviet religious policy reorienting churches' modes of operation, and elites' perception of power and organizational success (politicization).

(2) The *internalization* by church elites of the system's authoritarian political culture as a result of decades of close association with communist authorities (Soviet political culture).

(3) The *deterioration* of the means of producing and distributing high value religious services, which made churches resemble inefficient state-owned monopolies in the 1990s (non-competitive administrative structure).

(4) The *reduction* of church image and integrity as perceived by the population owing to the church's pernicious collaboration with the atheistic regime (credibility gap).

The path-dependent implication here is that the critical juncture event and the concomitant four constraints just listed place these churches on a particular trajectory. Extensive interviewing, surveying, and analysis of available data and trends suggest that the Russian Orthodox Church and other religious institutions, heavily influenced by their association with the Soviet state, are embedded within a similar historical and post-Soviet context that structures their actions and leads them to oppose religious pluralism. The legacies of Sovietism act as reinforcing mechanisms that influence churches even in the absence of the repressive regime that instilled them. Church leaders, rather than abandoning the traits learned or forced upon them by communism, have instead shown an alarming degree of continuity with the Soviet past. The next chapter will expose church aversion to religious pluralism and competition as partly the result of "shared institutional and policy legacy from Soviet rule" (Luong 2002, 36).

Rational Church Theory

Insights from rational choice theory will assist in revealing the other piece of the puzzle, namely the features of the transitional period or the immediate-strategic context that also shapes outcome. Modelling ecclesiastic behavior against the principles of rationality and utility maximization is a unique and promising framework for the study of religion (see Iannaccone 1997). In particular, the rational choice approach helps to understand the influence of market dynamics by providing insights on religious monopolies, the economic approach to market structure, macro-organizational behavior, and individual-level affiliation patterns. Recent work on applying this approach to religious behavior has yielded much and serves as a useful tool in unravelling individual decision-making in the context of post-Soviet constraints and opportunities. The calculated political choices of churches and the distinctive developments of the religious sphere since 1991 conform remarkably to assumptions generated by proponents of the approach. Many of these churches view the religious environment similarly to how secular leaders view politics, as zero-sum power relations. As such, these churches can reasonably be "thought of as religious firms competing for adherents in a structured marketplace" (Finke 1997, 46). A top priority of traditionally dominant churches is to maximize their own religious influence in society. This idea conforms to a central tenet of rational choice theory that religious producers are always viewed as optimizers who "maximizing members, net resources, government support, or some other basic determinant of institutional success" (Iannacconne 1997, 27).

The approach has generated many valuable insights on the religious behavior of both parishioners and clergy. In chapter 3, I will employ these and other assumptions to construct a theoretical scaffolding to explain church actions on religious freedoms as rational responses to the constraints and opportunities found in the religious marketplace. Assumptions springing from my research include that religious conflict and tension will increase in a society where the dominant church perceives a decrease in its relative power; formerly co-opted churches feel more threatened by the activities of foreign groups than churches that have long maintained independence from the state; market growth will be concentrated among new entrants and highly specialized religious groups; and religious mobility is disproportionately higher among sophisticated believers than among the general population. These assumptions and others developed by sociologists applying the theory to religious activity in other parts of the world, will be channeled to explain the decision calculus of churches operating in the post-Soviet space.

Elite Power Perception

Decision calculus is bound heavily by an individual or institutional perception of power change. Because religious leaders are committed to either maintaining or enhancing their organization's influence, perceived shifts in relative power motivate church hierarchies to take up reactionary strategies (Luong 2002, 7). The Soviet past serves as a basis for these churches' "institutional preferences and assessments of relative power" (ibid., 50). The leaders' perception of shifts in their relative power and their willingness to take up reactionary strategies are shaped by the interaction between the structural-historical and immediate-strategic contexts. Such an interaction causes some churches, that worked closely with the Soviet apparatus, to perceive a loss in their 'religious power' relative to other groups, and this then motivates them to adopt an anti-pluralistic agenda and advance it in the political arena. Where a church's perception of its power is stable or increasing, relative to other churches, they are less likely to adopt a confrontational posture. Thus both "perceptions and strategies are the product of the interaction between the structural-historical and transitional contexts" (ibid., 34).

The hierarchical structure of these organizations, as well as the character of church-state interaction in the region, makes religious elites, not the laity or parish-level clergy, the prime actors in formulating, bargaining, and implementing church policies, which impact institutional design. The commonality of experience under communism and the similar nature of the transitional religious free market experience, enables an examination in both a cross-regional and rational choice context. Indeed, the shared Soviet and post-Soviet experiences across traditional dominant churches of the region allows for testing this theoretical approach. Although the subject of inquiry is the Russian Orthodox Church, there is value in expanding the scope to ensure the accuracy of the methodological scaffolding and the hypotheses. The path-dependent model will be applied against the experience of two test case churches: the Lithuanian Catholic Church, with arguably the most tolerant record on religious diversity among former USSR republics; and the Georgian Orthodox Church, with perhaps the most restrictive viewpoint on religious freedom and tolerance of minority religious organizations. These two churches, along with the Russian Orthodox Church, share a history of repression and paralysis under the Soviet regime and each experienced profoundly the consequences of the fall of that system. They represent the culturally dominant, traditional religion in their respective country and have been inseparably connected to the history and identity of their nation for centuries.

The range of experience between the three churches best demonstrates the correlation between the degree to which the cause occurred (in this case subservience under communism) and the degree to which the effect occurred (in this case the prevalence of an anti-pluralistic agenda). The similarities of the Orthodox churches, including a close ethno-religious identity in society, a history of interdependence with the state, nearly identical theology, and a similar pre-Soviet history will assist in holding exogenous factors constant. Yet the slight differences in the independent variable and corresponding influence on the dependent variables among the two churches will assist in identifying explanatory factors.

Inductive reasoning regarding the experiences of the two Orthodox churches strongly suggests the presence of a systematically-related causal relationship between the dependent and independent variables. Holding exogenous factors constant between Orthodox Churches and the Catholic Church is more problematic. Indeed, the staggering dissimilarities in theological, historical and organizational conditions make controlling variables impractical. The path-dependent approach of this study, however, will assist in limiting the factors playing upon the dependent variable. Ultimately the two case study churches will help evaluate a model that should prove valuable in understanding and contextualizing present-day Russian Orthodox Church actions vis-à-vis other religious organizations operating within its self-proclaimed canonical territory.

Definitions & Research Methods

Several terms and concepts employed throughout this book are defined differently in the press, academia, and among church leaders. For consistency and accuracy during extensive interviews conducted with church elites, as much as possible, I ensured that respondents based their answers against the following definitions.

Religious Pluralism: The multiplicity of religious organizations operating within a society, the abundance of which depends upon market features, not state interference.[1]

Religious Liberal Society: An institutional design which affords every religion and individual equal rights to practice and propagate their religious beliefs without encumbrance by state or other entities. As Francoise Champion notes, "This involves allowing for the individuality of each religion and not turning the specific features of the dominant religion into the norm" (1999, 42).

Traditional Religions: Religious organizations that are accepted, with or without legal recognition, by the state and citizenry as having contributed most to the historical development of the nation—a church that not only commands the most religious adherents among the populace, but has been historically tied to the majority ethnic group of a nation through a common linguistic and social heritage.

Non-traditional Religions: Religious organizations that are not currently recognized by the state as having contributed to the historical development of society and that are not designated traditional by the state.

Sovietization: The process by which individuals, organizations, and institutions conformed to the Soviet social, political, and cultural model—an ideology rooted in the central tenets of Marxist-Leninism, which include authoritarianism.

Politicization: The process by which individual and organizational objectives shift from non-political to political characteristics. The organization, as well as its leaders, gradually begin to place more reliance upon political means to achieve desired ends than traditional avenues of influence.

Years of interviewing and surveying executive level religious officials across the former Soviet Union form the empirical research foundation for this book. In addition to face-to-face conversations, a standardized

---

[1] The term "religious pluralism" has been interpreted in Western scholarship in numerous ways to reflect various realities. This paper will not delve into the debate regarding the scope and boundaries of religious pluralism, but instead will use this simple description.

questionnaire was utilized in order to control for language peculiarities across religious denominations. This method allowed for precise comparison of answers from all respondents on myriad questions. I also conducted an extensive survey, which included a synthesis of interviews and questionnaires, on religious affiliation patterns among converts and adherents of The Church of Jesus Christ of Latter-day Saints in Russia. In addition, numerous conversations occurred with hierarchs of the Russian Orthodox Church Outside of Russia, the Lutheran Church, and the Orthodox Old Believers. Over one hundred lengthy interviews were conducted and twice as many questionnaires returned in five nations of the former Soviet Union. These conversations with clergy, officials, and parishioners were conducted with the understanding that attribution would be assigned. However, in light of legislative and societal changes in the region that have transpired between the fieldwork and the printing of this book, I have decided to anonymize most identities.

This volume is organized with the goal of better appreciating factors affecting the Russian Orthodox Church's posture on matters of religious pluralism. Assumptions are presented in chapters 2 and 3 which establish the theoretical framework necessary to evaluate the historical and contemporary factors that explain a church's support for restrictive measures such as the Yarovaya laws. First, a path-dependent model of institutional behavior accounts for the way in which Soviet legacy continues to influence church choices on matters of religious liberties. This structural-historical context is followed by a look at the post-Soviet period through the lens of rational choice theory to identify constraints confronting religious leaders in the immediate-strategic context. The two contexts help in conceptualizing present-day factors influencing the behavior of religious elites.

In chapters 4 and 5, these factors will be tested in the two case study churches of the Georgian Orthodox Church and the Lithuanian Catholic Church. They represent extreme examples on the religious tolerance spectrum. This contrast will help illuminate chapter 6's discussion of the Russian Orthodox Church's journey from the chaotic 1990s to its resurgence and what it all means for church policy on religious pluralism. Chapter 7 summarizes implications for the Russian Orthodox Church, the wider region, and assess lessons learned from using a rational choice framework to examine religious behavior in post-Soviet countries.

A church's history and disdain for religious freedoms and diversity is largely inconsequential without a willing partner in government. The state, not the church, ultimately passed the draconian 2016 measures. So, to truly understand the demise of religious pluralism in Russia, church-state interaction needs to be understood. The concluding chapter does this and acts as a somewhat stand-alone essay that gives the book a practical relevance beyond the religious sphere. I provide a more geopolitical perspective on the topic by examining the church's role in the Kremlin's notorious disinformation campaigns. I argue that the reason church appeals for a command religious economy have only recently fell on sympathetic ears in the Kremlin is explained by understanding the church's assimilation into state influence operations. Since the Crimean annexation, elements of civil society, not typically associated with information confrontation, such as Non-Governmental Organizations (NGOs), the Russian Orthodox Church, and academia have increasingly functioned as 'voice multipliers'. The Kremlin finds great utility in enlisting these entities to reverberate its messaging. The 2016 measures likely represented an act of reciprocation for the church's assiduous efforts in Putin's all-of-government approach to national defense.

2. Legacies of Sovietism
Structural-Historical Constraints

> "There is no certainty that, even if the church opened a dialogue with society about the most important thing—not culture, peace-making and charity, but Christ on the cross and the resurrection—it would be heard and understood" (Cited in Orlov and Kotzer 1998, 160).

This pessimistic assessment was uttered by Patriarch Aleksei II shortly after the collapse of communism. It was indicative of a general foreboding felt among the many senior Russian Orthodox leaders in the church's ability to appeal on a spiritual level to the public. They were not ignorant to the debilitating consequences of decades of atheistic propaganda and the dismantlement of church ministerial resources. This Soviet inheritance also included a palpable estrangement between the church and society as parishioners drifted away from organized religions during years of atheistic indoctrination. While individual religiosity had undoubtedly been altered by the Soviet experience, so too had many churches. Bishop Jonas Kauneskas of the Lithuanian Catholic Church maintained that his church had to become "reacquainted with the populace after years of isolation" (Interview 2004. Vilnius, 23 Dec). Other clergy indicate that, in large measure, their churches started from scratch after 1991. In explaining the legacy of Stalinism on the present-day Bulgarian Church, Sabrina Ramet noted that the church's "willingness to accommodate the regime cost it the trust and loyalty of many citizens" (1998, 281). This derision felt by many segments of society toward established churches was just one of the obstacles that traditional dominant churches inherited from what the Russian Orthodox patriarch at the time called their "spiritual Babylonian captivity" (Cited in Orlov and Kotzer 1998, 160). The intrusive and destructive nature of Soviet religious policy changed many churches into entirely new creatures. Thirty years on, the influence of Soviet policy and practices on institutional design and church-state and church-society relations has proven remarkably durable.

This chapter examines the mechanisms by which institutional legacies from the Soviet era have continued to the present day. The extent and strength of that legacy, however, depended on Soviet-era decisions and circumstances. A careful examination of the historical record, current policy, and the thoughts and actions of individual clergy suggest that the decision on the part of the churches to either bend to the will of the Soviet state or struggle against it was a watershed event that resulted in structural transformation, with present-day ramifications. Paramount among these structural transformations was the politicization of churches, which resulted in the restructuring of those institutions' perception of power. Aside from the politicization process, several other constraints such as inefficient bureaucratic structures and schismatic elements that plagued churches after the fall of the USSR were triggered by this critical juncture choice. This history lesson is pivotal because it assists in understanding the present-day policies of church hierarchies by placing them in the context of the past. The trigger event resulted in a structuralist path-dependent process that explains how the "institutional legacies of the past limit the range of current possibilities and/or options in institutional innovation" (Hausner and Jessop 1995, 6). Decisions made during the Soviet era affect the parameters of the decision space for churches today. This process-tracing methodology helps demystify present-day choices of the Russian Orthodox Church.

It is vital from the onset to underscore that the intent is not to pass a moral judgement on the actions of persecuted church leaders, but to understand the implications of those actions on church policy formulation after 1991, particularly as it relates to religious pluralism. Many have been quick to condemn, opining that those churches that decided upon the collaboration policy option, "betrayed their own interests in favor of the government's" (Pushkarev *et al.* 1989, 72). In reality, the decision was much more complicated as Russian Orthodox clergy were quite literally compelled to submit to Soviet dictates at gunpoint. Their motives are impossible to discern and may very well have been more noble. Instead of standing in judgement, their choices need to be examined because of the explanatory value they hold in understanding the diversity of policy on issues of religious pluralism in the post-Soviet space.

Theoretical Approach

An analysis of the 20th Century institutional history of the Russian Orthodox Church or any dominant church in the region presents a daunting methodological challenge. Within a century these churches experienced several state-regime changes, an intrusive state-imposed cultural and organizational restructuring, and vacillations between conditions of state-favoritism and state-oppression. The unravelling of such a fluid institutional history requires an equally dynamic approach that pulls from insights from historical and sociological institutionalisms as well as from agency-based models. We must begin with the principle that churches, like all institutions, are not naturally occurring, but display a "nature-like longevity" (Goodin 1996, 207). Hegel described this dual nature characteristic of an institution as being made by man, but taking on a "second nature which is often as impossible to change as the law of gravity" (ibid.). This overriding concept of Historical Institutionalism is essential in explaining the mechanisms by which the Soviet legacy continues to influence the institutional choices of certain churches. It rests on the notion that individuals act within institutional arrangements and that these arrangements are a result of history and develop over time. Applying this to the post-Soviet space, David Stark explains that instead of studying a transition, we are in fact examining transformations, "in which new elements emerge through adaptation, rearrangements, permutations, and reconfigurations of existing organizational forms. Instead of institutional vacuum we examine institutional legacies" (1996, 993-995). Because churches did not enter the post-Soviet era with a clean slate, a comprehensive analysis of the present-day religious environment and policy preferences of church elites requires a full accounting of the institutional history in the transformative communist-era.

Historical Institutionalism, therefore, is interested in organizational configurations and institutional change over long periods of time. Importance is placed on the "asymmetries of power associated with the operation and development of institutions" (Hall and Taylor 1996, 7) and understanding the "overarching contexts and interacting processes that shape and reshape states, politics, and public policymaking" (Pierson and

Skocpol 2002, 694). It takes history and process seriously, and therefore naturally inclines toward a structural rigidity with less concern for the interaction of individual behavior and institutions (Hall and Taylor 1996, 7). Sociological Institutionalism, on the other hand, stresses that institutional "forms and procedures should be seen as culturally specific practices" (ibid., 14). In contrast to a means-ends rational methodology, sociological institutionalists underscore "the highly-interactive and mutually-constitutive character of the relationship between institutions and individual action" (ibid., 15). The approach emphasizes the embeddedness of values and how culturally constructed conceptions of power, influence, and success are seen to be more important than organizational configurations.

Of course, these approaches are not mutually exclusive, and scholarship has begun merging the two to account for dynamic arrangements. Peter Hall and Rosemary Taylor indicate that in response to criticisms of being overly rigid, Historical Institutionalists have adopted a cultural amendment to their approach. In a veiled concession to Sociological Institutionalism, it recognizes that "behavior is not fully strategic but bounded by an individual's worldview" (ibid., 7). Hall and Taylor assert that "the time has come for a more open and extensive interchange among [these approaches]" (ibid., 24). While certainly more complicated than a single-approach study, there is a growing consensus in academia that an integration of structuralism and behaviorism is necessary for scholarly inquiries. If ever a subject matter demanded such a theoretical amalgamation, it is the examination of churches that endured Soviet repression. The state did not only attack the churches' infrastructure and organization, but also its culture—thereby transforming institutions structurally and culturally.

The debate between social and historical institutionalism is simply a subset of the larger structural-agency debate that pits those who believe that structure shapes outcome against behaviorists, who emphasize the role of individual agency. Wisely, that debate is gradually becoming obsolete as evermore scholars appreciate that a flexible mingling of the two is needed in most academic investigations. Bob Jessop's Strategic Relational Approach postulates that structure and agency are so interconnected that to separate them and chronologically plot them on an institution's historical map is impracticable (See 1990). Or as Justus Uitermark noted, "strategies and structures are co-constitutive of each other, implying that it is impossible to draw an ontological line between them" (2005, 139). Colin Hay explains that instead of understanding agency and structure as two sides of the same coin, it should be thought of two distinct metals which constitutes the alloy from which the coin is cast. (Hay 1995, 189). This realization becomes all the more apparent to the subject matter at hand as we move from Soviet to post-Soviet and into the 21st Century. Institutional choices and changes were so dynamic as to make any over-reliance on a single approach untenable. I assert that a behavioralist model nested in a structural-historical context is the most suitable platform to properly view and account for forces at play on traditionally dominant churches. Therefore, the behaviorist approach of rational choice will help explain post-Soviet actions and agendas. However, that approach alone is insufficient to contextualize the entire decision space as it is limited in its ability to "provide us with the intellectual tools to ascertain either who is actually sitting at the bargaining table or how they got there" (Luong 2002, 39). This chapter will do precisely that by showing that the parameters of those leaders' decisions as well as the options available to them are bounded by historical occurrences.

Path-dependent Framework

The concept of path dependence refers to a "property of contingent, non-reversible dynamical processes that can properly be described as evolutionary" (David 2000, 1). It suggests that decisions of policy makers or decisive events establish particular directions of change and exclude others in a way that shapes institutional arrangements for years. A path-dependent process is one in which a move in a certain direction causes further moves in that same direction, thus creating a reinforcing mechanism that locks-in an institution's trajectory. This process-tracing approach which "unfold[s] through a series of logically sequential stages" (Mahoney 2001, 6) helps explain how differing historical events or policy choices lead to the creation of contrasting structural patterns. These in turn result in divergent outcomes in areas as diverse as regime types, electoral systems, or agendas on religious pluralism.

The sequential stages in the path dependent framework include:

1. **Antecedent conditions** which define the base line against which the decisions available to the actors are made. Essentially this consists of the aspects of the history of the institution and its environment previous to the critical juncture.

2. **Critical junctures** are turning points in an institution's history that are "characterized by the selection of a particular option (e.g. a specific policy, coalition, or government) from among two or more alternatives" (ibid.).

3. After a critical juncture occurs, enduring structural and institutional arrangements take shape. This structural persistence or forging of a legacy has two components. First is the **mechanisms of production**, which are the initial structuring, and shaping of institutional design and arrangements. Second is the **mechanisms of reproduction** where the legacy is solidified or "perpetuated through ongoing institutional and political processes" (Collier and Collier 1991, 31). This process of structural reproduction evolves when "institutions create vested interests, and power holders within these institutions seek to perpetuate their own positions" (ibid., 35). In this way, the structural adjustment that occurs after a critical juncture locks in a certain path and consequently narrows the range of possible outcomes.

4. The strength of a newly-formed institution over time "triggers a chain of causally linked events that, once in motion, occur independently of the institutional factors that initially produced it" (Mahoney 2001a, 114). Such reactions and counterreactions are called **reactive sequences**. They can be thought of as the indirect consequences of the critical choice period.

5. The utility of a path-dependent model for scholars is in the identification of causation. Variance in outcomes can be traced back to a singular point, i.e. critical juncture and its enduring arrangements. Differing historical choices result in contrasting **outcomes**. In short, a path-dependent

approach stresses how the decisions of key actors at significant moments create new institutional arrangements that shape future behaviors.

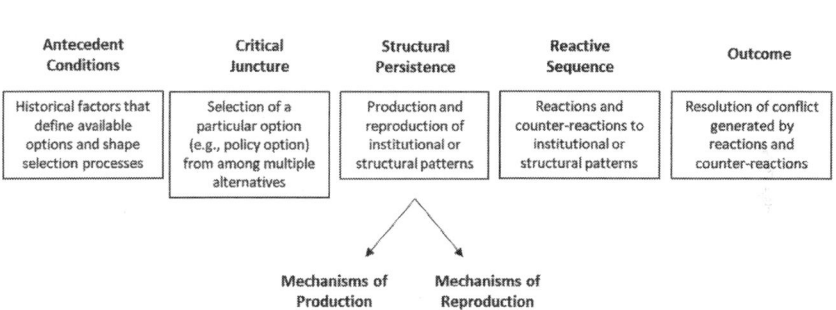

Figure 1. Path-Dependent Framework (Mahoney 2001a, 114)

Path-Dependent Explanation of Religious Pluralism

Lenin's 1918 decree on the separation of church and state ushered in Soviet religious policy in Russia and by extension in the republics. However, it was not until the reign of Stalin that rhetoric was fully backed by action. In 1927, Stalin made his intentions clear:

> "The party cannot be neutral towards religion, and it conducts anti-religious propaganda against all religious prejudices because it stands for science. . . .The party cannot be neutral towards the disseminators of religious prejudices, towards the reactionary clergy, who poison the minds of the laboring masses. Have we repressed the reactionary clergy? Yes, we have. The only unfortunate thing is that they have not yet been completely eliminated" (Quoted in Conquest 1968).

Although ideologically driven, religious policy was not always as consistent as Stalin implies. William Fletcher noted the policy was "at times embracing measures of expedience dictated by the times and circumstances" (1971, 2). Notwithstanding this fluctuation, pre-glasnost religious policy can roughly be divided into two phases. The first attempted at the wholesale destruction of the historically dominant churches in each republic. It began shortly following the revolution in areas under Red Army control—and therefore did not affect equally all churches that would eventually be found within the boundaries of the USSR. The persecution was "justified ideologically under the guise of class morality and the dictatorship of the proletariat" (Nielsen 1994, 2). Religious buildings were demolished, clergy killed, and smaller church organizations were given privileges at the expense of dominant churches in an effort to break the stronger churches' hold on society. In Russia alone, ten thousand Russian Orthodox churches were closed in a single year (Pushkarev et al. 1989, 55). An integral, and too often forgotten, component of this early policy was the establishment and support of rival religious organizations. The Bolsheviks would prop up schismatic elements in an effort to undermine the dominant church.

Eventually authorities recognized the impossibility of eradicating deep-rooted religiosity as well as the need to solidify public support for the war effort. In the second phase, the state decided to absorb the church and to transform it into a tool of the state. The transition from a policy of outright annihilation to one of control was applied at various times in the republics, but generally commenced during World War II. The communists decided to turn the church, like the new Soviet man, into a new Soviet church, one which was not permitted to have beliefs or ambitions contrary to Soviet political culture. The 'divide and rule' strategy was reversed and a reunification of schismatic groups initiated to centralize control. In his study of the formation of Soviet religious policy, Bohdan Bocuirkiw identified these two policies as divergent strains of thinking within Soviet leadership. He labeled the earlier strategy as fundamentalist, which presumed that it would be feasible to entirely eradicate religion from society. The other more pragmatic policy sought to Sovietize the church, "both for reasons of international security and for the sake of the regime's legitimization among the believing masses" (1973, 41). Although there was significant vacillation between these two approaches, the latter approach prevailed. Nonetheless, a particular church's status in the system "depended upon its usefulness to Soviet domestic and foreign policy" (Nielsen 1994, 19).

The state orchestrated a gradual transformation of many of these churches wherein priests became KGB informants, theology quickly meshed with Marxist-Leninism, and hierarchical rhetoric staunchly aligned with Soviet polices. The creation of a supervisory apparatus around the churches to watch the hierarchy and influence decisions enabled this transformation. Ecclesiastical appointments had to be approved by the Council of Religious Affairs (CRA), which wielded broad jurisdiction over churches. The Council was created in 1965 out of the Council for the Affairs of Religious Cults and the Council for the Affairs of the Russian Orthodox Church. CRA officials worked closely with KGB agents in clergy surveillance and recruitment. The success of this managed transformation depended upon the authorities' ability to win over priests. Arunas Streikus explains how this transpired:

"During the first decade of the Soviet occupation the most effective recruitment technique was threatening the target with punishment for real or imaginary crimes against the Soviet regime. Later, when resistance had declined and almost all the priests against whom it was possible to compose cases of a political nature were already in labor camps, this approach became less effective. The KGB therefore began to make more use of other techniques: appealing to the self-interest of priests or morally discrediting them. Priests recruited in these ways were also found to be more reliable than those simply frightened by the threat of punishment" (2006, 65).

The minutes of a 1961 KGB meeting shed light on the Soviet recruitment strategy, in particular, and Soviet religious policy intentions, in general. Arunas Streikus writes that a KGB leader in 1961 stressed that:

"Important elements in the successful recruitment of clergy were 1) to analyze thoroughly the personal features of the candidate; 2) to make sure he was not a 'religious fanatic' (if he was, attempts to recruit him would be a waste of time); 3) to prepare and carefully verify compromising material. Besides, he added, for priests it was usually very hard to endure recruitment, especially the need for a written promise to collaborate. He therefore proposed the gradual involvement of priests once they had been recruited" (2006, 65)

While some churches resisted the transformation through open rebellion or covert support of religious dissidents, many religious organizations settled into their Stalinist church role. Regardless of the policy choice, the repressive tactics of the early stage continued at the grass roots level and anti-religious propaganda commenced on a wide scale. Mass executions may have ceased, but murder and imprisonment remained commonplace as tactics to assimilate or destroy religious organizations.

Critical Juncture and Antecedent Conditions

Although situations varied in each country, the majority of historically dominant churches faced the same basic choice during the second phase of Soviet religious policy. They could either yield to state conditions and taskings or resist the intrusion of Soviet policies and ideologies and face harsh consequences. In many of the co-opted churches, this critical juncture was not a rash or quick decision by a church council or a primate. Rather, it developed over many years with considerable vacillations, infighting, and periodic attempts at resistance. In Russia, for example, the 1927 'Declaration of Loyalty' by Sergius certainly marked the start of accommodation on the part of the church, but the consolidation of senior church leaders behind a subservient role for the church vis-à-vis the state was not complete until the early 1940s. Tatiana Chumachenko ascribes the turning point to the 4 September 1943 meeting between Stalin and three Metropolitans (2002, 189). In the midst of the Great Patriotic War, the Metropolitans signed a concordat that normalized church-state relations to a degree. The choice was more than just an acquiescence to recognize the state and swear loyalty to it. The Russian Orthodox Church had been familiar with such a Petrine model of church-state relations from the Tsarist era. Soviet conditions, on the other hand, required the unwavering "acceptance of all the regime's demands for virtual submission" (Spinka 1956, 62).

The arrangement was no quid pro quo, but master-servant. In return for 'bending the knee' and losing almost all decision-making autonomy, the churches received little in return (Ramet 1998, 227). They were not repaid with a relaxation of persecution, the freeing of imprisoned clergy, or the reopening of more than just a token number of churches. They were, however, allowed to exist as an official organization and top-tier church leaders lived a somewhat privileged life not too dissimilar from that of party elites. For the Russian Orthodox Church, concessions by the Soviet government after World War II gave the church more freedom than they had ever experienced after 1917; yet the religious laws of 1918 and 1929 were not repealed. Indeed, although less dramatic than the Stalinist religious purges, the gradual closing of churches and monasteries, and the propagation of anti-religious material remained widespread under the leadership of Khrushchev and Brezhnev.

For those churches that were unwilling to bow to Soviet threats, such as the Lutheran Church of Estonia or the Catholic Church of Lithuania, survival was considerably more problematic. By adopting the resistance policy choice, these leaders pitted themselves directly against the central authority. Arrests and persecutions of church leaders ensued. The dismemberment and forced merger of the Ukrainian Greek Catholic Church with the Russian Orthodox Church serves as an illustration of a church that resisted Soviet take-over. The arrest of all church leaders on 11 April, 1945 did not compel the church to break communion with the papacy. Not until the mock Synod of Lyiv, were selected priests compelled to declare as void the Union of Brest. The church was subsequently forced to join with the Russian Orthodox Church. Yet this unwanted union was never a happy one. Catholic priests who resisted were punished for their rebellion for the remainder of the existence of the USSR. Indeed, the church was the largest banned religious institution in the world and fostered an extensive underground network of church activities and religious dissent (Fein, 1989). Similarly, the Catholic Church in Lithuania contrasted clearly with the accommodationism of other churches and was described by the state as early as 1965 as a "serious opponent, subtle and experienced" and one that is "openly hostile to the Socialist system" (Conquest 1968).

The decision on the part of church hierarchies to resist or conform to Soviet policy was undoubtedly rooted in antecedent conditions. The pressures and influences playing upon religious leaders before and during this critical choice period were myriad. At first glance, confessional difference appears most deterministic, particularly as explanation for the differing patterns of historical church-state interaction. Hans Kung's research into what he labelled as the paradigms of Christianity reveals distinct confessional differences between Catholicism and Eastern Orthodoxy (Byzantine) with regard to church-state relations. The Byzantine paradigm is characterized by the church's legal incorporation into imperial state law in which secular power dominates spiritual authority (Madeley 2000). It is also historically entangled in the "political and military conflicts of the secular power, often giving theological legitimization to wars, even inspiring them" (ibid., see Kung 1994). His model, which has also been referred to as Petrine, is attested to in the fact that "in none of the nations in which Orthodoxy was the religion did the churches ever enjoy true independence" (Remond 1999, 24). Rene Remond adds "to this specifically historical fact may perhaps be added a spiritual tradition turned more towards union with God than to sustaining the body of society, thereby implying a passive acceptance of temporal events" (ibid.).

The Roman Catholic paradigm, on the other hand, is one of total loyalty to the Pope as "absolute ruler, lawgiver and judge" where the church "presents itself as a completely independent ruling institution" (Madeley 2000). While Orthodox churches have a long history of close interaction with state organs and association with nationalism, since the 1800s, Catholicism has been more associated with resistance and individual rights. In explaining the diversity in Soviet church-state relations in the Baltic States, Nils Muizneks notes that a history of resistance among Catholic entities created a church structure conducive to dissident activities: "Unlike their Lithuanian counterparts, Latvian dissidents lacked an organizational base such as the Catholic Church" (1997, 381). Steve Bruce adds to this point his belief that the Soviet-era disparities between the two confessions are a consequence of distance from the Soviet regime. The international structure of Roman Catholicism and its emphasis on papal authority has enabled the church in Poland, Czechoslovakia and Lithuania to "call on the spiritual and political aid of the Vatican in trying to resist the communist party" (Bruce 2000, 43). Historical patterns of church-state interaction indicate "Orthodox churches have been far more amenable to infiltration and far more disposed to subordination than Catholic churches" (Ramet 1989, 39). With the notable exception of the

Hungarian Catholic Church, that worked closely with the state, this assumption appears accurate in depicting patterns in the Soviet sphere.

Historical and theological differences between Orthodoxy and Catholicism undoubtedly played an important role in determining which direction churches took at the critical juncture. Yet variation in church postures among Orthodox branches demonstrated that confessional differences were not the only factors at play. At the same time, the argument that Orthodox Churches always break towards submission and state-direction does not hold up under scrutiny. As Ramet notes, a Stalinist church differs from the Petrine model in several ways. Foremost is that while the latter is "merely deprived of power in which it once shared, a Stalinist church has lost all decision-making autonomy and has been reduced to a mere agency of the state" (Ramet 1989, 277). Although at times draconian, Tsarist religious restrictions revolved primarily around political pragmatism and not around zero-sum calculations inspired by atheistic malice. Bolsheviks, on the other hand, sought the systematic elimination of religious suppliers and the eradication of religiosity among the populace. Consequently, the mass closures and demolition of church buildings and the widespread deportations and executions of clergy, which accompanied Soviet rule, did not have historic precedents for Orthodox churches and, therefore, allowed for divergent Soviet experiences.

Even in the tsarist era, religious intolerance was not a forgone conclusion. Scholarship on imperial Russian policies on religious tolerance is extensive and includes Paul Werth's work in which he describes the tsarist era as "a multiconfessional Orthodox state—that is, a polity that established several religions while constituting only one of them as dominant" (2014, 5). Maria Salomon Arel notes that "despite clashes with Catholic forces, Western Europeans who chose to make Russia their home in the 16th and first half of the 17th centuries generally found themselves in a remarkably accommodating religious environment compared to what they knew in their native lands" (2016, 16). Religious freedoms began to be restricted for non-Orthodox Christians thereafter, but fluctuations in policy occurred until the Bolshevik revolution.

While theology and history were certainly influential antecedents, church leaders were also influenced by immediate political considerations. One such consideration was the degree to which the various churches experienced the first stage of Soviet religious policy. The situation in Armenia serves as a case in point. Annexed shortly after the revolution, it was one of the first to feel the repressive hand of Soviet religious policy. During the 1920s and 1930s, vast numbers of clergy were killed and hundreds of churches destroyed. The persecution climaxed with the murder of Catholicos Khoren I by secret police in 1938. When faced with the institutional choice of continued persecution or cooperation with the state, the weakened church selected the latter. After the Second World War, the reopening of a handful of churches coincided with the "church leadership embarking upon a policy of close collaboration with the state" (Anderson, 2003, 148). The Baltic States, on the other hand, were assimilated into the Soviet Union relatively late. Although church closure and clergy persecution occurred, an increase in international scrutiny made any attempt at the wholesale destruction that occurred in the 1920s untenable after the war. This contrasts with the Russian Orthodox Church where 163 bishops in 1930 were reduced to just four within a decade (Fletcher 1997, 81). It is fair to conclude that for those churches that experienced the full onslaught of communist oppression, the desire and the mechanism to resist were seriously weakened.

The influences of these and myriad other antecedent conditions made the collaboration path an appealing one for many churches. For instance, while many leaders that opted for collaboration with the state saw it as a means of preventing their church's demise, they were also keenly aware that their own survival was in jeopardy. The prospect of martyrdom is without question a powerful determinant. The balance between agency and structure in a decision-maker's policy formation is heavily prejudiced toward agency when self-preservation enters the equation. Out of all the traditional churches, the fact that only the Lithuanian Catholic Church, the Ukrainian Greek Catholic Church and, to a lesser extent, the Estonian Lutheran Church made a determined and sustained effort to resist is evidence of the pressures exerted upon these individuals. Indeed, these early leaders were strongly coerced into choosing the subservient path. In Russia, for example, Patriarch Sergius was imprisoned and authorities threatened to shoot 117 bishops if he did not comply with their demands (Pospielovksy 1984, 67). Indeed, William Fletcher has argued that a subservient role was the only realistic posture many of these churches could have taken (1997, 81).

The nature of these antecedent conditions naturally leads into the structure-agency debate. Does action determine structure or does structure determine action? Did the historical patterns of church-state relations (Byzantine vs. Catholicism) determine whether resistance or collaboration was chosen? Or was the decision by the actors influenced mainly by immediate tactical conditions? It appears that structure and agency interact in a fluid manner and a definitive answer concerning where one begins and the other ends cannot be empirically determined. Jessop's Strategic Relational Approach and its emphasis on the fusion of structure and agency appears to be well-suited for this dichotomy (See 1990). That being said, the answers to the above questions, at least for the purpose of examining the Russian Orthodox Church's approach to institutional design, are largely irrelevant. An "infinite explanatory regress into the past" (Mahoney 2001, 7) is of little concern as the critical junctures clearly marked a new starting point for these churches.

That critical choice was pivotal because it led to institutional change and restructuring and, therefore, determined the path trajectories of these institutions for years to come. In analytical terms the critical juncture is pivotal in assessing and predicting final outcomes and thus has a neutralizing effect on antecedent conditions. James Mahoney notes that "Although the choice itself may have been caused by prior events, it is the variables activated by the choice, not the antecedent conditions that led to the choice, that predict final outcomes" (2001, 7). This antecedent-neutral starting point is also useful as there is little consensus in academia concerning tsarist Orthodox tradition and democratic norms. Recent experience and perhaps some cultural bias in the West have led some scholars and politicians to surmise that the two have always been at odds. But many well-versed scholars have argued recently that this may not be the case. For one, Aristotle Papanikolaou asserts a theological Orthodox foundation supportive of liberal, democratic principles (2012, 1-12). The role of Orthodoxy in several Eastern European nations, as well as recent trends in the newly independent Orthodox Church of Ukraine, seem to support this idea and dispel any generalizations related to Orthodox Christianity and totalitarianism.

Structural Persistence and the Legacy of Religious Totalitarianism

The critical juncture for the churches occurred during the early Sovietization period when the hierarchy of these churches, under varying degrees of duress, decided on one of two paths: (1) to resist overtly and covertly the encroachment of Bolshevism on their churches' structural and institutional integrity or (2) to gradually become subservient to the regime. For the latter, structural incentives were such that many churches adopted both the institutional and attitudinal traits of the Soviet regime. Historical Institutionalism suggests that these same structural and attitudinal traits "endure in the absence of the processes that initially led to their establishment" (Mahoney 2001, 8). Extensive fieldwork has helped extract the following sources of continuity from a church's past, which are pertinent to the post-1991 religious environment.

Church Politicization

For churches that acquiesced, Soviet policies gradually altered identity in a way that institutionalized political affiliations over public ones. Church leaders began to increasingly measure institutional success against a backdrop of political maneuvering based on power and influence. Essentially, institutions adopted the political culture of the Soviet regime. Of the three categories of political culture described by Almond and Verba, subject political culture comes nearest to describing that particular culture:

> "Here there is a high frequency of orientations toward a differentiated political system and toward the output aspects of the system, but orientations toward specifically input objects, and toward the self as an active participant, approach zero. The subject is aware of specialized government authority; he is affectively oriented to it, perhaps taking pride in it, perhaps disliking it; and he evaluated it either as legitimate or as not. But the relationships toward the system, the output, administrative, or downward flow side of the political system is

essentially passive, although there is a limited form of competence that is appropriate in a subject culture" (1963, 19).

Frederick Barghoorn has applied Almond and Verba's design to the political culture of the Soviet Union. He stressed the combination of low levels of subject competence combined with "participation directed ultimately from the political center at the top of the command structure" (Cited in Welch 1993, 75-76). In the Soviet system, the state imposed a unique and authoritarian institutional arrangement for governing church-state relations in which it positioned itself as the patron and, as with all Soviet organs, political power was highly centralized and distributed from the top down (Towster 1948, 391). Autonomous activities were strictly forbidden and social institutions were required to "act as 'transmission belts' ensuring the implementation of party directives among their respective membership" (White 1994, 5). This vertical command structure facilitated the intense politicization of institutions that participated in the Soviet political process—where politicization refers to the the transformation of goals and perception of success from a non-political to a political nature. By exerting control over a particular institution, authorities were able to re-direct the perception of power to be grounded in one's association with the communist political establishment. For instance, the source of a mayor's power was purposefully changed from his constituents to his political superiors. Industry leaders, likewise, gauged their success not in market terms, but by criteria set by Soviet economic planners. Churches changed from a focus that included filling the pews and providing spiritual nourishment to citizens to less lofty and less noble goals. Church leaders and clergy underwent an identity transformation in their understanding of their personal career enhancement and their church's success as a whole. This politicization was a deliberate process facilitated by the Council of Religious Affairs.

The CRA acted as patron, using handouts in the form of appointments and favors in return for obedience. Interactions closely resembled a gift economy, where exchange of favors were agreed upon quid pro quo. Reciprocity, of course, was almost always to the advantage of the individual and not to the church. As such, church leaders gauged their perception of power against the barometer of political clout and material comfort. Church leaders recognized that their survival and their church's existence were entirely dependent upon satisfying the Soviet regime. Opportunistic and careerist leaders jockeyed for positions and status by cooperating with the authorities as a culture of accommodation and religious lethargy became pervasive in many churches. Perhaps the most blatant example of this was the assistance by some leaders in seeking out and destroying dissident religious members and movements. Equally egregious was the practice of church leaders intentionally suppressing spirituality among their own church membership.

The primary mechanism for creating a new Soviet Church was a continuous process of controlled personnel turnover. This politicization process was expedited by a recruitment strategy that placed strict control over seminaries and meticulously screened potential clergy. As Lenin's statement suggested, the intention was to screen out committed, competent priests and stock the clergy with uneducated and less devote personnel who were willing to play by Soviet rules. Non-conformist clergy were forced out and those more amenable to cooperation were promoted. Jane Ellis described this process in accounting for non-resistance on the part of hierarchies:

> "One of the reasons why none of the present hierarchs is likely to take such a step is quite simple because the process of selection carried out by the CRA has been aimed at ensuring that precisely the kind of person who might do so has been excluded from any position of leadership" (1996, 263).

Indeed, as early as 1913 Lenin hinted at this strategy in a letter to Gorky. He opined that to undermine the church, communists should deal with "a priest who violates young girls" over a moral and educated clergyman (Cited in Pospielovsky 1984, 53). Many of these church officials were not only selected by the CRA, but their activities were also largely dictated by that agency. Dimitry Pospielovksy points out that the CRA used many of the clergy from the state-created Renovationist churches to stock subservient churches in the USSR. The Renovationist movement was disbanded in the 1940s, but several of its leaders who were unquestionably careerist, opportunistic, and supportive of the regime were given church positions in the Russian Orthodox Church and other national churches (ibid., 60-80). Ultimately, it is impossible to measure the level of religiosity of these men or to clearly discern their motives. However, an internal government report by the Council of Religious Affairs issued in 1982 sheds light on the character of hierarchs.

"Both in words and deeds [they] affirm not only loyalty but also patriotism towards the socialist society, strictly observe the laws on cults and educate the parish clergy and believers in the same spirit, realistically understand that our state is not interested in proclaiming the role of religion and the church in society and do not display any particular activeness in extending the influence of Orthodoxy among the population" (Ellis 1996a, 216).

Whether or not this loyalty to the state was forced or was willingly extended is unknowable. However, these leaders were groomed for decades in an institutional design created entirely by Soviet leaders. That post-Stalinist design encouraged political over public alliances. Soviet religious policies and communist political culture structured incentives in such a way as to motivate religious leaders to alter their institutional arrangements from the public to the political sphere and to invest in political identities rather than public ones.

This incentive-based system altered church elites' perception of power. The term "power" with regard to churches is better understood as the number and strength of what can be called channels of influence. These channels, whether political, cultural, social or legal are the means by which a church disseminates ideas and enacts policies. Prior to the onset of communist rule, Petrine churches had many channels of influence at their disposal. These ranged from religious education in schools, to political alliances with the ruling regime, to open access to the public for propagation of doctrine. For co-opted institutions, such as the Russian Orthodox Church, the legacy of the USSR is the weakening of many of these channels in favor of political modes of influence. This was particularly true in the 1990s. In his analysis of political change in post-Soviet Russia, Michael McFaul defines power as "the resources at one's disposal to realize one's preferred outcome in a specific issue area" (2001,

17). In terms of Soviet religious policy, the state attempted to control all resources at a church's disposal.

Religious elites of subservient churches gradually acclimatized to the new command-economy institutional design for religious life in the latter Soviet era. Design features included political machinations by senior church leaders and the repression of religious activity of unsanctioned religious groups. Church officials began to realize the increasing benefits of moving down the path paved by Soviet planners. Richard Deeg notes, "Overtime actors operating within the institutions that define a particular path become more adept and knowledgeable and use this to enhance the efficiency of the institutions" (2001, 9). Jane Ellis has noted that the subservient position of the churches gradually increased as their societal ties were cut. And that the "relations between church and state took on something of the nature of a bargaining relationship after the war: the church threw its weight behind the state during the war, and afterwards it assisted in the regime's drive for hegemony in Eastern Europe and in the subsequent peace campaigns" (1996a, 261).

Favoritism was the main means by which the state distributed political rewards to subservient clergy who were willing to stifle religious activity and vocally support the Communist Party. For the latter activity, clergy would often be called upon to deny Soviet oppression and fan the flames of the peace movements in international bodies such as the World Council of Churches. Metropolitan Filaret of Kiev stated in a television interview, "I am surprised that our Church and believers are considered persecuted. No one is persecuted for religious convictions in the Soviet Union . . . The attitude of the Soviet State to the needs of the Church are considerate and understanding" (Ellis 1996a, 209). Over time, the most accommodating clergy rose to positions of power and received political rewards, primarily in the form of personal favors for their vigor in supporting state policy. After the fall of communism, the perception of power shaped by the Soviet experience remained, and some church leaders continued to view church success through the prism of the previous system. Indeed, church leaders displayed remarkably little reticence in entering the political arena after 1991.

Church Administrative Structure

Churches also inherited a poor administrative apparatus for competing in the post-1991 religious environment. Speaking of Western Europe, John Madeley describes the process by which state-sponsored churches lose competitiveness:

> "Long-established mono-confessionalism also has its own pathologies, regardless of confession. Insofar as a virtual confessional monopoly in a particular territory has been maintained by positive state support on the one hand and the repression of challenges on the other, established churches might be expected to become less vital as organizations. They no longer depended for their sustenance on mobilizing support within society, looking instead to those in authority within the state to provide, pursuant to the bargain of mutual support between 'Crown and Altar'. Finke, Iannacone and others trace to this circumstance the 'hollowing out' of the established churches of much of Europe. Protected from the challenges of competition in an open religious 'market' of the sort which patently exists in the USA, many, if not most, of Europe's established churches are seen progressively to have lost the ability to maintain levels of commitment and loyalty without which they have tended to go into institutional decline" (Madeley 2016, 32)

The particular circumstances of subservient churches of the USSR were different, but the outcomes were largely similar. After 1991, many churches possessed monopolistic traits such as inefficiency and non-competitiveness because they were shielded from competition in a closed market. Indeed, the process of atrophy and the loss of competitiveness was all the more profound for state-supported Soviet churches because the sponsor, the Soviet state, was also dedicated to ruining and disestablishing the patron. Churches occupied the rare and unenviable position of having been persecuted monopolies. The hobbling of ecclesiastic competencies was not simply a by-product of state repression, but a methodical process on the part of authorities to weaken the church's ability to operate efficiently. In the free market of the 1990s, churches such as the Russian Orthodox Church were inhibited by these negative characteristics of monopolies, while at the same time not benefiting from legislative protection.

The organizational inefficiencies also stem from a Soviet strategy that emphasized the centralization of power within these churches and the weakening of parish level participation. The state wanted to work with and control only one entity and was not concerned with winning the political alliance of every parish priest. This was a direct reversal of the early Soviet religious strategy, stemming from the 1918 legislation that only recognized local congregations as legal ecclesiastical units. The Soviets later desired to centralize the control process to such an extent that the dominant churches were also seen to represent all denominations in a given country (See Simon 1974). Where religious hierarchical structures were not in place to control, as in the Muslim communities of Central Asia, organizational structures such as the Tashkent Directorate were created. This hierarchical organization and its post-1991 offshoots were inherently distant from the 'rank and file' follower of Islam. The dismantlement of the church at the parish level continued unabated in the 1990s and 2000s resulting in an estrangement forming between church leaders, local clergy, and parishioners.

In effect, the Soviet approach restructured many of these churches into a top-down organization. In the experience of the Russian Orthodox Church, the state forced into submission the Local Council, which was canonically superior and closer to the rank and file than the Synod and the patriarch. The Local Council was only convened three times under communism and its decisions and agendas were a "rubber-stamping function" (ibid., 110). By placing the Synod as the supreme religious authority, the church effectively "placed the pastor in a position of a hireling" (Bourdeaux 1995, 185). Furthermore, parish-level interaction between clergy and parishioners was significantly restricted. Many of the administrative problems faced by the Russian Orthodox Church post-1991 may partially stem from the severing of ties between local clergy and leadership. This was pivotal because it eliminated a historical strength of Orthodoxy, namely, that local clergy were close to the people and "more assimilated into the structure of society" (Madeley 2000). Survey data suggests that "Communist rule caused a weakening of church ties in the population and a decline in the social significance of church and religion" (Pollack, 2010).

Another structural consequence of Soviet oversight was the cessation of pastoral mobility. Churches were prohibited from moving priests to parishes where they were needed and as a result any pre-Soviet mechanisms for effective administration and alignment of resources quickly atrophied. Decision-making, by extension, was taken from the parish-level clergy and consolidated to often isolated and uninformed bishops. At the same time, the great shortage of priests forced bishops to ordain laymen or reinstate aged retired clergy to work in the dioceses (Davis 2003, 134). Tibor Fabiny detailed the "theological and moral deterioration" of the Hungarian Lutheran Church due to this phenomenon (2004, 11). He indicated that in a sense, the church "beheaded" itself by deciding to collaborate with the regime (ibid., 25). Decades of Soviet rule resulted in the creation of a new religious cadre with few tools to effectively administer spiritual care on the individual to congregational level. Local clergymen that only knew "frightful oppression and painful accommodation to the state" (Schleifman 1998, 159) were dramatically different from their pre-revolutionary predecessors. Many were trained more in Marxist-Leninist ideology than biblical studies. Soviet religious law prohibited all religious activity that was not sacramental or liturgical. Surveys regarding the religious knowledge of current priests show staggering ignorance, with many clergymen unable to define the central tenets of their religion. The Soviet press frequently portrayed such clergy in the Soviet Union as "avaricious, money grabbing, irreligious people who have joined the church solely for what they can get out of it" (Ellis 1996, 82). This description was certainly not accurate for the majority of Soviet-era priests. Nonetheless, decades of Soviet religious policy transformed clergy from having an embedded spiritual role in society to occupying a largely ceremonial one.

The centralization and breakdown of efficiency of church administration mirrored that of almost every other Soviet institution. In short, the Soviet-era severely weakened the production of religious goods and services. These churches after 1991 were not too dissimilar from newly privatized industries that had a weak chain of command, a shortage of capable employees, an underdeveloped distribution network, and a product unsuited for the post-Soviet marketplace. The recognition by many church leaders of their churches' non-competitive posture undoubtedly influenced church policy formulation in the transition.

Internal Schism

The legacy of Sovietism has also been felt in churches' internal constitution, often provoking schisms (Ramet 1998, 282). William Fletcher described how Sergius' proclamation in support of the state, bred resentment and dissatisfaction within Orthodoxy, which resulted in schismatic movements:

> "It was the change in the Church's position from political neutrality to acceptance of the Soviet political regime which initiated the rise of underground Orthodoxy as a whole. A number of important and influential Church leaders refused to submit to this change of course, and opposition movements formed around them which, whatever their numerical strength at first, were an immensely serious challenge to the Russian Orthodox Church from the point of view of the stature of their leadership. The movements which arose around the dissident hierarchs were soon to experience an immense growth, and would exercise a profound influence on subsequent development of underground Orthodoxy in the U.S.S.R" (Fletcher 1971, 274).

The internal disturbance arising from misgivings over church closeness to the state was exacerbated by the Soviet religious policy of the 1920s and 1930s that encouraged break-off movements. The Soviets created competitive movements and propped up schismatic bodies such as the Living Church and Renovated Church in an attempt to disestablish mainstream Orthodoxy. A leading Bolshevik stated, "We have nothing against the current schism. We should make use of it to tear the masses completely away from all clergy, from any church, from every religion" (Pospielovsky 1984, 163). This policy, however, was reversed in favor of a concerted effort to co-opt the dominant churches. The Soviet state demanded a reunification of all splinter movements under the central control of the subservient church. In many ways, this centralization policy only drove schismatic elements further away from the perceived compromised original church. After the critical juncture period, segments of the church that disagreed with the organization's links with an atheistic body went underground.[2]

Jane Ellis noted that statements by the hierarchs of churches "that complete freedom of religion exist[ed] in the Soviet Union have earned them stringent public criticism from some clergy and many lay members of the church believe[d] almost exactly the opposite" (1996a, 211). For many clergy, they had no alternative but to break communion with the church and "go into the catacombs" (Andreyev 1950). Orthodox splinter churches included the Russian Orthodox Church Abroad and the Catacomb Church. Variants of the True Orthodox Church also existed in Georgia and Belarus in response to corruption perceived in the national church. Father Subev's assessment of the Bulgarian Orthodox hierarchy mirrored that of many of these underground members: "Our church is sick and its disease comes right from the head. The diagnosis is dementia. The patriarch was appointed by the communists and has always served them faithfully" (Ellis 1996a, 283). After the collapse of communism, many of these groups initially showed a reluctance to rejoin their parent church. Even in cases where underground clergy and schismatic organizations have returned, they have demonstrated a propensity to threaten disunion at the slightest provocation, often resulting in church paralysis.

Interestingly, this process of Sovietization, inefficient administration and public dissatisfaction was also evident with Islam in Central Asia. Indeed, the Islamic leaders in Central Asia serve as the ultimate example of the subservient path because the hierarchies were not co-opted, but rather created to further Soviet interests. These Central Asian nations

---

2 There were essentially two waves of Soviet-era schismatic movements that were initially at odds with each other. The first wave was the Soviet supported Renovationists in Russia and the republics. These were pro-Soviet, anti-church establishment entities which the state used in its attempts to destroy the dominant religion. They were recognised and supported by the state and given property by the dominant churches. Many of these churches operated until the early 1930s when they were deemed no longer useful to the state because of progress made in the subordination of the dominant churches. The second wave, which occurred after the critical juncture, was the antithesis of the first. These splinter groups were anti-Soviet, and tried to keep intact the integrity of the church. They were, however, also anti-Patriarchate, but for reasons that were different from the earlier movement.

lacked a centralized Islamic organization prior to Soviet occupation. Sunni religious practices in the region were bound more by theological symmetry than a structural hierarchy. Soviet authorities promptly recognized the necessity of inverting this arrangement. The state could not control what did not exist. The Spiritual Administration of the Muslims of Central Asia established in 1943 began the unnatural institutionalization of Islam. The Muslim Board of Central Asia—also called Spiritual Administration of the Muslims of Central Asia and Kazakhstan (SADUM), included all five republics, and was formed in and operated out of Tashkent. Hafeez Malik writes that the board was established and a mufti was installed "in order to control the Muslim population through religion. That was the purpose of the Soviet policy. These boards were not created to promote Islam or to propagate Islam but to control the Muslim population" (1991, 11). In order to secularize Islam, authorities quickly replaced the Sharia religious law with Soviet legal institutions, substituted secular holidays for religious holidays, and restructured Islamic institutions so as to co-opt religious leaders and weaken Islam as a social force.

The religious dignitaries which stocked the muftiyat were selected for their political dependability. Because the muftiyat was a communist-created entity, the mufti was seen by many Islamic adherents as a Soviet stooge. Dissent was widespread and a divide appeared between official Islam, represented by the Soviet picked mufti, and unofficial Islam, represented by myriad groups which viewed the board as illegitimate. After 1991, the Tashkent based administration was subdivided into national muftiyats and the unofficial Islamic movements were able to gain international attention and Middle Eastern financing. Leaders in the national muftiyat had a vested interest in insuring that the status and prominence, which were afforded them in the past, be perpetuated into the transition. These boards continued to discharge their duties and served in a similar capacity as a mouthpiece for the state. The authoritarian regimes in the region, coupled with the very real threat of Islamic insurgency caused governments to relate to their respective muftiyat as the Soviet state related to the Tashkent Board. These boards differ very little in function or appearance from their parent organization. The Soviet-era divergence of official and unofficial Islam has persisted in the transition. Official or formal

Islam today loosely mirrors the Soviet-instituted structure of directorates and mufti recognized by governing authorities. Unofficial or informal Islam consists of the groups (IMU and Hizb ut-Tahrir) and movements (Wahhabism) that were thought to be a threat to the security of the state. Both sides of this divide are adamantly opposed to one another.

The creation and subordination of the Kazakhstani Muslim organization is loosely representative of the other four descendants of the Soviet Tashkent-based board. While still Party First Secretary, Nursultan Nazarbayev withdrew the Kazakhstan Sunni community from the Muslim Board of Central Asia and installed Ratbek hadji Nysanbayev as Kazakhstan's first independent mufti. However, few considered him independent of the state and many accused him of fleecing church funds and improper contact with the Soviet and Kazakhstani state security apparatus. Collaboration between Nazabayev's government and the Administration has been extensive. Legislative attempts have been made to increase the influence of the Spiritual Administration over all Islamic activity. That body has resorted to heavy-handed tactics to gather all operating mosques under its jurisdiction. For instance, the Union of Muslims of Kazakhstan, a non-state organization, has experienced intense discriminatory measures stemming from its unwillingness to be absorbed by the Administration. The Union's head, Murat Telibekov, states that a 2002 national security "law strengthens state control over the life of believers. And the muftiyat, which follows the will of the government, has not missed the opportunity to exploit this" (Rotar 2005).

For Christian churches, much of the internal discord of the Soviet era has also carried over and resulted in churches having to expend energy and resources on these disputes at the expense of focusing on the restoration of societal ties. The decades-long struggle between rival Orthodox churches in Ukraine is the most well-known example of post-Soviet schism. That country had no less than three Orthodox churches vying for the allegiance of Ukrainians. While this dynamic will be explained in more depth in later chapters, it is enough to say at this point that the long and contentious process that eventually led to the January 2019 autocephalous status of the Ukrainian Orthodox Church had its roots in the Soviet era.

Credibility Crisis

The pattern of church-state interaction under communism has also affected churches' reputation among would-be parishioners. Sabrina Ramat notes the importance of "credibility and even legitimacy in the eyes of the people. A church, after all, is judged not merely by the plausibility of its doctrines or the stability (or adaptability) of its rituals, but by its political behavior" (1998, 276). The tendency to view churches during the Soviet-era as compromised and corrupt stems from both intense anti-church propaganda and a church's own statements of support to the regime which "then it followed that the Church, despite its protestations of nationalism and love of homeland, was a servant of the enemy" (Ramet 1998, 276). Jane Ellis described how:

> "Many members of the church continued to have to suffer very great hardship as a consequence of their faith, and the subservient church leadership not only failed to help them but denied publicly and repeatedly that they were suffering for their beliefs" (Ellis 1996, 262).

One larger legacy of the Soviet-era on the general public after 1991 was a "predisposition to distrust" (Mishler and Rose 2001, 32). A 2001 ten-nation study on public trust in institutions concluded that the "overall pattern in post-communist countries is one of severe skepticism bordering on outright distrust of current institutions" (ibid., 41). More specifically regarding churches, the survey found that the trust placed in religious entities was low with 39 percent of respondents distrusting the institution. Although religious organizations ranked above most other institutions, they had a lower level of public confidence than both the media and the military. This distrust was found to stem from dissatisfaction and frustration with institutions and not from an underlying culture of mistrust. In explaining political trust, the study determined that institutional explanations better suited the Soviet and post-Soviet era than cultural theories (ibid., 39-40).

Research also shows a correlation between distrust and a church's level of engagement with the Soviet state. Hank Johnston noted that religiosity is relatively high in countries where the dominant church was actively involved in resisting the Soviet regime and in the fight for independence. He points to both Poland and the Czech Republic where the role of the Catholic Church in opposing the Communist State resulted in the church maintaining or even strengthening its role after independence (1994). Similarly, Barbara Strassberg writes that the Catholic Church has been influential in the political history of Poland; and after 1945, it acted as the catalyst for opposition to the Communist party (1998, 350). Polish Catholicism, therefore, became inseparably associated with nationalism, freedom, human rights, and democracy as the country moved from communism to democracy.

But for subservient churches, there was no peace-diffident after 1991 as distrust lingered. This crisis of credibility is vital as it may precede the actual breakdown of an institution. Claus Offe discusses how institutional collapse may be proceeded by entities failing to:

> "[..] inculcate the norms and preferences that condition the loyalty of members. In this case, institutions stop to "make sense" to member and to be "taken seriously" by them or by the wider social domain for which an institution claims validity and consequently the institution loses support and recognition. Scandals and cases of corruption in which representative agents of an institution become seen as betraying core values are particularly powerful causes of the sudden loss of an institution's credibility (1996, 219).

He further states that institutions may break apart because of their "manifest failure in performing the functions with which they are charged" (Offe 1996, 220). Former subservient churches were certainly not doomed for collapse after 1991, but the consequences of the critical juncture choice likely had detrimental effect on post-1991 activities. This in turn made them vulnerable in the new religious environment. Offe explains, "Institutions may decay because alternatives emerge which allow for the satisfaction of those needs and the fulfilment of those functions over which the institution used to hold a monopoly" (1996, 219). Immediately after 1991, many believers and former rank and file members of the historically dominant churches appeared disenchanted with the church and were thus more susceptible to proselytization. This legitimacy gap experienced on the part of co-opted churches has proven a key determinant in their position toward religious protectionism.

Conversely, those religious organizations that were resistant to state domination and politicization maintained their credibility in the eyes of the people. Bohdan Cywinski wrote of such churches, which "deprived of political power, it possesses only moral authority—and in this lies its strength . . . Its moral authority is inversely proportional to its participation in political power" (Cited in Ramet 1998, 276). By opting for the resistance policy choice, these churches retained a degree of moral authority and as a result found themselves on firmer ground with the public in the more open post-Soviet marketplace.

Church Political Culture

Correlated with the politicization of the clergy was the steady conversion of church culture to harmonize with communist political culture. Here, political culture is defined as the "attitudinal and behavioral matrix within which the political system is located" (White 1979, 1). Almond and Powell suggest that a group's political culture determines, "the conduct of individuals in their political roles, the content of their political demands, and their responses to law" (1978, 25). The close interaction between co-opted churches with the Soviet political machine led many clergy to adopt to varying degrees Soviet political culture. Frederick Starr states that post-communist leaders have been shaped by their "personal, communal, and national pasts, and are applying on the job whatever truths they have derived from that historical experience" (1994, 4). This emphasis on the inertia and continuity of Soviet political culture can partially explain the stagnation of liberalization in a broader since in the region (Molchanov 2002, 19). The carry-over attitudes in post-Soviet communities are routinely referred to as the old Soviet mentality. From the judiciary to electoral systems, all former Soviet republics, even the three EU members, have found it hard to shake off the old way of doing things. Paramount among the values learned through socialization into an undemocratic regime were authoritarian and autocratic inclinations (Mishler and Rose 2001, 2). One observer of the religious sphere in the region notes that in many countries "the traditional churches are the last appendage of Soviet power" (Interview 2005. Anonymous, non-Orthodox leader, Tbilisi, 20 Nov).

The legacy of the Soviet period on church-state relations has been described as one of "legal and illegal state surveillance of religious life and active intervention of the state authorities in church affairs" (Plokhy 1999, 10). It was also a period of active cooperation between the two entities. The combination of state favoritism, the enforcement of anti-democratic polices, and the selection of accommodating leaders resulted in the prevalence of authoritarian and anti-democratic leanings among some church leaders. These learned traits are significant because after 1991, the majority of churches did not experience any sort of reshuffling of church executives. Subservient leaders that rose to positions of authority during the communist-era are, by and large, still lead churches. In detailing the difficulty of abandoning a subject political culture and adopting a participant political culture, Almond and Verba stated that "a successful shift from a subject to a participant culture involves the diffusion of positive orientations toward a democratic infrastructure, the acceptance of norms of civic obligation, and the development of a sense of civic competence among a substantial proportion of the population" (1963, 27). As we will see in the ensuing chapters, some of these clergy have carried over the Soviet value system into the transition and have become "the new oppressor, trying to hound out foreign churches and missionaries competing to save souls" (Dixon 1997).

Conclusion

In summary, four areas of continuity from the Soviet experience can reasonably be assumed to be possessed, in some degree, within formerly subservient traditional churches:

1. A politicization of the church in which church leaders increasingly resort to political channels of influence and view organizational gains in terms of political access (Church Politicization).
2. A poor administrative structure for competing in post-1991 religious environment (Church Administrative Structure).

3. An insecure external and internal foundation due to a perceived diminishment of church credibility and legitimacy (Internal Schism and Legitimacy Gap).
4. A hierarchy and clergy that harbor authoritarian, autocratic and, discriminatory tendencies (Church Political Culture).

The purpose of this chapter was not to be a definitive account of the effects of Sovietism on churches, but to extract those sources of continuity that impact clergy attitudes towards religious pluralism. The institutions that were influenced the most by the subject political culture had a more difficult time adopting to the present participant culture. Almond and Verba wrote:

> "The mixed subject-participant culture, if it persists over a long period of time, also changes the character of the subject subculture. During the democratic interludes the authoritarian-oriented groups must compete with the democratic ones within a formally democratic framework. In other words, they must develop a defensive political infrastructure of their own. While this does not transform the subject subculture into a democratic one, it certainly changes it, often to a significant degree" (1963, 26).

The machinations of many traditional churches post-1991 suggest that authoritarian-oriented subject subcultures did, in fact, encounter difficulty operating within a democratic environment. The defensive posture of co-opted churches in competing with other institutions in the transition shows a great deal of continuity with the Soviet past.

Almond and Verba assert, "Political cultures may or may not be congruent with structures of the political system" (ibid, 21). Indeed, this is precisely the dichotomy that existed in Russia for many years after 1991. Once oriented to a subject political system, Russia changed, quite literally overnight, into a participant political system. Yet remnants or political subcultures from the previous subject political culture remained. "Even the most fully developed participant cultures will contain surviving strata of subjects and parochials" (ibid, 27). The nations of the former Soviet Union would certainly not be classified as the most fully developed participant culture. These hold-out subcultures include, among other institutions, several of the historically dominant churches. Thus, with regard to co-opted churches, they are stuck in the subject political culture and its orientation towards the "specialized structure of the central authoritarian system" (ibid, 27). In Russia, the authoritative subcultures, to include that ingrained in the Russian Orthodox Church, endured long enough to witness and participate in Vladimir Putin reconstituting authoritarianism across the nation.

The actions of formerly subservient churches have validated the paramount concept of Historical Institutionalism that "political identities can become as 'sticky' as the institutions that foster them, and thus, ironically, can even outlast these policies and institutions" (Luong 2002, 101). History is a clear determinant of action. For historically dominant churches, the critical juncture that was determinative of that history was the decision between the collaboration policy choice and resistance policy choice. For those churches that chose the former, the 'stickiness' of the past has made it difficult to "purge their mindset of the operative assumptions and behavioral habits needed to survive in the communist order" (Ramet 1993, 353). Dimitry Pospielovsky, in describing the Russian Orthodox Church in the transition, notes that it "has failed to find in itself the living force to lead Russian Society morally or spiritually, as was hoped by both believers and non-believers when the collapse of the Soviet State had become obvious" (Quoted in Davis 2003, 245).

The four elements of the Soviet legacy are essential to understand post-1991 developments. This is because the the degree to which a church was co-opted by the Soviet state is negatively correlated with a church's success in the new religious market and its posture on issues of religious pluralism. Simply, those churches that were heavily subservient and experienced, to an intense degree, the legacies of Sovietism have consequently been less competitive, its members more susceptible to proselytizing, and its leaders more willing to rely on political subsides and state protectionist measures to restrict market access. The experience of many of these churches under communism is analogous to prisoners of war undergoing torture. Military studies have shown that while every soldier will eventually break, those soldiers that resist the longest have a better survival rate in captivity. The reason for this is that they keep a degree of self-respect and honor in the eyes of their peers by resisting.

Conversely, soldiers that give in easily are less likely to cope well in captivity. Similarly, as will be demonstrated in the next chapter, the success of churches after captivity in a new religious environment is determined by previous choices. Ramet described one such church that broke, as being "weak, divided, it's very ranks depleted by decades of counter socialization, and shorn of virtually all credibility." The church has been in "no condition to evangelise effectively, having to concentrate its energies on solving its own internal disputes" (1998, 283).

LEGACIES OF SOVIETISM 59

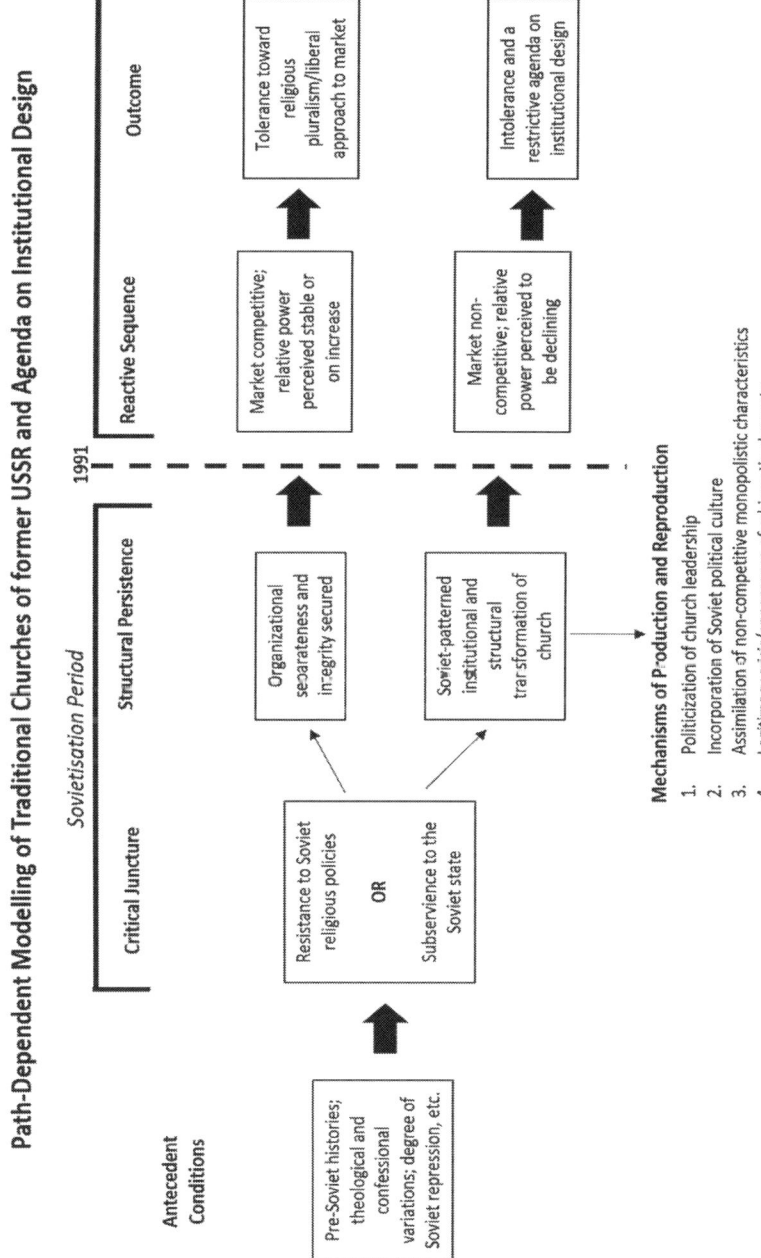

Figure 2. Path-Dependent Model of Churches in former USSR

3. Post-Soviet Market Features
The Immediate-Strategic Context

With 70 years of Soviet legacy ingrained into church DNA, clergy almost literally stumbled from Soviet captivity into the wild unknown of a free-market economy. While circumstances differed, the regulatory framework and general environment which greeted churches contrasted remarkedly with institutional arrangements that were present under Soviet rule. A suppressed religious market was replaced by the abrupt infusion of diverse religious groups. Their presence profoundly altered the spiritual landscape. Anthony Gill notes that at no time or place in the history of the world has a religious marketplace changed so quickly and dramatically as in the former Soviet Union (1998, 188). This new religious playing field, shaped largely by the presences of new entrants, served as an exogenous shock to most churches. Even denominations considered more open, such as Catholic churches of the region, had never experienced Western-style pluralism to such an extent. With regard to church-state interaction, the new market features made the previous power arrangements with the state obsolete.

This chapter explores how this drastic change in market structure has influenced political strategies of churches as it relates to religious pluralism. Special attention will be paid to the contours of the new market structure and its effect on the balance of power or influence among churches. As noted in chapter One, the perception of relative adjustment in power by a particular church is rooted both in constraints inherited from the Soviet past and the challenges presented by a free-for-all religious marketplace. The two converge to provide the context against which elites shape church strategy.

As we move into the immediate-strategic context of the post-Soviet religious environment, a transition to a more agency-based framework is required. The rigidity of a purely structural model is inadequate to properly grasp decision making processes, particularly on matters of religious pluralism and liberties. The study of religious elites, like most aspects of metaphysics, has always been problematic for social scientists. For centuries academic inquiry shied away from in-depth analysis of religion, viewing it as irrational and therefore impossible to study or define. Serious science, replete with observables and testable hypotheses, was never applied to religious behavior in any comprehensive way. Fortunately, beginning in the 1990s, a novel approach to the study of religion appeared that provided a working framework in which such a metaphysical realm could be studied with increased methodological rigor. In so doing, it has brought religious behavior out of the clouds and the vagary of spiritual experience and into a more manageable and verifiable realm. This approach conceptualizes the religious sphere in terms of goods and services, supply and demand, and producers and customers. Religious organizations and movements ranging from the powerful Roman Catholic Church to a start-up congregation in a residential apartment are considered as suppliers of a religious commodity in a structured marketplace (Finke 1997, 46). If we take as a constant that "church workers are motivated by the same sort of self-interest that motivates secular workers" (Iannacconne 1997, 40), then economic theories relating to markets, competition, and regulations can help us understand factors playing on churches since 1991.

This chapter will employ a rational choice framework to nest the Soviet legacies of the previous chapter into post-1991 market dynamics. The religious situation in the former Soviet Union can best be understood when conceptualized as the united behavior of religious consumers and producers interacting in a religious economy (ibid., 27). From this theoretical basis, useful insights emerge on demand-side phenomena occurring among Russian citizenship as well as the supply-side behavior of the Russian Orthodox Church and other religious entities. The common historical experiences of many of these large churches as well as the similar nature of the post-Soviet religious marketplaces lend themselves to an examination of these churches in both a cross-regional and rational choice context.

In his landmark book, Anthony Gill points out that "rational choice explanations require specification of the actors, their preferences (or goals) and the constraint they face" (1998, 49). I will examine the goals of church hierarchy, the obstacles they encounter in achieving those goals in the transitional society, and how religious protectionism is seen as a way to alleviate the problems caused by those constraints (ibid, 50). The underlining premise is that many formerly co-opted church hierarchies are embedded within a similar socio-cultural context, formed by the intersection of past and present constraints, that structure their actions and lead them to oppose religious pluralism. Religious market structure undoubtedly influences church political strategy on myriad issues. Since 1991, the dramatic transformation in the market structure has led some of these "formerly hegemonic religions to use the political arena to protect their spiritual territory from aggressive newcomers" (ibid, 188).

Rational Choice Framework

For years, scholars from various social science disciplines have applied the economic theory of rational choice to better understand the behavioral patterns of individuals and institutions in numerous contexts. The underpinnings of the theory can be condensed into three assumptions:

> Assumption 1: *Individuals act rationally, weighing the costs and benefits of potential actions, and choosing those actions that maximize their benefits.*

> Assumption 2: *The ultimate preferences that individuals use to assess costs and benefits tend not to vary much from person to person or from time to time.*

> Assumption 3: *Social outcomes constitute the equilibrium that emerges from the aggregation and interaction of individual actions* (Iannaccone 1997, 26).

The theory is predicated on the rationality and uniformity of individual behavior. An individual's choice, with all other things being equal, will tend to maximize pleasure or gain and minimize pain or loss. This same cost-benefit rational calculation is applicable both on the demand-side and the supply-side. For example, all business firms when faced with similar circumstances will opt for the path that maximizes profits and minimizes costs. This explains why economies experience "capital and labor flow from low-reward to high-reward uses" (Arrow and Colomatto 1996, XIV). The utility maximization principle is allied with the assumption that individual judgement with regard to evaluating a cost/benefit choice is always constant. As a result, the actions of individuals can be generalized to predict a variety of systemic social outcomes. The choice process has three fundamental elements: rational calculation, individual preferences, and exogenous constraints. Anthony Gill's simplified equation states: Choice = f (rational calculation, preferences, and exogenous constraints) (1998, 195).

If preferences are held as constant and individuals and firms always maximize benefits, then a rational choice model "must explain changing behavior in terms of changing constraints" (Iannacconne 1997, 28).

> Corollary: *Behavioral changes (over time) are the consequence of changed constraints; behavioral differences (across individuals) are the consequence of differing constraints* (ibid.).

Rational choice theorists are primarily concerned with constraints on an individual's or institution's behavior. These constraints can take a variety of forms. They can be internal or external as well as immediate or historical. Behavioral changes, therefore, are modelled as optimal reactions to varying circumstances (ibid., 27). And interpersonal or inter-institutional differences are understood as being caused by differing constraints. The legacies of communism, as put forth in the previous chapter, can best be understood as post-1991 constraints on church behavior. In addition to these legacy constraints, other fetters, independent of Soviet history, have materialized post 1991 including but not limited to increased competition, secularization trends, and laity interfaith mobility.

Rational Choice Methodology of Religion

Before delving deeper into the consequences of these constraints, the theoretical scaffolding of rational choice theory needs to be built around the behavior of churches and their adherents. Those theorists that apply rational choice to the study of religion reject the irrationality of belief and subscribe to Hume's view that "a passion can never, in any sense be call'd unreasonable" (Cited in Allingham 1999, 1). They assert that a theory of religion should be guided by empirical research and rest on methodological individualism which examines social phenomenon from the viewpoint of individual decision makers. Laurence Iannaccone maintains that the study of religion must be approached like any other societal phenomenon and "provide theoretical explanations for observed empirical regularities" (1995, 78). The approach sprung from what proponents consider to be the complete failure and inadequacies of previous theories of religious behavior. Rodney Stark points out that previous models were predicated on the irrationality of religion and therefore, social scientists studied religion half-heartedly and without a great deal of scientific rigor. For one thing, the early theorists were strongly anti-religious and approached the subject subjectively as "childishness" (Freud 1927, 88).

The approach, much like rational choice theory in general, has not gone without criticism. Many academics believe that because religious belief is such an indistinct social experience, rationalistic explanations are impractical for analysis. Steve Bruce, perhaps the most outspoken academic opponent, maintains that "sociological explanation for such a broad phenomenon as religion over such a broad range of countries is impossible" (1999, 115). But even Bruce acknowledged that the approach, which treats religion as a commodity and assumes maximizing utility, has value in certain societies that have largely been secularized (2008, 98). Most post Soviet nations, particularly Russia, fit that description.

The framework for the social scientific study of religion accepts the core guiding principles of rational choice theory and the corollary influence of changing constraints. (rationality + constant preference + changing constraints = outcome). Rationality is believed to underlie consumer and producer decision-making processes. The utility maximization principle is equally applicable to both the behavior of average religious consumers and churches. Notwithstanding slight variations in preference, consumers of religious goods and producers of spiritual commodities typically act according to their interests. Nonetheless, while religious producers are always seen as optimizers, the taste of consumers is dependent upon socialization and past experiences.

Of course, the usage of an economic theory to study sociological phenomena seems inherently contradictory, especially with the inexact nature of religious belief. Economists emphasize analytical power, while sociologists place importance on the descriptive closeness to social reality. As Siegwart Lindenberg notes, "Economists thus generally are unwilling to forego their highly simplified (and therefore often very unrealistic) models in favor of more realistic but analytically less powerful models, and sociologists generally are unwilling to forego descriptive richness" (1992, 4). The Method of Decreasing Abstraction helps bridge this divide and provides a path for rational choice theory to explain more abstract phenomenon. It combines the analytical power of the economic approach with the descriptive advantages of sociological and psychological approaches (ibid.). It succeeds in doing this by beginning with a very simplistic model and then incrementally making it more realistic. Siegwart Lindenberg summaries the method:

> "The method of decreasing abstraction (i.e., decreasing simplification) attempts to achieve theory driven analyses and empirical accuracy by taking model building to be a sequence of versions of theory in which empirical accuracy is stepwise approached, while the early versions of the theory provide analytical power" (1992, 6).

The framework, therefore, consists of a core set of guiding ideas (in this instance the three assumptions outlined previously) and bridge assumptions (supply-side assumptions to follow) that span the divide between the core and reality.

Rational choice theory has generated interesting and productive bridge assumptions on the demand and supply-side of religious economies. For my purposes, only assumptions and predictions germane to the subject matter at hand will be drawn out. Because the subject of this study is religious organizations generally, and the Russian Orthodox Church more specifically, supply-side assumptions will be emphasized. My paradigmatic approach relies on a microeconomic model of behavior, in which rational-actors form the cadre of religious firms that produce and distribute religious commodities in the form of metaphysical answers to philosophical questions in a competitive marketplace (Gill 2005, 10). While my focus will be on "entrepreneurs of faith" (Schmidt 1998, 72), several demand-side assumptions are essential in understanding the post-1991 religious environment. To help illustrate the following demand-side assumptions in practical applications, I appeal to my personal interactions with a number of Russian believers during my work in Siberia in the mid-1990s. Their names are changed, but their stories are true.

Demand-Side Assumptions

> Demand Assumption 1: *Individuals and households purchase religious commodities by combining money inputs (that pay for physical goods and services) with inputs of their own time* (Iannaccone 1997, 30).

Rational choice theories of household consumption revolve around the purchase of commodities and the rewards individuals derive from them. Religion is viewed as a good that people purchase (or produce) through monetary and time inputs, but its rewards are generally immaterial. A rational choice axiom states that "some desired rewards are limited in supply, including some that simply do not exist (in the physical world)" (Stark 1997, 7). As the attainment of salvation is rarely achieved in this life, people seek compensators for what Azzi and Ehrenberg call "afterlife consumption" (1975, 427) in the form of religious commodities, i.e. promises, forgiveness of sins, eternal perspective, comfort, and other fulfilling nonmaterial goods. Stark distinguishes religious compensators from religious rewards, "because one is the thing wanted, and the other is a proposal about gaining the reward" (1997, 7). Religious compensators explain the path by which the desired rewards may be obtained, through a long ritual process. Supernatural compensators can include rewards in the afterlife, release from suffering, and experience of total inner-bliss (Sherkat 1997, 69-71). Expenditures to obtain these compensators and to ultimately receive the desired rewards consist, among other things, of church attendance and contributions (Iannaccone 1997, 31). Rational choice theorists, therefore, maintain that people deliberating on the purchase of a religious commodity or on which religious firm to patronize are "individuals engaged in a rational process" (Neitz and Mueser 1997, 151). And as such, conclusions can be made on the collective activities of consumers and producers.

For instance, the idea of input substitution appears applicable to religious purchases. Empirical studies have shown that low-income families are more likely to be engaged in time-intensive religious practices while high-income households will substitute money for time. Church contributions among the rich have been found to be higher as a percentage of income than in low-income households. Income levels have in turn been linked to commodity preference. High-income households generally attend denominations that "rely strongly on the services of professional church employees, require less-time consuming rituals and hold fewer and shorter meetings" (Mangeloja 2003, 8). Religious contribution has also been correlated with what Laurence Iannaccone calls religious human capital.

> Demand Assumption 2: *As individuals and households consume religious commodities, they also accumulate a stock of religious human capital that enhances the satisfaction they derive from subsequent religious activity* (Iannacconne 1997, 32).

Religious human capital consists of a person's religious knowledge and skills in assisting the church and transmitting their spiritual experience to others. Laurence Iannaccone, who pioneers this new approach to religious activity, maintains that an understanding of religious human capital helps explain trends in "religious intermarriage, conversion ages, the relationship between church attendance and contributions, and the influence of upbringing and interfaith marriage on levels of religious participation" (1990, 297). Most significantly, the willingness of a person to convert to a church or switch denominations is reflective of a desire to match one's religious capital to a suitable supplier. In this and numerous other ways, "human capital shapes patterns of religious affiliation" (Iannaccone 1997, 32). For instance, low levels of religious capital among believers is corelated to religious choice based primarily on socio-cultural influences and not a result of long and thoughtful investigation. Those with little religious capital tend to be indifferent to suppliers' performance and will largely remain in the church in which they were born. Conversely, a rigorous assessment of a producer's competence and a propensity toward switching providers usually accompanies high religious capital.

Elena of Krasnoyarsk illustrates the importance of religious human capital in customer choice. A deeply spiritual mother of two, with a religiously indifferent husband, in 1995, she was relatively wealthy and an active participant in her Krasnoyarsk Orthodox community. An avid Bible reader, she was an enthusiastic parishioner with an extraordinary high level of religious capital. Yet she belonged to a church that provided little outlet for her to give meaningfully of her time. When introduced to a new, high-demand religious movement, it took only two weeks for her to abandon the faith of her birth. She was more than happy to give a significant portion of her income and over ten hours a week of her time to a new entrant church. Her experience exemplifies that, notwithstanding the low religious human capital of the Russian public after decades of atheism, a small segment of people with high human religious capital existed and were vulnerable to proselytization. Most religious market share developments post 1991 revolved around this cohort of believers possessing a high level of human religious capital (See Sherkat 1997). This small, but significant interfaith mobility, particularly in the 1990s, was not lost on the Russian Orthodox Church. Elena's local Orthodox priest was almost certainly aware of her religious choice.

> Demand Assumption 3: *For consumers searching for religious goods, the character of the producer stands as proxy to the quality of the product* (Hechter 1997, 151).

Since religious commodities are intangible, the reputation and image of religious firms is primarily what shapes consumer choice. Michael Hechter writes:

> "The accuracy of many promises made by a priest cannot be checked readily, since they often refer to events taking place in the hereafter. This assessment problem can be eased if the priest is also engaged in activities where his performance and trustworthiness can be monitored; he may earn a reputation for reliability, and this by association renders his less tangible promises also more reliable" (ibid.).

The demand for religious goods, therefore, is highly performance elastic. Furthermore, the degree of elasticity increases proportionally with the religious human capital of an individual or society. This assumption converts the legitimacy gap of the Soviet-era for co-opted churches into a present-day transitional constraint. A church made up of Soviet-tainted clergy is unlikely to be an appealing choice for consumers, especially those that are selective about their choice of a religious provider. When offered an alternative, Elena jumped at the chance of abandoning the Russian Orthodox Church. Her disloyalty was likely explained, in part, by a mistrust of the church. My research among former Orthodox adherents-turned-converts to non-traditional churches indicates a high degree of distrust of former priests. For most other individuals, the trust factor is irrelevant since those with less sophisticated religious taste or with less desire for intense religious participation will be influenced more by socio-cultural factors than the observable performance of church employees. Paul Froese, using a rational choice model examined Hungary where the state established a policy of a 'church within socialism'. He explained that the credibility of the Catholic Church was eroded by collaboration with the communist government to such an extent that when religious freedoms expanded after Hungarian independence, people nevertheless did not flock back to the Church (See Froese and Pfaff 2001).

> Demand Assumption 4: *Collective production tends to reduce the risk and raise the value associated with religious activities (Iannaccone 1997, 35).*

Religious commodities tend to be much riskier than other commodities because they promise much, but the benefits are in doubt as they are typically only delivered after death (ibid., 32). As such, there is great uncertainty in the value of religious goods. Consumers are naturally skeptical of producers' motives and techniques; this results in a high degree of selectivity. Those suppliers that reduce the risk of consumer fraud are more attractive and competitive. Attributes of a low-risk firm include volunteer clergy and "collective activities, which provide continuous assurance through the enthusiasm, devotion, conviction and testimony of fellow members" (ibid., 35). Parishioner participation, therefore, has a bearing on risk and satisfaction.

Churches differ markedly in terms of collective production of religious commodities. They range from ritual congregational to highly collective. Iannaccone labels them as "high cost" sectarian groups or "easy going" mainstream churches (ibid.). Ritual congregational churches consist of paid professional clergy, impersonal religious ceremonies, low-intensity demand on consumers and susceptibility to free riders. In the nations of the former Soviet Union, Orthodox Churches and the Armenian Apostolic Church are widely understood to be ritual congregational institutions. On the other end of the spectrum are highly collective churches, which demand much from the laity and, in some cases, are run by the membership. They limit free riding through exclusivity, are time intense, reduce the risk of religious commodities and prohibit member participation in competing religions (ibid., 37). In addition, they are characterized by "strict behavioral standards, dramatic conversions, high rates of church attendance and giving, resistance to social change, small congregations, and lower-class and minority appeal" (Iannaccone and Stark 1994, 743). Examples of these churches are Jehovah's Witness, Krishna's, fundamentalist Christian denominations and The Church of Jesus Christ of Latter-day Saints.

In collective churches members participate in both the consumption and production of religious commodities. Ritual congregational churches are "organized around client/practitioner or buyer/seller relationships", which collective churches are organized in such a way that "all members are, to varying degrees, co-workers and co-consumers" (Iannacconne 1997, 39). The Catholic churches would presumably fall somewhere in the middle of the two extremes. Viktor of Novosibirsk illustrates the appeal of a more collective experience for certain individuals. A middle-aged man with deep conviction in Christianity, he found little fulfilment in being a bystander at Orthodox services. He rarely attended, preferring instead to read his Bible at home. When confronted with a new entrant church that demanded hours a week of unpaid work and financial offerings, Viktor had little hesitation in joining. He had found a church that matched his religious profile. His devotion found expression in his active participation in the production of the religious experience.

This distinction between ritual establishment churches and high commitment sectarian churches is essential to understanding the dynamics of the post-Soviet religious economy. In their landmark book, *The Churching of America*, Finke and Stark conclude that in a pluralistic market, rigorous sectarian groups will grow at the expense of less-demanding established churches. They explain this as a sect-church cycle in which sectarian groups, which traditionally have a high level of tension with the socio-cultural environment, tend to experience a higher rate of growth as well as a higher level of commitment from parishioners than static churches, which are characterized with a low level of tension with society and lackluster commitment from laity. They continue by asserting that an institutional evolutionary process occurs by which sects convert themselves into mainstream churches by reducing demands on members and lessening societal stress. The mainstream churches become so relaxed that they lose members to high-cost groups. William Bainbridge explores this inability to compete. He asserts that traditionally dominant religious movements follow a natural long-term cycle in which they become "low-tension churches, thereby losing commitment from the members; weakening ties in these churches feeds an unchurched population; and out of that in turn are recruited adherents to sects or new religious movements which provide high intensity religious compensators" (1995, 6).

The post-1991 marketplace witnessed this sectarian–mainstream divide to the extreme. Indeed, it could be argued that no religious market in history rivals the stark distinction between mainstream and sectarian churches in transitional states. The legacies of Sovietism reinforced traditionally dominant churches as static figurehead institutions that provided a low return on investment. This is contrasted with the efforts of highly enthusiastic 'high cost' sectarian groups who promise a great return on investments, low consumer risk, and cause significant societal tension. Sectarian churches, in contrast with mainstream churches are proselytizing firms that seek to capture market share by spreading their message to as many people as possible (Gill 1998, 10). Although membership in these churches is relatively small, their missionary efforts represent a direct threat to certain mainstream denominations due to the quality of members being 'poached'.

> Demand Assumption 5: *In a large congregational church, a minority of members provide the majority of time and money input that adds to the health of the institution.*

Surveys have shown that in large churches, nearly 80 percent of money and time inputs are contributed by 20 percent of adherents. Even a cursory look proves that this holds true for the Russian Orthodox Church. The majority of people claiming allegiance to traditionally dominant churches in the former Soviet Union are titular members. They are cultural consumers as their affiliation stems from tradition more than collective participation within the church. Those supporters who do contribute to the church's wellbeing through time and money inputs, and who usually have a high level of religious capital, tend to be more prone to switch spiritual association. Elena of Krasnoyarsk is a case in point. This explains why mainstream churches that claim the vast majority of the population can still feel threatened by the marginal success of sectarian groups. The overall flight from the Russian Orthodox Church to new entrant groups after 1991 was a mere one to two percent—but those that fled held a disproportionate amount of religious human capital. Their loss was felt more than their numbers would suggest. The intricacies of the sectarian-mainstream divide laid the groundwork for applying relevant supply-side assumptions to the transitional marketplace.

Supply-Side Assumptions

There are eight assumptions concerning the behavior of suppliers of religious commodities in open and closed markets that are germane to post-Soviet behavior. They consist of a synthesis of concepts from various religious rational choice scholars as well as some generated specifically for this book.

> Supply Assumption 1: *Churches are profit-maximizing firms specializing in the production of religious goods and services. Church workers are motivated by the same sort of self-interest that motivates secular workers* (Iannaconne 1997, 26).

Religious organizations should be viewed as rational profit-maximizing entities that are "maximizing members, net resources, government support, or some other basic determinant of institutional success" (Iannacconne 1997, 27). This business-like casting of religious leaders has, at times, been criticized. However, Anthony Gill provides a well-articulated defense of this assumption:

"Leaders of religious institutions are subject to many of the same concerns and constraints as their secular counterparts (e.g., politicians, labour leaders). Primary among these concerns is the need for their church to survive and expand—i.e., to preserve the institution and increase membership. In addition to proclaiming the Word of God, bishops are also bureaucrats. They devote much of their time and energy to deciding how to distribute scarce resources so as to serve their basic goals. No matter how divinely inspired the clergy may be, a church exists in a world of scarcity and can thrive only to the extent that its leaders use resources efficiently. The conditions that cause secular actors to modify their behavior in defence of their institutionally determined goals will likewise apply to leaders of religious institutions; clergy who act irrespective of their church's institutional health will find that they are presiding over a weak and irreverent organization with few believers in tow" (1998, 11).

The politicization and secularization of church leaders under communism further validates the principles of rationality and optimality. It has already been demonstrated that while working and compromising with the Soviets, these leaders became accustomed to acting according to means-ends rationality. At the same time, state authorities deliberately and systemically alienated clergy and senior church officials from parishioners—reorienting their focus from the pews to the corridors of political power. Consequently, the application of business-like characteristics to Russian Orthodox leadership is even more appropriate in light of the politicization and Sovietization which church elites endured.

Supply Assumption 2: *Church leaders weigh the costs and benefits of an action on their church's relative power before enacting a strategy.*

This concept is implied in the process-maximizing assumption but needs greater examination. Any significant change in church strategy implies thoughtful consideration of the ramifications of that strategy on church success. For instance, when a church contemplates a policy on religious pluralism, it must weigh the utility of a particular approach. When petitioning the state to argue for protectionism, church hierarchs must take into account the benefits derived from such an action, such as a reduction in competition as well as the cost. These costs might include public perception of the church as an anti-democratic institution. A church's view of its relative power is influential in this cost/benefit analysis. Churches that perceive a downward shift in their power related to a more pluralistic society will seek institutional arrangements "that retain as much of their previous distributional advantage as possible" (Luong 2002, 3). Leaders that sense a decline in their institution's relative power might conclude that the costs of an anti-democratic petition to the government are outweighed by the benefits, i.e., a halt or even reversal of the decline of that power through protectionism. This is essentially the case with many formerly co-opted churches, and in particular with the Russian Orthodox Church's enthusiasm for the 2016 measures. The motivation for religious leaders to lobby the state for religious restriction is a "desire to acquire or retain as much power as possible given their perceptions of how present changing circumstances are affecting their previous ability to influence the distribution of [religious] goods and/or benefits" (Luong 2002, 34). The post-1991 religious marketplace resulted in striking power shifts among religious producers, uprooting almost overnight the pre-existing balance of power. Several churches perceive their power to be negatively correlated with the increase in membership of sectarian groups. Because they assess their market share as decreasing, church leaders see protectionist policies as an appealing remedy. For those churches that perceive their relative power as stable or increasing, the costs of an authoritarian plea to the state outweighs the benefits.

Supply Assumption 3: *To the degree that a religious economy is unregulated, it will tend to be very pluralistic* (Stark and Iannaccone, 1994, 232).

When formerly controlled religious markets are opened, religious suppliers tend to increase through both domestic sources and foreign arrivals. The correlation of deregulation with an increase in religious pluralism has been studied in 19th Century America and post-World War II Japan. In the latter case, the liberal laws on religious activity imposed by the American occupiers disestablished Shitoism as the state church and resulted in the upsurge of religious groups (See McFarland 1967). Similarly, the post-1991 religious economy has witnessed an abundance of market entries from abroad and re-entries of Soviet-oppressed groups in the wake of deregulation. It has been suggested that as early as 1995, more than

3,000 missionaries from 25 western churches had entered the former USSR (Elliot and Corrado 1997, 336).

> Supply Assumption 4: *To the degree that a religious economy is competitive and pluralistic, overall levels of religious participation will tend to be high. Conversely, to the degree that a religious economy is monopolized by one or two state-supported firms, overall levels of participation will tend to be low (Stark 1997, 17-18).*

This assertion runs somewhat counter to established secularization theory which maintains that there is a correlation between an increase in modernization and a rise in secularization, i.e. a decrease in religious activity. As people become more educated and sophisticated, they no longer need religion. Other researchers maintain that pluralism has a negative effect on church membership and that religious monopolies can be associated with high rates of religious mobilization (Bainbridge 1995, 2). Yet the secularization theory runs into empirical roadblocks. For one, it fails to explain the highly religious American outlier. Proponents also exaggerate the competitiveness of European religious markets. Stark and Iannoccone "account for the apparent secularization of many European nations, by stressing supply-side weaknesses—inefficient religious organizations within highly regulated religious economies—rather than a lack of individual religious demand" (1994, 230). Paul Froese found a causal relationship between religious restrictions and religious activity when investigating the post-1991 religious revival in Hungary. He hypothesized that religious activity fluctuates, not according to the secularization model of shifting demand, but as a result of religious competition (2001, 251). Religious activity, therefore, is purported to be a direct result of religious supply. Bainbridge's research found that "in a culture with a dominant religious tradition, the emergence of sect movements increases the proportion of the population affiliated with religious organization" (1995, 2). The religious revival in the former Soviet Union, therefore, was not entirely due to an increase in demand but also in supply. Demand had simply been made dormant by the anti-religious policy of the Soviet State. In turn, as a religious market increases in pluralism and competitiveness, it will become more efficient, i.e., churches will appear that provide a "higher ratio of return to investment" (Finke 1997, 53). In such a competitive atmosphere, churches must provide a high return on investment or they will see a decrease in their market share. This increase in efficiency is due to firm specialization.

> Supply Assumption 5: *To the degree that a religious economy is pluralistic, firms will specialize* (Stark and Iannaccone, 1994, 232). *To the degree that firms specialize, religious tension will increase.*

In a competitive market, producers must tailor their products to the needs of specific segments of the population. People seek diverse products as a result of diverse taste, because religious consumers seek compensators that match their religious capital. Since religious monopolies fail to meet the religious needs of every segment of society, new firms specialize to meet the demand. In an open market, religious consumers with diverse religious capital, who were once forced to be under the umbrella of a monopolistic firm, can choose among many denominations. Religious mobilization, therefore, is increased in competitive economies. What this assumption suggests is that even without an inherited comparative disadvantage from the Soviet era, traditionally dominant churches would have seen a small exodus of members to other groups. The comparative disadvantage resulting from the Soviet legacies detailed earlier only exacerbated the exodus.

This process of firm specialization and consumer mobilization results in the second aspect of the assumption—societal tension due to denominational polarization. Bainbridge notes that congregational churches reinforce the existing social status of its members and that these churches usually consist of members with relatively high social status. Meanwhile, sects provide compensatory status to poor segments of society.

> "To the sect member, possession of wealth and high education are not badges of honour; rather, faith in God and membership in the sect are the noblest qualities, conferring subjective status. In the extreme, the sect will define as sinful the consumption habits of members of the church congregation, while the church defines as presumptuous the status claims of sect members . . . Given

a modicum of religious freedom, the result is schism and the eruption of high-tension sect movements" (Bainbridge 1995, 5).

Russia in the 1990s witnessed a tremendous amount of such tension and religious discord. New religious entrants, uneasy with the label of sect, began to destabilize by their very presence, a religious scene already in serious tumult in the wake of Sovietism. Tensions ensued with the dissemination of hateful religious pamphlets, the burning of rival churches, and countless other negative phenomena. Indeed, the discord was manifested across the region as mainstream churches, whose norms mirror that of the prevailing culture, came into conflict with sectarian groups whose alleged deviant norms placed members at odds with the historical pattern of society (Iannaccone 1992, 278).

> Supply Assumption 6: *The capacity of a single religious firm to monopolize a religious economy depends upon the degree to which the state uses coercive force to regulate the religious economy* (Stark and Iannaccone, 1994, 232).

This assumption identifies the ultimate source of religious restriction, and by extension, the primary determinant of religious life in any given nation. Churches can only monopolize a market to the degree that the ruling regime allows. In this way, state-favored churches are analogues to business monopolies. Commercial hegemons thrive on the ability to control prices and exclude competition. Often this unfair and anti-competitive behavior is regulated by the state after considerable lobbying by non-state actors. Any regulation restricting competition naturally "changes the incentives and opportunities of religious producers and the options of religious consumers" (Spickard 1998, 100). State-supported monopolies, either business or religious, distort the market and restrict choices for consumers.

> Supply Assumption 7: *Government regulations on religious activity change the incentives and strategies of state-favored firms.*

Monopolies have little incentive to innovate or appeal to certain segments of society when consumers have no choice but to buy their products. This applies as equally to religious providers as it does to commercial establishments. Roger Finke notes, "Incentives for institutional change or popular appeal soon fade when churches find they can restrict their competition through suppression" (1997, 51). Under such conditions, hegemonic churches become inefficient in the absence of competition, which in turn may reduce overall levels of religious participation in a community. This is due to the monopolistic characteristics of institutions and the church-sect distinction referred to earlier. Anthony Gill notes, "Although monopolies guarantee that religious consumers cannot defect to other faiths, a lack of pastoral attention to its parishioners will weaken the popularity and credibility of the church" (1998, 68). As early as 1776, Adam Smith recognized the monopolistic characteristics of Church of England clergy:

> "The clergy, reposing themselves upon their benefices, had neglected to keep up the fervour of faith and devotion of the great body of the people; and having given themselves up to indolence, were incapable of making vigorous exertion in defence even of their own establishment" (cited in Gill 1994, 406).

Roger Finke's supply-side work on the deregulation of religious markets expands upon Smith's reasoning. When a controlled market becomes competitive, monopolies must "abandon inefficient modes of production and unpopular products in favor of more attractive and profitable alternatives" (Iannaccone 1995, 77). However, such a restructuring and institutional transformation is often unappealing to a firm accustomed to dominating a market. Drawing upon his own research on the American colonial established religions, Finke concludes that churches accustomed to privilege will inevitably, in a free market environment, seek to "suppress the activities of itinerants rather than compete with them" (1997, 50). Iannaccone writes that "a state-sponsored religious monopoly will provide only the appearance of piety—an inefficient clergy and apathetic pollution lie just below the surface" (1997, 40). He notes two types of religious regulation: subsidy and suppression. As will be seen, the Russian Orthodox Church benefited from the former from 1997 and only achieved state support for the latter from 2016.

While the comparison is not precise, churches which were subordinate to the Soviet state may be viewed as quasi-religious monopolies.

During most of the Soviet Union, particularly during the second Petrine phase, co-opted churches dominated the religious community and alternative religious choices were suppressed. Subservient churches were not classic examples of monopolies since they were not given free rein to propagate their own religion. However, on a political and institutional level they portrayed some of the same characteristic as business monopolies.

> Supply Assumption 8: *As major religious firms accommodate themselves to the secular culture (secularize), growth will be concentrated among the less accommodated firms. In market terms, growth occurs in areas with market openings* (Finke 1997, 55).

As already noted, commitment to a particular church is highly fluid. In a free market, people will switch suppliers to fit their taste. In the closed Soviet system, individuals dissatisfied with the Russian Orthodox Church did not embrace atheism, but simply stopped attending church. This is confirmed empirically by surveys that found that during communism, Russians left the "Russian Orthodox Church in droves, but did not abandon religion at the same rate" (Froese 2004, 38). After 1991, people returned to church, but to the church of their choosing. The appearance of consumer choice, firm specialization, demand-side mobilization, the church-sect cycle, and the monopolistic qualities of formerly state-sponsored religious firms account for this assumption being empirically validated in the former Soviet Union. While overall market share is still dominated by the traditional churches, growth in the market share of active parishioners immediately after 1991 appears to have been skewed towards non-traditional churches.

These eight supply-side bridge assumptions lay a foundation for a discussion at the intersection of the structural-historical context and the immediate-strategic context and its consequences on religious pluralism. While the topic of this book is Russia, broadening for a moment the discussion geographically helps to accentuate trends.

The Religious Marketplace in the Former Soviet Union: 1991–2020

The fluidity of the post-Soviet period makes any cross-regional generalizations difficult. The fifteen nations of the former Soviet Union are entirely sovereign entities and the commonalities between the former Soviet republics lessen with each passing year. The academic practice of studying these nations as a group is quickly becoming impractical. Even so, when it comes to the treatment of religious pluralism from independence to the present day, several region-wide trends are discernible.

With the fall of communism, all fifteen Soviet republics, with the exception of Turkmenistan, opened their religious markets to some degree. A departure from Soviet ideology brought "emancipation from any all-embracing doctrine" (Rousselet 2000, 65). New constitutions across the region bestowed freedom of religious activity for individuals and institutions. In most nations, especially outside of Central Asia, this *laissez-faire* policy was quite prevalent. Although not without some bickering between politicians and religious leaders, pluralism and tolerance became widespread. What resulted was a religious market that increased in competitiveness and the presentation of phenomena previously described, i.e., increase in religious participation, proliferation of new firms, firm specialization, religious mobilization, and a rise in religious tension. Public polling data and historical records attest to these features during the 1990s and do not require in-depth explanation here.

It took about five years for a correction to begin. In 1996, market liberalization began to halt—particularly in Orthodox countries and in Armenia. The following governments signed amendments to their constitutions restricting, to a degree, the freedom of operation of religious organizations: Belarus—1996 amendment to Constitution, Russia—1997 Law on Freedom of Conscience, Armenia—1997 Law on Freedom of Conscience amended, and Georgia—2002 Constitutional Agreement between Church and State. The titles of the legislation are, of course, misleading and entirely for public consumption. The laws did not facilitate a full-fledged cessation of religious activity, but rather an ideological shift from impartiality to favoritism. The laws made clear a distinction between traditional religions and non-traditional religions and provided certain privileges to the former.

In many cases, the ambiguity of legislative wording allowed for subjective interpretation by local officials. This was particularly the case in Russia where certain local authorities took issue with the operations of Jehovah's Witnesses. These governmental restrictions were augmented by hostile rhetoric towards non-traditional churches in the media and in politics in the late 1990s. As a consequence, public opinion turned negative toward these groups. An opinion poll conducted in Russia indicated that 29 percent of respondents in 1999 believed that non-traditional religions should be allowed to operate freely as opposed to 57 percent a decade earlier (Cited in Rousselet 2000, 61).

Within this torrent of change, the experiences of national churches were once again remarkably analogous to commercial firms navigating the economic transition. When the Soviet closed-economy liberalized after 1991, foreign products saturated the market. Trade liberalization allowed domestic consumers to experience an increase in choice, while domestic producers of goods faced fierce competition. The market, instead of governments, largely determined commercial winners and losers. Consequently, formerly state-owned firms had to be restructured, downsized or simply shutdown. The survival rate of firms depended upon factors such as agility to change, the competitiveness of the particular market and political access to state protection.

The religious market similarly underwent a shock therapy transformation in which state controls were relaxed, subsidies were abandoned, and the market liberalized to allow for the proliferation of numerous domestic and foreign religious suppliers. Variances existed across the region, but Western influence and a visceral reaction to Soviet repression motivated most nations toward a level of religious pluralism that often exceeded even pre-Soviet historical or societal norms. Religious consumers suddenly had more choices than many wished, and traditional suppliers swiftly found themselves in competition for market share, which they had become accustomed to dominating. This religious shock therapy radically altered the structure and incentives of religious economies. Roger Petersen correctly surmised that many of "these hierarchs came to view their church's dominant status as a part of the natural order" (Petersen 2001, 35). Vedran Horvat described how in the transition, traditional churches that are "often confused with the new rules of the transitional game, resort to agreements with pro-national governments in order to retain their previous positions" (2004, 11-12). In describing some dominant churches in the transition, Tamas Kodacsy says that many of them live off the goodwill of their state sponsors and few are self-supporting (2004, 36). In the Central Asian nations, which never opened their markets to the extent of Christian-dominated countries, incremental restrictions occurred throughout the 1990s. The Baltic nations, on the other hand, have kept their markets pluralistic and transparent. Even within the Orthodox block, the degree of religious restriction and of ecclesiastical pressure on governments varied.

An analysis of the religious setting in these nations, within the parameters of both the Soviet past and the demand and supply-side assumptions of the transitional period, reveals institutions that have been in perpetual flux for a century. The complexity of the situation can be simplified by understanding that institutional design and choice is shaped by the changing contours of the religious marketplace structure. This is because as market structure changes, it in turn shapes the religious elites' perceptions of shifts in their relative power. Luong writes, "The engine of institutional change is a shift in asymmetrical power relations, or more specifically, perceptions of the degree and direction in which relative power has shifted among established and emergent actors alike" (2002, 49). By conceptualizing the convergence of Soviet constraints and transitional circumstances on churches' perceptions of their relative power, we can better frame it in economic imagery.[3] Here the business analogy

---

3   Luong further explains this as the "dynamic interaction between the structural-historical context and the immediate-strategic context which directly shapes actors' perceptions of shifts in their relative power as the game proceeds, and hence, their bargaining strategies" (2002, 25). "The dynamic interaction between the transitional and structural-historical contexts creates perceptions among actors concerning the degree and direction of shifts in their relative power, which, in turn, have a direct influence on their preferences and strategies. Because these perceptions are derived under unstable or transitional circumstance, they are largely based on subjective rather than objective considerations" (ibid., 29).

remains useful, particularly when discussing monopolies and former Soviet subservient churches.

A command economy places different constraints on business behavior than does an open market economy. Similarly, the monopoly-type religious configuration under communism produced different constraints on traditionally dominant churches than did the current religious free-market (Supply Assumption 7). Historically dominant churches held a monopoly before 1917, but the Soviet State reinforced that position for co-opted churches (Supply Assumption 6). In the absence of competition and with close church-state interaction, the dominant churches during communism lacked the motivation or the ability to expand their base of participation; instead, they spent their "resources protecting the monopoly" (Warner 1993, 1045). As described in the previous chapter, co-opted churches' production and distribution infrastructure atrophied under communism. Indeed, the incentive structure, which the Soviet system created for church leaders, was not only dissimilar from present-day incentives, but was its antithesis. Soviet planners designed church-state and church-society institutional arrangements with the intent of disestablishing and destroying the church through inefficiency and irrelevance.

With the fall of communism, these same Soviet institutions experienced an identity crisis and began searching for new points of reference. For traditionally dominant churches the transition "represented an exogenous shock to status quo asymmetrical power relations" (Luong 2002, 15). The monopolistic power of formerly co-opted churches has been challenged by the infusion of other religious firms (Demand Assumption 3 and 4). Stark and Iannaccone, write, "Other things being equal, new and unconventional religious organizations will prosper to the extent that they compete against weak, local conventional religious organizations within a relatively unregulated religious economy" (1997, 134) (Supply Assumption 8). These unconventional religious groups increased steadily in the region after 1991. An *East-West Church & Ministry Report* survey indicates that the membership of sectarian groups tripled in the region from 1993 to 1998 (Filatov 1993, 1). The demand-side assumptions have demonstrated the fluidity of consumer choice and mobilization in a competitive market. In such an environment, time and money inputs will move from low-reward to high-reward religious uses. In other words, religious markets are just as harsh and competitive as business markets. Inefficiency and ineptitude are quickly exposed and punished with a decrease in business and capital. Formerly hegemonic firms must swiftly restructure and adapt to the new market structure. Religious leaders that don't abandon "inefficient modes of production and unpopular products in favor of more attractive and profitable alternatives" (Iannaccone 1997, 27) will experience a decline in market share (Supply Assumption 5). The legacies of Sovietism, however, made a quick restructuring of administrative and ministering resources competitive problematic (Demand Assumption 3). A history of hegemonic rule that produced a complacent clergy, among other things, prevented such a transformation and resulted in these churches' inability to compete. As a result, the perception of their power shifted downward in the midst of a religious pluralistic environment in which competition appeared between the various churches over each other's constituents (Supply Assumption 3).

The strategic response that many churches have employed to remedy this downward shift in relative power is to petition the state for protection from what they considered unfair overseas competitors in their canonical territory (Supply Assumption 2). The enacting of such a protectionist strategy is not only a product of legacy and immediate constraints, but also the result of the politicization and the autocratization of church leaders as discussed in the previous chapter. Institutional choice, therefore, is "deeply rooted in the Soviet system" (Luong 2002, 52). In the post-1991 market structure, the burden of monopoly and the legacies of Sovietism have shackled these religious firms competitively. Many of the dominant churches of the former Soviet Union, that for decades lacked incentives for "institutional change or popular appeal" (Luong 2002, 51) because of protection from competition, have resorted, not to new strategies of competitiveness, but to old tactics of political maneuvering. The type of restrictions sought ranged from total embargos to what could be referred to as non-tariff barriers, such as 50-year registration requirements. However, the church's role in enacting religious restrictive legislation is advisory, not determinative. The final arbitrator is the state. In addition, religious decision-makers must also weigh the cost to their church's image of promoting unfair restrictions on competitors. Anthony Gill notes, "Under more competitive circumstance, religious leaders must consider their political decisions more carefully in order to avoid alienating large groups of important church goers" (1998, 188). Where church and state goals fuse, the two entities will cooperate. The trend toward reversing the religious liberties granted after the euphoric aftermath of the fall of communism can be explained by the confluence of church and state incentives.

Contextualizing Institutional Choice

The institutional choices of religious elites during the early days of Sovietism placed churches on various path-dependent trajectories. Enduring structural transformations which followed the critical juncture have been perpetuated through ongoing institutional and political processes. These churches were thrown into entirely new church-state and church-society institutional arrangements after 1991. In the transitional environment, the degree of continuity with the Soviet past has been correlated with the critical juncture choice. Yet the institutional design fostered under communism has not been the sole determinate of institutional choice. It must be viewed in light of transitional circumstances. Therefore, institutional outcomes differ across the region according to varying Soviet and transitional constraints. Luong succinctly captures the dual influence of past and present circumstances on institutional design:

> "Individuals engaged in the process of designing new institutions utilize both the previous institutional setting (or the structural-historical context) and present dynamic circumstances (or the immediate-strategic context) in order to assess the degree and direction in which their relative power is changing, and then develop strategies of action based on what they expect their influence over the outcome to be vis-à-vis other actors" (Luong 2002, 14).

Outcome is not determined by either Soviet structural legacy or present-day marketplace circumstances alone, but by the interplay of the two. Features of a free religious market economy, such as firm specialization, fierce competition, and decreased government protection are interpreted differently by churches due to their structural histories. The last two chapters have attempted to place in context a church's perception of its relative power by framing it as the intersection of Soviet institutional setting and transitional dynamic circumstances. By contextualizing church behavior as the amalgamation of Soviet and transitional circumstances, the institutional choice of church elites can be understood, particularly as it relates to accounting for the differences of opinion on religious pluralism among churches.

Applying this logic to the Catholic Church of Poland is illustrative. Ramet has noted that the Polish Church played a central role in the resistance movement against the Soviets (1998). Consequently, the church kept a great deal of autonomy from the state and respect in the eyes of the people. The clergy retained a close connection with society and post 1991, displayed few monopolistic characteristics. The competitiveness of the church is manifest by the lack of success of sectarian groups in Poland. Missionaries from The Church of Jesus Christ of Latter-day Saints have operated in Poland since 1992 with almost no success compared to operations in neighboring nations. The Polish Church has not perceived a downward shift in its power, nor has it been threatened by the activities of other religious groups, and has, therefore, devoted little attention to blocking the market entries of sectarian churches. Furthermore, political developments in Poland, such as European Union accession and a populace largely ideologically aligned with the United States' notion of freedom, translate into a restrictive agenda on the part of the Catholic Church carrying very high opportunity cost.

Several years of research into religious affiliation trends and extensive interviewing of clergy in Ukraine, Georgia, Lithuania and Russia suggest the following implications arising from this structural-historical and immediate-strategic model:

> Finding 1: *Those church leaders who were trained, appointed, and worked during the Soviet-era for a co-opted church are more authoritarian in their views towards the activities of other religious groups.*
>
> Finding 2: *Formerly co-opted churches will be less competitive in the post-1991 marketplace than those churches that were not subservient to the Soviet state. Sectarian churches will be more successful in formerly co-opted church territory than in areas where the dominant church resisted the Soviet state.*

Finding 3: *Ecclesiastic leaders that worked closely with Soviet authorities are more willing to engage in political machinations to achieve institutional aims than are leaders that resisted Soviet policy.*

Finding 4: *Leaders of formerly co-opted churches will feel more threatened by foreign and domestic sectarian groups than church elites that resisted the Soviet state.*

Primary Finding: *There is a deductive correlation between the degree of Soviet subservience of a church and its willingness to pursue a policy of religious protectionism through political interventionism.*

Deciphering the motives behind an individual's choice is rarely straightforward. It is doubly difficult and multifaceted with an institution. However, a path-dependent theoretical framework for understanding institutional choice has been articulated thus far in this book which is both highly sequential, yet simple. The critical juncture under communism determined which path churches would follow. For those that decided on the path of subservience, a reinforcing structural transformation took place that has carried over into the transition and has resulted in competitive disadvantages. Those few churches that travelled the path of resistance experienced a completely different institutional history and have found the post-Soviet market structure to be much more favorable. To this point, this book has described churches as either totally subservient or entirely independent of the Soviet State. This was done for literary clarity. But, as is usually the case, reality has many shades of grey. Even so, extremes can assist in understanding the spectrum on which most churches—including the Russian Orthodox Church—fall. For this reason, it is useful to appeal to the model built in the past chapters to examine first the clear intolerance of the Georgia Orthodox Church to non-traditional religious entrants and then the acceptance, or at least indifference, of the Lithuanian Catholic Church to such entities.

4. The Georgian Orthodox Church
A Case Study in Authoritarianism

Situated prominently on one of the many hills surrounding Tbilisi is a granite statue referred to as Mother Georgia. She holds in her right hand a sword; a goblet of wine in her left. The symbolism is unambitious: all visitors to her land who are friendly will be offered the cup of hospitality, while those considered unfriendly will be met with the sword of hostility. The message is especially apt to the subject at hand. Few nations after 1991 wielded the sword of defense as firmly and aggressively towards undesirable religious groups as did Georgia. That the Georgian Orthodox hierarchy advocates privileges for its organization, promotes restrictions on all other organizations, and benefits from its favored position is unquestioned. Unlike the rhetoric in other nations where hostility towards competitors on the part of traditional churches is often kept oblique out of fear of being perceived as too tyrannical, Georgian Orthodox officials largely dispel with pretense. Indeed, the situation in Georgia is instructive because region-wide trends such as the consolidation of collective national identity around the traditional religion, the rise in ethnocentrism, and attempts at religious monopolization are manifest so extreme in Georgia.

Georgia is also unique in the omnipresence of religious nationalism in post-Soviet society and politics. Religion is seen in Georgia as more tied to national identity than even in Russia. A 2018 poll found 57 percent of Russians found religion to be a key component of national identity compared to 76 percent in Georgia (Pew 2018). This phenomenon partly explains why the country experienced the greatest affiliation swing from atheism to Orthodoxy of any country in the former Soviet Union. From 1970 to 1995, the percentage of Georgians aligned to a religion went from 47 percent to 80 percent (Barrett 2001). This quick societal reset was made possible by the historic association of the church and the nation which congealed during sixteen centuries of co-habitation. After 1991, a mutually beneficial relationship rapidly grew between church and state in which the latter sought legitimization and the former sought protection of its social and legal prominence. The consequences of religious nationalism and church-state converging interests allowed the church to become remarkably ubiquitous throughout the nation. At the same time and not entirely unrelated, non-Orthodox churches suffered mistreatment. Remarkably, the pro-western Rose Revolution of 2003 and subsequent Western-oriented presidents did not substantially alter the institutional arrangements that are so advantageous to the traditional church and so disadvantageous to all other religious denominations. As recently as 2020, an independent survey of the country found that "Non-Georgian Orthodox religious communities repeatedly face obstruction from local municipal councils and national state bodies such as the State Agency for Religious Issues to building new places of worship. Such problems affect communities such as Muslims, Jehovah's Witnesses, Catholics and Protestants" (Gavtadze and Chitanava, 2020).

The Critical Juncture

In 1917, the short-lived Menshevik government granted complete freedoms to the Georgian Orthodox Church and restored the church's autocephaly, which was abolished in 1811. When the Red Army invaded Georgia in 1920 and the nation was formally annexed by the USSR, these moves were quickly reversed. In what would become a pattern for future Soviet occupations, Bolshevik planners systematically began attacking and dismantling organizations and institutions which posed a threat to Marxist ideology. Authorities recognized the church as an obstacle to the establishment of a communist centralized system owing to it being "a political institution with an independent social base" (Jones 1989, 293). Stephen Jones notes that authorities fully appreciated the Georgian Orthodox Church's "support for ethnic separateness and hence a [potential] barrier to the integration of the Georgian population into the Soviet Union" (1989, 293). The state placed strict controls over all churches and began widespread persecution consisting of church demolition, clergy imprisonment, and execution, in addition to extensive anti-religious propaganda. Particularly ruthless attention was given to outspoken, defiant clergy (Interview 2005. Anonymous, GOC official, Tbilisi, 19 Nov).

The Georgian Orthodox Church was one of the less-fortunate churches in the region as it came under Soviet control much earlier, during a time when international awareness of Soviet repression was virtually non-existent. Constraints on Bolshevik oppression during and shortly after the civil war were few. Stalin appeared particularly obsessed with incorporating his homeland into the Soviet system. Unlike the Russian Orthodox Church, the Georgian Church did not experience a notable revival during and after World War II. For these reasons, savage persecution resulted as 2,500 Orthodox churches in operation before 1917 were reduced by the mid-1970s to just 40. This one-in-sixty ratio was more severe than even Russia where one-in-seven churches survived (Reddaway 1975, 15). In the 1920s and 1930s, Soviet laws and oppression effectively reduced the church to "an organizational shell" (Jones 1989, 294).

The dilemma faced by the Georgian Orthodox Church during this atheistic onslaught resembled that of other traditional churches: commit to overt struggle and risk the church's complete martyrdom or collaborate and conform to the demands placed upon it by authorities. Empirical evidence suggests that the Georgian hierarchy very quickly decided to pursue the latter option. Like other national churches in the Soviet Union, the Georgian Orthodox Church adopted a "patriotic attitude and was rewarded with state recognition of its canonical status" (Jones 1989, 294). Church leaders and state authorities developed a quid pro quo operating arrangement whereby the state ensured the hierarchs' survival, extravagant lifestyle, and supported the church's autocephaly status, which was recognized by the Russian Orthodox Church in 1943. In return, church leaders cooperated with Soviet infiltration of the church, accepted intrusive state oversight, and championed Soviet policy at international religious gatherings after it joined the World Council of Churches (WCC) organization in 1962.

Stephen Jones detailed how this initial compromise in the case of Georgia was virtually a total sell out. He paid particular attention to the three Soviet patriarchs, Eprem II, David V and Ilya, and their interaction with religious dissident Zviad Gamsakhurdia, who would eventually become the first president of independent Georgia. Gamsakhurdia led a small group of dissidents who both criticized the church and attempted to preserve its integrity. He described Eprem II, who ruled until 1972, as "an increasingly pliant tool of the Soviet authorities" who transformed the church into "an obedient organ of Soviet religious policy" (Jones 1989, 298). Eprem reportedly said, "When Moscow plays the piano, we must dance to its tune" (Jones 1989, 298). Notwithstanding a relatively meagre dissident movement early on, the critical juncture decision occurred early in the 1940s and enabled the Sovietization of the church to progress quickly. Research suggests that the pragmatic attitudes of lower-level clergy mirrored that of the patriarchate. Parish-level clergy played only a minor role in dissident activities and, in fact, were widely viewed, in and out of Georgia, as corrupt and totally subservient to Soviet authorities. In addition, interviews with clergy who served during communist rule, reveal a highly subjective interpretation of Soviet-era church action.

The Historical Context: Soviet Legacy

While the church hierarchy undoubtedly viewed the initial compromise with the Soviet state as a necessary concession for survival, authorities over religious affairs perceived it as an opportunity to debilitate the church through attrition. Severe persecution continued with the purging of recalcitrant clergy even as authorities coerced pockets of holdout clergy to collaborate. That collaboration was cemented into the church by means of a state-controlled clergy recruitment process and an incentive structure built to cripple church operations. In path-dependent language, this process acted as a mechanism of production and reproduction in which an institutional alteration of the church occurred over several decades. Beka Mengeashvili, the former Ombudsperson over religious affairs in Georgia, opined that this transformative process produced after 1991 a church that embodies "the last legacy of Soviet power in [his] nation" (Interview 2005. Tbilisi, 24 Nov). Mengeashvili, who is arguably one of the most knowledgeable people in Georgia on the nation's religious environment and the activities of the Georgian Orthodox Church towards other denominations, maintains that to understand present-day church activities without a thorough consideration of Soviet-era church developments is impossible.

"Of course, there is a correlation between the extremism we have seen in the Church since 1997 and the KGB infiltration of the church under communism. What the church is doing is not in the Georgian character. After 1991, Georgia looked to the West, the only thing that has looked backwards has been the [Georgian Orthodox] Church" (ibid.).

Mengeashvili continues by noting that by 1991, the entire Georgian Orthodox Church cadre had been recruited and schooled within the Soviet-established religious scheme. During the 70-year occupation, a complete personnel changeover took place within the church, overseen by a hostile Soviet apparatus. For instance, the Georgian section head of the Council of Religious Affairs attended all church councils and was repeatedly accused of "interfere{ing} not only in the placing of priests and especially bishops, but in various minor matters of church life" (Quoted in Jones 1989, 304). Even the election of present-day Patriarch Ilya is now widely accepted as being Soviet orchestrated. The mechanism of church transformation employed by Soviet authorities and detailed in chapter Two had adequate time to be worked to near perfection in Georgia.

Church Politicization

The concept of a Soviet religious policy is a contradiction in terms. The policy was, of course, anti-religious at its core. While atheistic propaganda in Georgian society and clergy persecution are well known, the efforts of the Soviet state to ruin the church from within have received less attention. Authorities were assiduous in crippling both church image and its effectiveness by replacing the merit-based leadership promotion with a patronage system. The patron-client relations placed the local Council of Religious Affairs as the sponsor and church leaders as the beneficiary. The incentive structure for church leaders was purposely made secular and individualistic, making concessions by the state beneficial to individual clergy and not the church as a whole. For instance, priests who assisted in limiting religious devotion or reported on clandestine religious activity were allegedly given preferential treatment in the form of access to apartments and cars. At the very least, the more cooperative clergy were shielded from persecution. The incentive-based structure, therefore, encouraged self-interested behavior over church-interests. As a result, there emerged a general disinterest in increasing the health and spiritual foundation of the church. This was best illustrated in the leadership of David V. Jones explains:

> "The Georgian Church under David V was an easy prey for government manipulation. David V did not exploit the growing interest among Georgian youth in religion and failed to fill the ten vacant eparchies. The quality of services, the priesthood and the seminary students declined and little attempt was made at restoration work. Real control of the church lay with Metropolitan Gaoiz, who exploited his position for personal gain" (1989, 304).

Metropolitan Gaoiz's actions would become so egregious that he was eventually arrested in 1979 and sentenced for fleecing church funds (Ibid., 302). To facilitate a comprehensive conversion of clergy from a church or even metaphysical interpretation of success to one based on personal wealth or political access, the KGB set up a personnel acquisition filter for the Georgian Orthodox Church. This recruiting system assessed not potential job performance or competence, but rather connections, incompetence, and pliability to authorities' agendas. It was impossible to pass through seminary and become a Georgian Orthodox priest without first being screened by the KGB. In contrast to a conventional meritocratic employment screening, Mengeashvili states that the KGB screening process "filtered out the competent, honest, and devoted candidates and allowed in only the corrupt, greedy and inept seminary students" (Interview 2005. Tbilisi, 24 Nov). Another observer of the religious sphere concluded, "The leadership of the church and the common priest were certainly connected with the KGB. If you confess to your priest an illegal act, the police will come knocking at your door that night" (Interview 2005. Anonymous, non-Orthodox leader, Tbilisi, 20 Nov).

The filtering processes coupled with the Soviet incentive system produced a church leadership comprised of political pragmatists. Previously forced to sustain Soviet policy at international religious gatherings, the same leaders today have no reservations in entering the political fray and actively lobbying for policy. Many officials maintain that the church and state should work hand in hand to ensure the spiritual health of society. The church sees its role as more than just consultative, but as an active partner with the government in regulating the spiritual affairs of the nation. One particular parish-level priest noted that, "The Patriarch has made it clear that the church and the nation are one, but the church should lead the religious life of the nation" (Interview 2005. Anonymous, Tbilisi, 17 Nov). Additionally, most priests interviewed believe that the church has a very strong influence on government decision making, even outside the specific realm of religious institutional design.

The politicization of the church was manifest in the activities of the Jvari organization from 2004 to 2006. Founded by the Georgian Hierarch, Paata Blushvili, the group was dedicated to purging the nation of non-orthodox religions. Violence was their primary means of policy implementation. They organized mob attacks against non-traditional groups in close coordination with local authorities (Corley 2004a). Blushvili made the organization's goal clear, "We're just defending our faith. The Jehovah's Witnesses and all these other groups are criminal sects—they should be banned" (Corley 2003). When asked their opinions of the Jvari organization, church leaders are quick to add their support. A Georgian Orthodox priest asserted, "Their efforts come from a desire to keep Georgia clean from harmful elements" (Interview 2005. Anonymous, Tbilisi, 17 Nov). The group espouses anti-sect inclinations similar to those of former parliamentarian Guram Sharadze. He founded a political party which holds as its central tenet the elevation of the Georgian Orthodox Church in society and politics, and the outlawing of non-traditional groups. The interconnection of Sharadze's backers and church clergy is such that it is difficult to determine where the party ends and the clergy begins. In the early 2000s, parliamentarians of other parties such as Eldar Nadiradze, Khatuna Khoperia, and Vakhtang Bochorishvili likewise worked with church officials in proposing religiously restrictive legislation. The latter noted that extremist priest Basil Mkalavishvili "appeared [because] we were unable to restrict different religious denominations by civilized methods" (Liberty 2003). When questioned regarding church meddling in the political process, clergy were entirely unapologetic.

While hierarchical-level relations with government organs have proven extensive, lower-level, parish-to-mayor and priest-to-municipal-police-officer connections seem even more deep-rooted. Large and small-scale persecutions of religious minorities have revealed a disturbing pattern of cooperation between local clergy and local officials, particularly from 1991 to 2006. The June 2003 arson attack on a Baptist church in the village of Akhalsopeli is a case in point. The mob that destroyed the building was allegedly organized by local Orthodox priest Bessarian Zurabashvili. No charges were ever filed and local authorities appear to have been culpable in the attacks (Corley 2004). In describing his tactics on national television, Mkalavishvili explained how he would often forewarn law enforcement officials before his mobs mounted an attack. He said, "Thank goodness, there are people in our security and police services, wishing to help me; they understand how dangerous these sects are for Georgia" (Liberty 2003).

Soviet Administrative Structure

The slow and methodical KGB personnel filtering process resulted in another post-Soviet constraint—an inefficient ministry structure. The church became a weak supplier of religious commodities due to it being shielded from competition and as a result of its interaction with laity being severely restricted. Furthermore, the clergy was staffed with men hand-picked to erode the church's competence at preaching and proselytizing. Standards of deportment were intentionally lax. For instance, within a year of his ascension to power, Ilya II was presented with a document from a fellow hierarch detailing the allegations among clergy of "homosexuality, trading in church candles, embezzlement of money earmarked for church repairs and drunkenness" (Kobahidze 1997). In the 2000s, a senior official in the Public Defender's office, estimates that eight out of ten priests have never read the Bible (Interview 2005. Anonymous, Tbilisi, 24 Nov). Father Vassily Kobahidze, Press Secretary for the Patriarchate, complained that "unfortunately we have few educated clergy . . . It is much easier to say the television is 'Satan's box' than it is to preach the faith on television. It is much easier to say that everyone will perish than it is to preach the salvation of people" (1997).

Restrictions on administrative functions and accountability under Soviet rule set a pattern that continues today. Priests and deacons were rarely supervised or retrained in the 1990s and into the 2000s. Mengeashvili notes, "There are no controls placed upon the church, so it has developed into a totally corrupt entity, the only thing that is controlled is the freedom of speech, if you have anti-patriarch or pro-liberal tendencies you are punished" (Interview 2005, Tbilisi, 24 Nov). Few serious attempts at restructuring the church to enable better ministering have occurred. Even suggesting that the church requires reform is grounds for punishment. The Kobakhidze affair is a case in point. In late 2004, the Holy Synod sanctioned Basil Kobakhidze, a charismatic Deacon who called for inter-faith dialogue and internal church reforms. Kobakhidze and two other priests, Zaza Tevzadze and Michael Asatiani, accused the patriarchate of remaining silent on religious persecution, conducting political machinations to obstruct a treaty between the government and the Vatican, and being "fraught with corruption and nepotism" (Peuch 2004). Kobakhidze described the Synod's rebuke of his action as "an act of retaliation against one of those [few] priests who dare openly say that the Georgian Orthodox Church is in a catastrophic state" (Ibid.). At the time, there was widespread condemnation by priests of Kobakhidze's attempts to reform the administrative structure of the church (Interview 2005. Anonymous, GOC official, Tbilisi, 19 Nov).

When asked, many Georgian clergy refuse to see any correlation between Soviet repression and the church's inability to properly discharge its spiritual duties to the populace. Officials even now assert that while other religious organizations are not a threat to the church, they do endanger the entire Georgian nation. One high ranking official stated that "these western sects are a sickness on our Georgian soul" (Interview 2005. Anonymous, GOC priest, Tbilisi, 21 Nov). There is ample circumstantial evidence to suggest the church was not market-competitive after 1991. But the lack of a genuinely free marketplace after 1991 to the present-day does not afford an opportunity to see what the consequences of Soviet legacy would have been with new market entrants.

Legitimacy and Organization Unity

Corruption and political subservience in the church were widespread and well known to the public. David Koridze, a senior investigator wrote the most detailed account of the 'red clergy' of Georgia in the report "On the Crimes Committed in the Patriarchate of Georgia", which was sent to the Central Committee of the Party. The report was leaked out to the West and was subsequently published and analyzed in Religion in Communist Lands. Noted was the 1973 election of the new patriarch that "took place in illegal circumstances" (Jones 1989, 301) and was allegedly rigged by the KGB. Koridze listed the "offences committed, from the robbing of the patriarchate and the illegal appointment of David, to the illegalities being carried out with the knowledge and assistance of the Commissioner for Church Affairs, D. Shalutashvili, for which help he has received many bribes in money and presents" (Reddaway 1975, 15). In addition to KGB participation in the election of the patriarchate, the events surrounding the arrest of Zviad Gamsakhurdia also suggest strong church-state cooperation (Jones 1989, 304).

In the 1970s, Gamsakhurdia and a few other dissident church members established a secret Christian court to investigate the actions of church leadership. The KGB broke it up and arrested most of the members of the court (see ibid., 302). Church leaders including Patriarch David and Metropolitan Gaioz supported the persecution of the late 1970s both overtly and covertly. The Georgian Communist regime covered-up church-police collaboration and forced Koridze into early retirement for his work on the report. Jones concludes that the campaign against Gamsakhurdia revealed "close cooperation between government and church authorities" (ibid., 341). The election of current Patriarch llya in 1977, who "publicly professes loyalty to the regime and its policies" (ibid., 303), produced little change in direction. An observer of the Georgian Church in the 1970s stated that the consequence of such corruption was that "a proportion of the believers have stopped going to church and have started to pray in specially created sects" (Reddaway 1975, 16).

Upon independence, the public and especially the new President Gamsakhurdia, were deeply suspicious "of a hierarchy seen as tainted by its past association with the Soviet regime" (Jones 1989, 301). He opined that the "disillusionment with [the Patriarch's] leadership led to a significant drop in church attendance and to the closure of churches, one after the other" (Quoted in Jones 1989, 298). However, the restricted religious market in the 1990s prohibited any legitimacy gap from being manifested in the prosperity of other groups. In the 1990s, the clergy had a well-earned reputation for shaddy behavior. Accusations of bribery and dishonesty were directed, not only at the patriarchate, but at clergy on every level. These included drunkenness, black market profiteering, providing authorities with information obtained from confessionals, and reporting clandestine religious activity (Interview 2005. Anonymous, non-Orthodox leader, Tbilisi, 20 Nov). Yet the church's current standing in society is favorable. In a 2019 public survey, the church had the highest performance rating of institutions, with 64 percent stating it was good or very good (Thornton and Turmanidze 2019). Even so, this was a drop of 25 points since 2016. In Georgia, 85 percent of citizens refer to themselves as culturally Orthodox and 50 percent attend church regularly (Alisauskiene 2016). The high regard of both the church and Patriarch Ilya can possibly be explained by economic factors and nationalistic sentiment. However, it would be difficult to contend that religiosity and activity is not high in one of the most restrictive markets in the region. The situation in Georgia, therefore, calls into question the supply-side assumption of a positive relationship between religious pluralism and religious vitality.

While the public reputation of the church is obscured by a closed marketplace and a fervent retreat into religious nationalism, the credibility of church leadership is challenged on rare occasions from within the church. Interestingly, these ideological challenges to the patriarchate have come from both directions—a small group of liberal-leaning clergy urging reform and a larger movement encouraging a more anti-ecumenical isolationist approach. The former exists less as a grouping and more as scattered priests, who feel isolated and discontent in a church that strongly condemns dissent. One such conscientious priest, Orthodox father Georgi Chachava, was reportedly attacked by fellow priest David Kvlividze "for his liberal views and readiness to work with other Christian churches" (Corley 2004). As mentioned, the more senior Basil Kobakhidze was officially punished for his ecumenical speech and suggestions that the church is in need of internal reform. These two priests are the exception to the rule. Indeed, the dearth of introspective church dialogue serves as further evidence of the comprehensive Sovietization of the church.

The other much larger and more prominent segment of the clergy are radicalized to such a degree that they abhor all interfaith dialogue and advocate an across-the-board ban on all non-Orthodoxy groups. This group's influence is manifest in schismatic rhetoric by church leaders. Parish priests and even bishops are all too willing to threaten separation from the church if their demands are not met. An example of this was the events that led to Patriarch Ilya's withdrawal of the church from the World Council of Churches. He had served as president of that organization from 1979 to 1983 and was regarded as a champion of inter-faith dialogue. However, in 1996, numerous parishes wrote an open letter to him declaring that "ecumenism is heresy" and begging him not to "rend the robe of the Church of Christ by schism." After more direct threats of severing "Eucharistic communion" with the "mother church", Ilya had little choice but to act (Open 1997). Father Kobahidze admitted that "about seventy percent of the faithful, to one degree or another, are infected with schismatic ideology" (1997)—a comment he made in August of 1997 at the height of the ecumenical debate. That debate has turned out to be the defining event in the transitional period for religious liberties in Georgia. From 1991 until the church's withdrawal from the WCC, the church's agenda on religious freedoms was ill-defined and persecutions rare. After the withdrawal, the 70 percent of the clergy Father Kobahidze alluded to, emboldened by their success, began steering the church toward a more hostile agenda on religious pluralism and freedoms. After 1997, extremists like Mkalavishvili and groups, such as Jvari, began operation. Attacks on religious minorities increased to levels unparalleled in other former Soviet republics, although anti-sect incidents have abated somewhat since 2011.

Church Political Culture

Conversations with church officials, as well as statements and behavior by the clergy, indicate that Soviet political culture found resonance among church leaders. As noted earlier, this culture is characterized by disrespect for the rule of law and an aversion to democratic liberalism. Among those Church leaders interviewed, there is firm opposition to liberalizing the religious sphere. They unanimously agree that the plurality of religious organizations operating in Georgia will harm society. Priests categorically and unapologetically assert their disdain for all other religious groups, including Catholics. The clergy's hostility towards America is also reflective of church ideological culture. Orthodox leaders open espouse distaste for America and what it historically represents. A particularly outspoke priest states, "The largest problem facing the church is America" (Interview 2005. Anonymous, GOC priest, Tbilisi, 18 Nov). This is in spite of the fact that the majority of Georgians have a great admiration for the United States. An extensive survey found that of all the countries in the world, Georgians believe they can rely on the US the most. The survey also found that 60 percent of the sample believed that the spread of religious sects will be a threat to the country during the next five years. (Sumbadze 2003). In contrast to this, when asked what has done the most harm to the spiritual health of their community during the past century, Western influence was mentioned by Orthodox clergy more often than Communist occupation or Marxist indoctrination. Conversations with priests reveal that democracy, equalitarianism, and liberalism are not strongly-held values among clergy.

Attacks on human rights organizations, most notably the Liberty Institute, serve as an illustration of the clergy's orientation. The Liberty Institute criticized the ultra-Orthodox conservative Member of Parliament, Guram Sharadze, who proposed a bill in 1999 to ban all non-traditional groups in Georgia. His attempts were supported by many Orthodox priests (Interview 2005. Anonymous, GOC official, Tbilisi, 19 Nov). Although unsuccessful, his anti-sectarian rhetoric continued and he was successful in bringing a case against Jehovah Witnesses that eventually resulted in that group being de-registered. In a July 2002 televised debate with Liberty Institute director Levan Ramishvili, Sharadze was accused of spreading intolerance and violence and of previously being a KGB informer. A few days later fifteen men ransacked the headquarters of the institute and attacked the director, who was severely beaten, as well as other members of the staff. At the time, the attack was called "one of the most vicious assaults on human rights defenders ever seen in the former Soviet Union" (Human Rights Watch 2002). It also demonstrated close collaboration between Sharadze's "Our Georgia" movement and Mkalavishvili Orthodox extremism. The two groups demonstrated together on numerous occasions. During one of these, Sharadze was heard to say, "I am going to achieve in the streets whatever I could not achieve in parliament, and I do not mean just demonstrations only" (ibid.). Ombudsman Beka Mengeashvili noted:

> "Although Basil is currently sitting in jail, his opinions reflect those of many priests in the church and government officials. The government would give to him the addresses of sectarian churches so he could know where to attack.

Almost every priest agreed with his methods. The media were clearly in favor of his actions. He symbolizes the feelings of the Georgian Orthodox Church priests. Even the Patriarch was indirectly favoring him. On Public TV he was heard to say 'the imprisonment of Basil Mkalavishvili will open the door for new religious movements" (Interview 2005. Tbilisi, 24 Nov).

In the aggregate, the consequences of subservience to Soviet rule have been significant on the Georgia Orthodox Church. These legacies have converged in the transition to produce a church mentality in which Metropolitan Atanase Chakhvashvilil, at the time the second-most-senior Orthodox Bishop, could declare on public television that all sectarians should be killed. He mentioned Baptists and Pentecostals among others that should be "shot dead" (Corley 2002). He called for the banning of all non-orthodox groups as well as the human rights group, Liberty Institute. He suggested that the only logical way to deal with minority faiths is to declare war on them. The political and social conditions in Georgia during the transition have not allowed for such a religious genocide to occur. However, conditions have been sufficiently favorable to allow the church to be the predominant non-state actor in devising the transitional religious institutional design.

The Immediate Context: Post-Soviet Marketplace

Legal Framework

The legal framework for religious activity in Georgia has fluctuated greatly since 1991. The country did not experience a free market phenomenon after 1991 to the degree of other post-Soviet republics, particularly Russia. Although the first Constitution stipulated complete freedom of religion and upheld the rights of citizens to practice and express their religiosity, it also acknowledged the special place the Georgian Orthodox Church occupies in society. A Constitutional agreement, or concordat, between the state and the church was approved by parliament in 2002, which "recognizes the special role of the Georgian Orthodox Church and devolves authority over all religious matters to it, including matters outside the Church" (Freedom 2004). The Orthodox-state concordat merely codified arrangements that have existed *de facto* since the mid-1990s. The concordat affords the church oversight in the distribution of religious literature, the construction of religious buildings, provision for church involvement in public schools, exemption of clergy from military service, and allowance for the active involvement of Orthodox chaplains in the military (ibid.). The church also holds the distinction of being the sole religious organization in the country that has tax-exempt status. Legislation also allows the church to be closely involved in primary school curriculum. It has been reported, "In Georgia, classes often became denominational Orthodox instruction, with teachers taking children to pray in the local Orthodox Church" (Corley 2005).

It was not until the mid-2000s that the country began to pass more progressive legislation. Yet, nowhere in the former Soviet Union is there such distance between legislation and reality as in Georgia. In April of 2005, President Saakashvili signed an amendment that allowed all religious organizations to register with the state (Corley 2006). Nonetheless, few jumped at the chance and many of those who have registered believe that it "has not help[ed] [them] in any practical terms" (Interview 2005. Anonymous, non-Orthodox leader, Tbilisi, 20 Nov). Against the strong objection of the church, in July 2011, parliament passed legislation that permitted religious organizations to register as "legal entities of public law", as opposed to their previous lower status as "noncommercial legal entities of private law". This status, which is similar to that of a charitable foundation or an NGO, was considered unacceptable to some churches which refused to register. In 2018, the Constitutional Court declared as unconstitutional tax and property privileges granted to the Orthodox Church. The same year constitutional amendments guaranteed the "absolute freedom of religion," the separation of the Orthodox Church and the state, and equality for all regardless of religion (Freedom 2018). While these are encouraging moves, they occur against the expressed wishes of Orthodox church elites and without commensurate liberalization in practice. A former advisor to the Public Defender of Georgia, accurately summarized what favorable legal framework means for the church in practical terms, "The church's financial gains from its legal status are tremendous" (Interview 2005. Anonymous, Tbilisi, 24 Nov).

The liberal laws passed since 2005 have not been systematically implemented. For instance, serious violations against the freedom of belief for Muslims have occurred throughout Georgia in: Nigvziani in 2012;

Tsintskaro in 2012; Tsikhisdziri in 2013; Samtsatskaro in 2013; Chela in 2013; Kobuleti in 2014; in Mokhe in 2014; and Adigeni in 2016 (Gavtadze and Chitanava, 2020). The well-respected Forum 18 religious news service noted in Oct 2020, that the "systemic violations of human rights continue against those who do not belong to the dominant and politically influential Georgian Orthodox Church, even though the Constitution establishes high standards for human rights protection, Georgia's legal framework still includes some laws and regulations that unjustifiably restrict rights of non-Georgian Orthodox communities and create unequal conditions" (ibid.). A Sept 2020 report by the Public Defender of Georgia stated that notwithstanding progressive laws ensuring freedom of religion and belief to a high standard, non-traditional religious communities, unlike the Georgian Orthodox Church, are "disprivileged by discriminatory norms" (Lomjaria, 2020).

Church Structure and Policy Making Processes

The Orthodox hierarchy in Georgia consists of the 47-member Holy Synod led by Patriarch Ilya II. Metropolitans, archbishops, and bishops make up the Synod, which has the responsibility of selecting the patriarch, although this election as well as synod member selection were heavily influenced by state authorities during the Soviet era. An exhaustive examination of current Synod members' writings and public statements suggest that only five of the 47 members appear to have democratic, liberal inclinations. These consist of Bishops Melkisedek (Khachidze), Grigol (Berbichashvili), Abraam (Garmelia), Zenor (Garajuli), and Jobi (Akiachvili). One Georgian scholar estimated that if given the opportunity to vote freely, only ten to fifteen of the 47 would recognize the autocephaly of the Ukrainian Orthodox Church (Interview 2020. Gela Khmaladze, Kyiv, Jan).

Of all factors influencing the church's hostility towards non-Orthodox churches, money undoubtedly stands supreme. The church benefits greatly from legislative privileges, and freedom from oversight. The church's business interests are extensive and well hidden from the public. In the 1990s and early 2000s accusations were abundant of the church's participation in oil, vodka and cigarette trading (Mengeashvili 2005). While such assertions have not been substantiated and sources of income remain unclear, individual church leaders' wealth is on open display in Tbilisi in the form of new model Mercedes and opulent homes. In addition to unknown sources of funding, the state finances all Orthodox schools and seminaries and shares the bill for expensive new churches, which are appearing throughout the country. A year after the concordat was signed, the Vatican and the Georgian state were nearly ready to sign a similar document granting official status to Catholicism (Corley 2003a). Well-orchestrated Orthodox-led demonstrations derailed the concordat, which many in the church believed was a first step in the process by which the Catholic Church would gain Orthodox-like status (Interview 2005. Anonymous, GOC official, Tbilisi, 23 Nov). Because of the financial advantages of being a legalized monopoly, church protests against all outside religious activity appear more financially than ideologically driven. This is not to consign all church posturing on institutional design to a motive of money and greed. It would be safe to conclude, however, that the monetary benefits to the church as a whole and to individual hierarchs influence to some degree their decisions on religious liberties. The legacies of Sovietism, especially the 70-year transformation of clergy through the KGB filtering and secularization process, further reinforce the assumption that leaders approach the question of institutional design with practical self-interest rather than through moral or ideological consideration. The reformist priest Kobakhidze stated, "We simply criticize this clan of 20 to 30 people who concentrate in their hands all the power of the church and have turned archbishops and priests into slaves mainly preoccupied with keeping their salaries and social status" (Peuch 2004). In 2002, an observer of religious life in Georgia noted:

> "In many of the former republics of the Soviet Union, including Russia, the birth of freedom has brought with it religious tensions, particularly between the predominant Orthodox churches and newly emergent religions and sects. But Georgia is unique in the intensity of the violence toward religious minorities, and in the evidence of official complicity in the attacks" (Myers 2002).

Beka Mengeashvili also attributes the religious friction to Orthodox aggression:

> "I believe the largest problem facing religious life in Georgia today is the fact that a radical, fundamentalist strain of Georgian Orthodoxy has taken over,

high jacked the church. The most noticeable consequence of this is the radical hostile position which the church leaders have taken towards other faiths. The Church's animosity is equally strong towards all confessions and denominations" (Interview 2005. Tbilisi, 24 Nov).

The church withdrew from the World Council of Churches (WCC) in 1997 primarily due to the activism of hard-line conservative clergy. Five monasteries temporally broke communion with the Georgian Orthodox Church over the issue. They considered the Georgian Patriarchate to be too liberal. The patriarch himself admitted to Konrad Raiser, WCC General Secretary, that the reason behind his church's departure stems from internal forces threatening schism due to a "negative attitude towards the ecumenical movement" (Newbury 2006). Of the 150 Orthodox churches in the world, only the Bulgarian and Georgian branches are not current members of the WCC and the European Council of Churches. The consequence of the 1997 move towards extremism has been significant and resulted in religious tension and a black-market system within a monopolistic economy.

At the same time, parish-level clergy also influence policymaking indirectly. Indeed, the interplay between parish-level clergy and hierarchs on the issue of religious liberties is exceptionally dynamic. Parish-level initiatives appear to determine in large measure the ideological course of the church. The withdrawal of the church from the WCC is a perfect example. The patriarch admitted that he was forced to abandon an organization he had once led because of subordinate disdain for ecumenism. Since that time, the patriarchate has followed the lead of parish-level clergy in becoming radically opposed to the ecumenical movement. The antagonism toward religious pluralism and liberties has also been primarily driven by provincial and grass-roots clergy. For instance, the aforementioned Mkalavishvili and the Jvari organization were primarily parish-initiated movements. Interviews and analysis of public statements by senior and parish level Georgian Orthodox clergy suggest that parish priests and church headquarters officials see eye-to-eye on issues of anti-ecumenicism and the treatment of undesirable religious groups. This finding further attests to the comprehensive Sovietization of the church and that the agenda against religious freedoms is not the work of a hand full of officials in the patriarchate, but represents the mind of the vast majority of church clergy. Therefore, in contrast to Russian Orthodoxy, where the patriarch sets the tone for the church's religious attitudes and leaves it up to local church officials to implement such policy, in Georgia, the tone comes largely from the parishes and the patriarchate does the implementation.

Market Dynamics

In contrast to the situation in Russia and despite recent legislation, the religious market in Georgia has never fully opened. The type of missionary activity, that has energized the religious landscape in other former communist nations, simply does not exist in Georgia. Legal restrictions coupled with the fear of Orthodox persecution have meant that non-traditional activity is minimal. For instance, The Church of Jesus Christ of Latter-Day Saints, which before 2016 had over a thousand missionaries in Russia and fifty congregations, has just over a few dozen missionaries and one small congregation in Georgia. While more established churches have greater freedom of operation, legal privileges and government subsidies to the Georgian Orthodox Church have resulted in the Orthodox Church maintaining a dominant market share advantage. Notwithstanding legislation affirming Western notions of religious pluralism and church-state separation, the reality on the ground for minority religions is not too dissimilar from the 1990s.

According to recent polling, Georgia is the most believing nation in Europe with 99 percent confessing a belief in God (Pew 2018). More than 80 percent of Georgia's 3.7 million people identify as Orthodox Christians. But in Georgia, religious affiliation is not as nominal as it is in Russia. In Russia only 15 percent think religion is very important in their lives, with a mere 17 percent attending church at least once a month and praying daily. In Georgia, half of the population believe religion is very important in their lives and a third pray daily and attend church monthly (ibid.). At first glance, the populace appears out of sync with Orthodoxy clergy. A 2019 poll found that 71 percent thought protection of the rights of religious minorities was important or very important whereas only 9 percent thought it unimportant (Thornton and Turmanidze 2019). Interestingly though, other indications suggest a very conservative, unfriendly populace. In all of Europe, Georgians are the least accepting of same-sex marriage (only 3 percent). They are second after Greece in believing that their culture is superior to others. Georgians are also at the bottom of the list of people willing to accept Jews (25 percent) or Muslims (17 percent) as a member of their family (Pew 2018).

Persecution of non-Orthodox groups by both high-level leaders and parish clergy was a common feature of Georgia's religious landscape from 1991 to 2005. Non-orthodox religious groups complain that religious instruction in public schools is confessionally Orthodox (Corley 2003b) and that the church's permission is required to import religious literature (Corley 2003c). Such groups ranging from Old Believers to Jehovah's Witnesses have also complained that they are not allowed to build places of worship and that only Orthodox communities have legal status (Corley 2003d). The leaders of these religious organizations place the blame squarely on the shoulders of the Georgian Orthodox Church. A member of a minority religious group, a True Orthodox priest, observed that, "when the patriarchate got its concordat it became a monopolist and was able to obstruct everyone else" (Corley 2003e). Tatiana Chumachenko noted that "it was logical that Soviet leaders gave the Orthodox Church priority over all other religious confessions" (2002, 190). The hostility towards other churches has even spilled over into church relations with the relatively benign international ecumenical movement.

These macro-level obstructionist policies of the Georgian Orthodox hierarchy are coupled with highly visible persecution on the parish level. Orthodox priests have been accused of fomenting anger among their members and leading mob-like activities against non-Orthodox congregations and leaders. These activities have been reported as outright religious violence. Examples of such vigilante behavior are abundant. They include accusations against Orthodox priest Bessarian Zurabashvili for burning down a Baptist church in a rural village (Corley 2003f) and Father David's role in leading a mob to disrupt a Pentecostal gathering in Tbilisi (Corley 2003g). Such activities are rarely condemned or prosecuted by the state or Georgian Orthodox officials.

Local authorities' attitude towards Orthodox persecution of religious minorities range from indifferences to latent approval to participating partner. *Forum 18 News Service* reported:

GEORGIAN ORTHODOX CHURCH 109

"Between 1999 and 2003, Georgia suffered a wave of violence by self-appointed Orthodox vigilantes, with over 100 attacks on True Orthodox, Catholics, Baptists, Pentecostals and Jehovah's Witnesses in which believers were physically attacked, places of worship blockaded and religious events disrupted. Mob protests against religious minorities still continue. The authorities—who know the attackers' identity—have punished only a handful of people with relatively light sentences. In some cases, police cooperated with attacks or failed to investigate them" (Corley 2005a).

One example of Orthodox extremists attacking religious minorities occurred on 16 August, 2000 during the criminal trial of members of an Mkalavishvili mob, that attacked 120 Jehovah's Witnesses a year earlier. During a court recess, an angry group of 80 Orthodox fundamentalists under the direct leadership of Mkalavishvili stormed the courtroom and physically and verbally attacked the Jehovah's Witnesses and journalists. All of this was done without any intervention from the police or court officials. An observer noted:

"Immediately after the hearing, outside the courthouse, the Mkalavishvili mob attacked Liberty Institute representative, Giga Bokeria and Radio Liberty reporter, David Paichadze, kicking and punching them and then throwing rocks at them. When Bokeria and Paichadze manage to escape, the mob turns on Canadian lawyer, John Burns, local lawyer Mamuka Chabashvili, and foreign observers, beating them, tearing their clothing and stealing personal items. During this attack, courtroom security guards were watching but refused to protect victims from the mob. Lawyer Inga Geliashvili is present and pleads with the officers to assist the victims. The officers made no response and just continued to watch the attack" (Kopaliani 2000).

Accusations of police involvement in the persecutions are abundant. Although religious minorities complained on numerous occasions of beating, arson, and book burning, authorities allowed Mkalavishvili mobs to plunder with impunity. Confident in public and government support, the group would actually video record attacks on religious groups and distributes the recordings (Corley 2005a). Mkalavishvili was finally arrested in March 2004 after five years of organizing attacks on non-traditional groups. According to a religious freedom news outlet:

"Between 1999 and 2003, Georgia suffered a wave of violence by self-appointed Orthodox vigilantes, with over 100 attacks on True Orthodox,

Catholics, Baptists, Pentecostals and Jehovah's Witnesses in which believers were physically attacked, places of worship blockaded and religious events disrupted. Mob protests against religious minorities still continue. The authorities—who know the attackers' identity—have punished only a handful of people with relatively light sentences. In some cases, police cooperated with attacks or failed to investigate them" (Corley 2005d).

In his 2002 Christmas message to the nation, Patriarch Ilya warned the nation to shun new sects, listing among others the Catholic and Baptists churches. Beka Mengeashvili comments, "Most of the churches referred to as new religious groups, have actually been operating in the country for decades. The Jehovah Witnesses, Baptist, and Pentecostal churches have been in Georgia for a hundred years. They are already traditions" (Interview 2005. Tbilisi, 24 Nov). In Georgia there have been violent attacks and persecutions experienced by, not only the Jehovah's Witnesses and Pentecostal, but also by Baptist and Catholic congregations (Corley 2005c). The persecution became so severe in Georgia before 2006 that none of these denominations "believed that they could openly build places of worship" (Corley 2005b) Apart from the obstruction of building religious facilities, persecution also included "vandalism of Catholic graves, demands to remove non-patriarchal Orthodox literature from bookstores," (Corley 2004b) and legislative restriction of non-orthodox religious organizations. This assault on religious minorities is two-pronged. It is waged legislatively and politically in the corridors of power in Tbilisi as well as with rocks and Molotov cocktails in villages. While the former is sanctioned and carried-out by the Georgian Orthodox Patriarchate, the latter is the work of local parishioners and village clerics.

Many predicted that as a result of the November 2003 Rose Revolution and the toppling of Shevardnadze's government, conditions for religious minorities would markedly improve. However, Saakashvili's policies on religious freedoms were generally disappointing. Two significant steps that did occur included a more concerted effort to prosecute instigators of religious violence and an amendment allowing religious organizations to register with the state. The impact of both developments on the enhancement of religious rights has been negligible. Lutheran pastor Gary Azikov maintains, "Everything is as it was before the new government took over . . . nothing has moved forward" (Corley 2004). Also, True

Orthodox Father Zurab Aroshvili believes little has changed. When one of his parishes sought permission to construct a church, local authorities informed them that they must first receive permission from the Georgian Orthodox Patriarchate. His account reveals the continuing presence of the patriarchate in all religious decisions. "The authorities [told] our priest there . . . that they understand our plight, but officials say without patriarchate approval we can't give you permission, otherwise we would lose our jobs" (ibid.).

Even Western-oriented Mikhail Saakashvili gradually moved towards the Georgian Orthodox Church's interpretation of religious freedoms during his presidency. The temptation to draw upon religious nationalistic sentiment during the economic misfortunes of the 1990s and early 2000s was difficult to resist. Shortly after the arrest of Father Mkalavishvili, Saakashvili remarked on national television, "The Georgian state, not some local extremist who beats and raids people, should protect Georgia from harmful alien influence and extremism" (ibid.). Religious ceremonialism at government functions notably increased as the president repeatedly gave deference to the Orthodox Church, implying that nationalism and Orthodoxy are synonymous (ibid.). Although President Saakashvili, at first, kept his distance from the church, political realism and pragmatic necessity eventually eclipsed liberal idealism. This pattern of western-leaning politicians with liberal intentions retreating to Orthodox nationalism continues to this day. The church's influence on the state was most recently on display during the 2020 Coronavirus outbreak, when the church refused to participate in the lockdown and authorities had little power or resolve to force the issue (JAM 2020).

Georgia's religious freedom scores on the Pew Research Center's 2007 to 2017 improved in several key categories related to interfaith tensions. While limits on religious activity only improved by .3, interreligious tension violence improved from 5.6 to a 1.1; individual/social group harassment 4.2 to a 2.5; religious violence by organized groups 2.2 to 4.2; hostilities related to religious norms 6.0 to a 4.0 (Pew 2019). Yet this reprieve may be short-lived, as Georgia's ruling party appears determined to pass a restrictive religious law. The State Agency for Religious Issues (SARI) advocates a return to regulating registration and there are strong suspicions that SARI Chair, Zaza Vashakmadze, is positioning for such a law with the backing, albeit behind-the-scenes, of the Georgian Orthodox hierarchy (Gavtadze and Chitanava 2019). In early 2019, a group of 20 religious groups issued a letter that read in part, "A Religion Law may pose a high risk of creating in law an unequal hierarchy of religious communities, imposing certain restrictions on their activities, and creating barriers to registering religious communities" (ibid.).

Other factors suggest the recent respite in religious intolerance is not sustainable. There has been no serious movement to distance church from state. Instead, more formal avenues of communication and cooperation between church and state are being established. A February 2012 decree established a governmental commission with eight working groups discussing issues between the state and the Apostolic Autocephaly Orthodox Church of Georgia (Begadze 2017, 10). According to numerous well-respected individuals close to the Georgian Orthodox Church, the church remains a hotbed of anti-Western and pro-Russian sentiments. The church's refusal to accept the autocephaly of the Ukrainian Orthodox Church serves as stark evidence. This refusal goes directly against the agenda of the government and highlights the close association of the government of Georgia with the Church. Renowned for their hospitality, Georgians are best represented by the old Georgian saying, "The guest is a gift of God". Unfortunately for non-orthodox adherents, the spirit of that proverb does not extend to ecclesiastical hospitality.

Power Perception and Religious Pluralism

Church policy formulation on institutional design reveals an opportunistic church hierarchy, trained under Soviet patronage, with few qualms about resorting to overt hostility to non-Orthodox churches or to political bartering. Several factors have influenced the Georgian Church's perception of its power post 1991.

First, the rise of nationalism, particularly during the brutal times the country faced in the 1990s, afforded the church an opening to obstruct market liberalization. The church served as a source of national identity and stability amid the economic depression and political uncertainties that characterized the socio-economic circumstances of the first two decades after the collapse of communism. As Mikheil Shavtvaladze recently noted, "A major stimulus for the rise of religious nationalism in post-Soviet Georgia was the abrogation of communist ideology, and the demise of the Soviet Union created an ideological void that was afterwards rapidly filled with Orthodox Christianity" (2018, 59). Politicians habitually used religion as a tool for social and political action. Seeking to capitalize on the nation's ethno-religious identity and the interrelationship between nationalism and religion, officials sought to counter political fragmentation with religious commonality. Most government functions leaned heavily on religious legitimization. One priest, speaking of the 1990s, stated that, "religious nationalism, Orthodox patriotism exists also in Russia. But here, it is total. Some people sincerely believe in it. Others adhere to it only to make a career. Look at our government officials—they have traded all their portraits of Lenin for bibles and icons. Besides, this religious hysteria is not the work of isolated priests. It is the work of the patriarchate and the patriarch himself" (Quoted in Peuch 2004). Church leaders have become adept at enhancing church status by capitalizing on nationalistic sentiments.

Second, the Sovietization of the clergy also produced a cadre desensitized to democratic values. Local orthodox officials appear to have no reservations in tyrannizing non-orthodox congregations and a political culture exists that espouses "religious terrorism against the Jehovah Witnesses" (Mengeashvili 2005). Rhetoric from the patriarchate suggests that the patriarch and members of the Holy Synod are complicitous in creating an imperialistic and contentious religious atmosphere. Coupled with anti-democratic values is the tendency to resort to political means to achieve desired ends.

Lastly, the church almost certainly felt it would lose both adherents and national status in a free religious market. Furthermore, interviews conducted with church leaders suggested that many feared that a more democratic institutional design would result in calls for transparency of church financial dealings. Financial incentives are highly significant for the church to maintain the market's *status quo*. Rather than restructuring the church to compete in a religious market economy, the church at once skillfully used religious nationalism to advance its position in society and has effectively used behind-the-scenes machinations to secure legal privileges. The Georgian political landscape before 2011 appeared to place few constraints in the form of public or state disapproval on church agenda.

Research findings suggest that the church's Soviet past instilled within it a character that turned to political remedies, as a first resort, to solve institutional problems. The political instability and religious nationalism that abounded in the country after 1991 afforded the church an ideal opening to formulate an agenda on religious liberties completely unchecked by exterior considerations. Church decision-making is predicated on the assessment that the church's relative power would decrease in the presence of a free market. In the absences of a free and vibrant market, one can only speculate concerning what might occur under *laissez-faire* religious conditions. Would Georgians flock to new religious movements? Would a legitimacy crisis develop in the Orthodox Church? Might the patriarchate witness a dramatic loss of market share? The answers to these questions are difficult to answer. However, the dedication and fanaticism behind the Orthodox Church's opposition to other churches suggest that church hierarchs might answer affirmatively to these questions. The effort the church puts into preventing an open market suggests the very threat such a market presents.

5. The Lithuanian Catholic Church
A Case Study in Indifference

The experience of the Catholic Church in Lithuania serves as a counterpoint to the path travelled by the Georgian Orthodox Church. Nowhere in the Soviet Union did Communism encountered such a strong and established ideology as it did in Lithuania. The two institutions, with polar opposite remedies for the world's problems, were bound to collide in Lithuania. Fortunately for the church, that collision did not occur until the 1940s. Assessing the situation at that time, Soviet authorities likely accepted that the strength of the church as well as the religiosity of its adherents precluded its complete dismantling. The state, instead, put all its efforts into subjugating the church and transforming it into a socially insignificant anachronism (Interview 2004. Bishop Jonas Kauneskas, Panevezys, 11 Dec). Following the pattern that was set elsewhere, this was to be accomplished through the politicization of the leadership and the marginalization of the clergy. The former was accomplished with the help of a Soviet organizational structure built to encourage church leaders to invest in political identities. The latter was accomplished by severing clerical ties with society and through the methodical corruption of the church, primarily by means of an intrusive Soviet clergy recruitment policy. In contrast with the success achieved against the Georgian Orthodox Church, this destructive playbook ultimately failed in Lithuania. Antecedent conditions surely played a role in the church being much less malleable than the Soviet authorities had hoped. These conditions included the strength of the clergy's ties with the population, the durability of religious identities, and the prevalence of liberal ideals within the church. As a result, an ideological struggle ensued between Communism and Catholicism for over forty years. In the end, the church prevailed over a system that sought its destruction.

Empirical evidence suggests that this resistance mitigated any lasting institutional impact from the Soviet occupation and allowed those years to simply be a painful episode in church history rather than a defining moment that altered political identities, institutional arrangements, or church structure. Indeed, the Soviet occupation appears merely to have strengthened pre-existing identities and arrangements among Catholic elites. The success of the clergy in preventing a Soviet-style transformation or the corruption of their organization has clearly benefited the church post-1991 in competing and surviving in the transitional religious marketplace.

The Critical Juncture

The first Soviet occupation of 1940 and 1941 provided the church and its parishioners a foretaste of the religious repression to come when Soviet troops re-entered the country in 1944. Shortly following the reoccupation, the People's Commissariat for State Security (NKGB) Commissar over Lithuania sent instructions to his district chiefs informing them to "deal with the leaders of the Catholic Church with the aim of bringing them under our influence" (Streikus 2006, 64). These authorities required Catholic bishops to publicly denounce partisan resistance and support the state's plan for creating a national church with no ties to the Vatican. At first, the church hierarchy endeavored to avoid direct confrontation by stressing its policy of non-interference in politics. The church insisted that it would not condemn the rebellion nor would it support the partisans, telling its priests "to avoid contacts with the anti-Soviet underground, as that would provide the authorities with an excuse to accuse the church of disloyalty and would start unrestrained reprisals against it" (Streikus 2001, 87). The church hierarchy, led by a hand full of bishops, including Bishops Reinys, Ramanauskas, Matulionis and Paltaroko, believed that active resistance against the state through cooperation with partisans in the forest was an unwise course of action. Rather, they sought a measured rapprochement with the state, which would allow for the church's continued and uninterrupted operations.

This position of neutrality was untenable for at least two reasons. First, the Soviet authorities were fully cognizant of the influential standing of the church in the nation. The close bond between nationalism and religion "made the church a prime target of the Soviet campaign against Lithuanian national culture" (Misiunas and Taagepera 1993, 124).

Second, the religious identities of the church hierarchs forbade the church from compromising to the degree Soviet officials demanded. For instance, the Soviet prohibition on religious education and the restrictive registration initiative were considered too uncanonical for the hierarchs to support or even ignore (Chronicle 1981, XXXIV). Demands on the church were more severe than in Poland because of diminished international attention. One priest noted that "Soviet leaders' requirements were impossible for our bishops to fulfil" (Interview 2005. Anonymous, priest, Vilnius, 10 Nov). Bishop Juozas Zemaitis succinctly described the early hierarchs' precarious predicament with the rhetorical question, "How can water work with fire?" (Interview 2004. Bishop Emeritus, Marijampole, 14 Dec). It did not take long for a definitive impasse to occur.

The critical juncture was less a process than it was an event in Lithuania. 14 December 1946, for all practical purposes, was the day it transpired within the Lithuanian Catholic Church. On that day, Major Okhrimenka, the senior Soviet official over the church, presented three leading bishops with their final opportunity to cooperate with the state on Soviet terms. In his report of that meeting, Okhrimenka states that the Bishops "were made to understand clearly that as long as the episcopate and the clergy do not change their hostile position, the Soviet power will consider the church its secret and obvious enemy" (Cited in Streikus 2001, 88). Two bishops, Archbishop Reinys and Bishop Ramanauskas rejected the offer while the third, Bishop Paltarokas, accepted it with reservations. The Soviet response was quick and decisive. Two days subsequent to that meeting, Ramanauskas along with the equally defiant Bishop Matulionis were arrested. Archbishop Reinys was detained early the following year and died in a prison camp in Vladimir, Russia in 1953. The year 1947 witnessed the arrest or forced exile of other bishops and "by 1948, only one bishop was left in Lithuania—the ageing Bishop Paltarokas—but he still refused to denounce the Pope" (Misiunas and Taagepera 1993, 125). In his detailed analysis of early Soviet attempts at subjugating the Catholic Church, Arunas Streikus describes that:

> "Various types of pressure or inducement were used. The archbishop of Vilnius, Mecislovas Reinys, was promised that if he agreed to collaborate all his relatives who had been sent to places of deportation in 1941 would be

released. The bishop of Telsiai, Vincentas Borisevicius, was threatened with imprisonment because of his links with the freedom fighters. In order to persuade the vicar of the Kaunas archdiocese, Stanislovas Jokubauskis, the NKGB temporarily released from labour camp the famous statesman of the independence period, Fr Vladas Mironas, a signatory of the Independence Act in 1918 and prime minister in 1938-39, but who had been recruited as an agent while in labour camp, so that he could exert influence on the church hierarchy. Jokubauskis signed an appeal to clergy and believers urging them to end armed resistance, but refused to become a collaborator with the NKGB. The heads of other dioceses also withstood NKGB blackmail" (2006, 64).

While it is an impossible task to understand the thought processes of those early bishops, their martyrdom along with the deaths and exiles of myriad parish priests had two significant implications on the church's orientation. First, the more moderate attitude of Bishop Paltarokas permeated hierarchical decisions and behavior for the remainder of the occupation. It was by no means a policy of capitulation akin to what was adopted by the Georgian hierarchs or even the policy of pragmatism of other churches. Rather the early arrests had a sobering effect on the surviving leaders and made them appreciate that, at least superficially, they had to associate with the authorities. Active resistance and blatant disobedience were understood to be a ruinous strategy in the 1940s and 1950s. Prelate Barnardas Suziedelis concluded:

"If the clergy adheres to a reactionary course, we will be crushed. A way must be found to maintain contact with the authorities and achieve a modus vivendi with them" (Quoted in Streikus 2001, 89).

Many church leaders resolved to engage but not compromise with the authorities and to make the preservation of religion, and not the end of occupation, its central task (Streikus 2001, 89). The authorities' unlimited power of punishment during the 1940s and 1950s, however, meant that negotiations with the church were effectively conducted at gunpoint. Destalinization and increased international scrutiny of human rights violations starting in the 1960s caused negotiations to become less one-sided and afforded the hierarchs more opportunity to resist Soviet religious policy. Father Bitaytas of the Kaunas Diocese noted:

"Our church leadership resisted the state in every way they could, short of being arrested and imprisoned. In the early days this meant they could do very little because the authorities had no restraint on their repressive actions, but under Brezhnev and Gorbachev the church leadership was able to be a little more overtly defiant" (Interview 2004. Kaunas, 14 Nov).

The second ramification of early hierarchical resistance was that the critical juncture shifted the administrative leadership role of the church from first tier to second tier leaders. The heavy surveillance and paralyzed operational status of Lithuanian bishops made them largely figureheads. Bishop Kauneskas noted that because of the restrictions on their activities, early Soviet-era bishops showed their heroism not so much by what they did but by what they refrained from doing (Interview 2004. Panevezys, 11 Dec). Parish priests with exceptional skill and charisma filled this vacuum by taking up the responsibility of leading the resistance. In many ways they became the *de facto* leaders of the church, as the head priest of Vytautas Church in Kaunas opined. (Interview 2004. Kaunas, 16 Nov). Sigitas Tamkevicius and Jonas Kauneskas, who after 1991 would be ordained bishops, were leading religious dissidents and had disproportional degrees of power and influence considering they were mere parish-level priests. These priests and second-tier leaders led the fight in resisting Soviet religious policy and organizing dissident activities in the 1960s and 1970s (Interview 2004. Algimantas Kvedaravicias, Leader of Evangelical Reformed Church, Vilnius, 25 Nov). This increased in strength during the 1980s, influenced both by the Polish example and the opportunities that Gorbachev's glasnost and perestroika initiatives afforded.

At the parish level, priests, monks and the laity defied Soviet policy through secret religious ceremonies, street protests, the publication of forbidden literature, and myriad other subversive activities. Despite an intense recruitment campaign, by 1956 only 60 out of 900 working priests had been recruited (Streikus 2006, 65). Streikus explains that even recruited priests were not always dependable:

"It is clear from various KGB notes and reports that a considerable percentage of the recruited priests were not useful; some of them avoided passing on the more important information, some deliberately passed on disinformation, and some would coordinate their reports with the individuals on whom they were to in-form" (2006, 66).

In describing the Polish Catholic Church, Irena Borowik could have equally been depicting the Lithuanian branch when she said that the church "managed to mark out a part of the social environment within definite boundaries and establish itself as a macrosystem capable of contesting the state system on equal terms, both at the symbolic level and that of social mobilization" (1994, 136). Repression and restrictions drove religiosity and ceremonies underground. Citizens quickly viewed the church as a defender of the nation. In fact, the concept of the church and the nation became synonymous. Jeffery Haynes asserts that "the identification of the nation and Catholicism was so strong during the communist era that loyalty to the Church was viewed as a question of patriotism" (1998, 97-88). The religious struggle by the church became an important element of the overall resistance.

The Lithuanian Catholic Church's struggle and resistance against Soviet religious policy is well known and extensively documented. Discussions with Soviet-era religious officials simply reinforce the common perception of the church and its clergy as a rebellious organization fighting for freedom and religious liberties against the tide of Soviet repression and Marxist atheism. In the opinion of nearly every priest, both young and old, as well as those that served during the Soviet era or that commenced their careers after independence, there is unanimous admiration for the church's "dreadful struggle against communism" (Interview 2004. Alfonsas Svarinskas, Catholic priest, dissident, MP, Vilnius, 18 Nov). They feel that their church acted admirably under Soviet occupation and describe the relationship between the USSR and the church in adversarial terms (Interview 2004. head priest of St. Theresa's Church and Carmelite Cloister, 6 Nov). One emeritus bishop described the years under communism as an atheistic occupation (Interview 2004. Vladas Mickelevicius, Bishop Emeritus of Kaunas, 16 Nov). Most of the Soviet-era-martyred bishops and priests hold a near saint-like status in the church today. Pictures and busts of these persecuted clergy adorn the churches and clergy offices throughout Lithuania. One of the most influential Soviet religious dissidents in Lithuanian, the late Alfonsas Svarinskas, summarized the struggle this way:

> "The goal of the communists was to destroy the conscience of the people, that is to destroy religious belief. The church's aim was to safeguard, to protect the conscience and soul of the people" (Interview 2004. Vilnius, 18 Nov).

Father Svarinskas' history is representative of the experiences of many dissident clergy. Over the space of 45 years, he was arrested three times and spent a total of 22 years in Soviet work camps. The first arrest was for subversive behavior as a theology student. His second arrest and imprisonment was for what a Soviet prosecutor labelled, his "anti-Soviet attitude which runs like a red thread through all [his] sermons.... whenever [he] says 'godless', [he] intends it to mean the Soviet Government" (Chronicle 1989, 36). His last imprisonment was a result of his role in editing the underground journal, *The Chronicle of the Catholic Church in Lithuania*. Only through the personal intervention of President Reagan was he eventually released into exile. Although all but one Lithuanian bishop was murdered or exiled while Father Svarinskas was in prison and countless churches and monasteries closed, he remains adamant, as do most Lithuanian priests, that the "Soviet religious policy as carried out by the KGB was successful in destroying nearly everything in the church physically. They raped our church. But they did not succeed in ruining the church from the inside" (Interview 2004. Alfonsas Svarinskas, 23 Nov).

The church's critical juncture decision and success in preventing an institutional take-over by the Soviet apparatus is attributable to numerous factors. The relative late arrival of Bolshevism to Lithuania played a role. In contrast with the situation in Georgia and Russia, Soviet religious policy was not fully implemented in the Baltic States until after the Second World War. Although the church certainly felt the repressive policies of the Soviets, it did not experience the most egregious abuses of the Stalinist religious purges during the 1930s. Antecedent conditions were also a factor. The church's theology, historical role as a defender of freedom, and its independent hierarchical establishment, traced back to Rome, all undoubtedly influenced the critical juncture decision and the ensuing resistance. While the Vatican's presence in Lithuania was much less extensive than in Poland, the church's ties with Rome certainly accounted to some degree for the strength of the church compared to other Soviet-era churches. However, Christel Lane astutely attributes the position of the church, not to these factors, but to its struggle, "The better survival of the Lithuanian Catholic Church than other churches in the Soviet Union does not just reflect a slightly more lenient treatment by the political authorities, but is in large measure due to the greater vigour, vigilance and militancy of the church and its believers in the face of efforts to destroy it" (1978, 209). Similarly, Bishop Kauneskas stated that "resistance creates strength and our resistance served as a catalyst to strengthen our church" (Interview 2004. Panevezys, 11 Dec). The variations in Soviet-era accommodationism among the Catholic Churches of Lithuania, Poland, Croatia, Slovenia and Hungary demonstrate that Catholic tradition and practices by themselves were not definitive in determining the critical juncture outcome or the Soviet experience.

The Church struggled, not solely to defend the religious conscious of Lithuania against Marxist humanism, but also to secure its own institutional independence from Sovietism. Lengthy interviews in Lithuania reveal a church with pre- and post-Soviet experiences and a contemporary orientation that is the antithesis of those of the Georgian Orthodox Church. In stark contrast to the Georgian Orthodox Church, which as a state-favored church had little incentive for effective ministry, the Lithuanian Catholic Church never ceased striving to administer pastoral care. While the Georgian Orthodox Church's ties with the Soviet apparatus were deep-rooted, the Lithuanian Catholic Church stayed organizationally separate from the state. While the Georgian Church's institutional integrity was compromised, the Lithuanian Church's integrity remained intact. Finally, while the Georgian Orthodox Church was quickly co-opted by the state and consequently suffered half a century of Soviet encroachment and communist transformation, the Lithuanian Catholic Church resisted and fought against Soviet "sources of continuity" (Luong 2002, 51). The root of this contrast was the respective critical juncture of each church. This resistance on the part of the Lithuanian Catholic Church resulted in the Soviet institutional legacy having minimal significance on church identity, political orientation, or policy after 1991.

The Historical Context: Soviet Legacy

Church Politicization

As with the Georgian Orthodox Church, the Soviet system sought to politicize the religious sphere in Lithuania by reorienting religious elites' identities away from the laity and spiritual accomplishments and towards the state. The state "hoped they would weaken religious leaders' authority by creating the conditions in which both ordinary religious believers and priests would be as little dependent on the hierarchy as possible" (Haynes 1998, 90). They attempted to achieve this by first severing the administrative links between the hierarchy and parish-level clergy. Second, by thus segregating church leaders from the parish—and for that matter the Vatican—and with the help of a portfolio of incentives ranging from luxurious apartments to the acquisition of other denominations' property, the authorities hoped to have Catholic Church leaders in Lithuania view their successes purely in terms of bargaining with the state. While they were somewhat successful in accomplishing the former, their efforts at the latter were severely frustrated. The Soviet incentives for cooperation, which were remarkably effective among opportunistic Georgian clergy, largely failed to entice Lithuanian Catholic leaders to change their loyalty. Father Ceponis of Vilnius notes that "The [Soviets'] mistake was that they did not count on the church leaders being truly religious. . . they believed their allegiance could be bought easily" (Interview 2004. head priest of St. Nicholas' Church, Vilnius, 3 Dec). The imprisonment of the early bishops and of countless other clergy during the Soviet occupation compelled leaders to negotiate with the state. However, these negotiations were only a result of repressive coercion and were not tantamount to capitulation. Few individuals, within and without the church, dispute this assertion (Interview 2004. Father Edvardas, Palaimintojo Jurgia Matulaicio Basilica, Vilnius, 27 Nov). Indeed, opinion patterns suggest that more than 90 percent of Catholic clergy approve of the actions of church hierarchs under communism and maintain that the state was unsuccessful in infiltrating and controlling church leadership. Another factor, which prevented a politicization of the Lithuanian hierarchy, is simply that the hierarchy hardly existed. The quick capitulation of the Georgian Church meant that nearly all the church elites were still in their respective posts. The liquidation of the Lithuanian leadership in the late 1940s and the inability to re-staff vacant positions meant that the face of the church was represented by a relatively small number of men.

The primary incentive offered to the church for cooperation was a seat at the bargaining table to determine Soviet-era religious institutional design. Although this privilege was largely an illusion, obedient churches were favored over insubordinate churches and a hierarchy of churches resulted. In this way, the state intentionally fostered and reinforced political "cleavages by creating asymmetrical power relations, and hence political competition" (Luong 2002, 39) between religious groups. Because the Catholic Church opted for insubordination, it sat out this competition and was never entangled in the Soviet matrix of political bargaining and power. This is partly evident before and after 1991 by the church's amiable relations with other denominations in Lithuania. The church's decision to forgo deep or meaningful dialogue with authorities meant that the Soviet experience did not engender or fortify political identities among church elites.

The state's inability to persuade church leaders to support the peace movement or to distort the true nature of the Soviet regime at international conferences manifests the failure of the state to transform church leaders' identities from the religious to the political. Bishop Zemaitis stated, "While other church leaders were confessing the good of the USSR in conferences, our bishops were escaping these same conferences. The KGB would hand pick priests to attend, but even they would not speak of imaginary freedoms" (Interview 2004. Bishop Emeritus, Marijampole, 14 Dec). Soviet incentives such as career advancement or property had few takers within the church during the 1960's. Only the threat of imprisonment kept most leaders from subversive behavior. The KGB activities against lower-level priests were even less successful. Special attention was paid to recruiting seminary students, but in 1955 only 3 out of 77 had been successfully recruited and by 1980, 7 out of 50. This led the KGB to report that "an absolutely unsatisfactory situation exists in the field of infiltration and recruitment of agents in the Catholic seminary in Kaunas" (Streikus 2006, 66). Arunas Streikus writes about the complete disintegration of Soviet recruitment pretensions on the church in the 1980s:

> "It was becoming ever more difficult for the KGB to find new collaborators among the clergy. After the emergence of an underground press, it became easier for those who were being blackmailed to escape KGB traps. . ... After an alternative mechanism for the preparation of priests started to function, in the shape of a secret seminary, it was more difficult to recruit agents among the ordinands too" (2006, 66).

An exhaustive list of acts of resistance, underground activity and stubborn defiance by leaders of the church could be cited as further validation of their unwillingness to operate in the political arena. Bishop Matulionis' memorandum of 1945, adequately encapsulates the church's Soviet-era church-state doctrine:

> "The Catholic Church coexists with different forms of administration only if the execution of its entrusted mission to humanity is not hindered; however, it will never agree to be a tool of secular power" (Streikus 2001, 101).

This hierarchical-level resistance and the unsuccessful Soviet attempt at politicization of the Lithuanian Catholic Church is evident from conversations with Catholic clergy post 1991. The majority of church leaders believe that the church's success depends not on state access or protectionism but on its ability to better organize and consolidate the church's temporal and spiritual resources. Officials cite institutional goals, which require non-political means to be accomplished. They show little interest in being anything but the conscience of the people. While most would agree that the church should be privileged for its historic role in Lithuanian society, few wish the church to engage in political bargaining and most agree that the church should not endorse political parties or candidates. Among Catholic elites, 85 percent believe the church should abstain from direct participation in the political process.

Even the historical link between Lithuanian Catholicism and nationalism as well as the pervasive nationalistic feelings among church clergy is apolitical. Conversations with religious elites reveal that many high-level clergy distrust their president and parliament, but are proud of the ideals of freedom and human rights that the nation represented for so many years during the dominance of the Soviet Union. One priest remarked, "My patriotism is in the nation not the state" (Interview 2004. head priest of St. Raphael the Archangel's Church, Vilnius, 20 Nov). Another priest noted that during the years of communist repression, "the flag was forbidden to be shown in public or private so believers would discreetly display the colours of the flag in furniture and in the fabric of wall hangings" (Interview 2004. Father Miroslav, head priest of the Church of the Holy Spirit, Vilnius, 24 Nov). While a strain of nationalism is clearly strong among many, particularly older priests, the church as a whole has not been as pre-occupied as has the Georgian Orthodox clergy in leading the creation of a post-communist national and ethnic identity.

The lack of politicization stands in stark contrast to analogous non-subservient churches, such as the Polish Catholic Church. Both churches resisted Soviet religious policy, but differing circumstances allowed the Polish Church's opposition movement to take on a greater political character. The more lenient social and political atmosphere in Poland allowed the church to work within the political system, such as participating in local level elections to strengthen its own position and oppose totalitarianism. This activity politicized the church to some degree and accounts for the political mannerisms of the church in the early transitional years. The hesitancy on the part of the public to accept the church as a political player, minus a heroic cause such as the dismantling of a tyrannical regime, led the Polish Church to experience a lessening of its politically influential Soviet-era standing. While this foray into politics was short-lived, it nevertheless demonstrated the appeal of churches' for political avenues of engagement. The Lithuanian Catholic Church, on the other hand, never engaged in in Soviet-era politics and, therefore, had less desire or competency to seriously dabble in politics post 1991. The church's present perception of its power and influence remains firmly rooted in its connection with society and its ability to deliver spiritual fulfilment and not in church-state relations.

LITHUANIAN CATHOLIC CHURCH 127

Soviet Administrative Structure

In addition to attempts at hierarchical identity transformation, the Soviet state deliberately and systematically attacked the church on an administrative level in order to weaken its ability to operate and provide proper pastoral care to its parishioners. This was done, to a certain degree, to every church; however, the ineffectiveness of atheistic propaganda on the Lithuanian population, coupled with the church leaderships' unwillingness to be a pliable tool of the state, necessitated a focus on destroying church effectiveness and on weakening its ties with society. The plan required the controlled turnover of clergy with conformists and KGB-informants replacing defiant priests.

The initial plan of Soviet religious planners was to marginalize parish-level clergy through the creation of religious community committees (dvatsatka) with plenary powers over activity and property in parishes. Clergy were excluded from the committees, which were intended to be stocked with atheists (Vardys 1981, 33). In 1947, the state attempted to force this Soviet organizational model on the church by registering all church personnel and property. The aim of registration was "to break down the leading role of the clergy in the church" (Streikus 2001, 92). This action replaced the clerical structure of the church with religious communities run by layman. The registration initiative was adamantly resisted by all elements of the church, and only after another round of arrests was it implemented piecemeal. The plan actually backfired on the state to a degree since only the most religiously committed parishioners became members of the church committees, "and in this way they did not become tools for the interference of the Soviet authorities into the life of the parishes. On the contrary, they even contributed to the modernization of the church and encouraged the laity to take a more active part in the life of the church" (ibid., 94). The registration, however, allowed the state to control the movement of clergy between parishes and forced the church to significantly curtail new priest acquisitions.

All seminaries were closed with the exception of the Kaunas Seminary and all appointments of priests from that seminary had to be screened by the Director of Religious Affairs in Vilnius. By streamlining and controlling the flow of new priests, the state believed it could fill the ranks of the clergy with either subservient priests or uncommitted and inefficient ones. Bishop Kauneskas of Panevezys explains, "In 1975 the KGB started to place subservient priests, gay priests and even unhealthy priests into the clergy in order to weaken the moral standing of the church. I was kept from joining the priesthood for 14 years. Only when the KGB learned of my deteriorating eye-sight did they allow me in" (Interview 2004. Panevezys, 11 Dec). He explains further that even compromised priests assisted in the resistance:

> "If I had illegal religious material the KGB would confiscate it and arrest me, but they would look the other way if a priest friendly to the state had such literature. Therefore, we would purposely store things with such priests. I honestly believe that there was not a single priest who, of his own free will, was fully cooperative with the KGB. Many of the informant priests were in actual fact blackmailed into compromise" (ibid.).

Another famous religious dissident who spent decades in Siberian prison camps was also unwilling to condemn priests who cooperated with the state. "Many of these priests were simply scared to be sent to Siberia; they had no desire to ruin the church or be its enemy" (Interview 2004. Petras Plumpa, Soviet-era dissident, Vilnius, 12 Nov). One Catholic priest described the obstacle that the Soviet recruitment policy faced in Lithuania, "Soviet attempts to interfere directly with the church were doomed to failure because priests were unwilling to bow to a secular atheistic power" (Interview 2004. Anonymous, senior Catholic priest, Vilnius, 31 Oct).

Although the majority of priests were far from tools of the state, some Soviet appointed clergy were clearly KGB informants. The infusion of these priests primarily occurred from 1975 to 1985. These so-called 'compromised' clergy were zealously pursed and extracted after independence in a very public campaign to cleanse the church. Many believed that a "reformation had to occur in the church in order to rid her of the effects of communism" (ibid.). Petras Plumpa, a political and religious prisoner for 23 years was instrumental in this internal reformation. While working for the Services of Safety of the Lithuanian Republic, he scrupulously examined and passed on to church leaders, KGB archival documents which detailed that agency's contacts in the church. In a very transparent way, these documents were released to the public and most of the heavily compromised clergy were dismissed, forced into retirement or given undesirable posts. Plumpa explained his role:

> "I was given the responsibility of finding the information with which the Vatican was able to cleanse the inner vessel. After the war and until the mid- seventies when I began my second prison term, one third of the church leaders were imprisoned and the rest persecuted. From 1975 onwards, the KGB started a new method. If you can't cut the head off, then determine what goes in the brains. That is to say they tried to infiltrate the church by appointing agent-priest and bishops throughout the country. This is why the reformation in the church was necessary and why the church asked for my help. I went through the KGB documents and decided which priests were agents and which priests were just under pressure. It was all mostly clear. However, many priests were not agents but just scared to be thrown into prison" (Interview 2004. Vilnius, 12 Nov).

Bishop Kauneskas, one of the three surviving members of the Catholic Committee for the Defence of Believers' Rights, concluded in 2004 that "The church did a very good job of sifting through the clergy after 1991. I would say we have fewer than one hundred priests out of thousands who were Soviet informants" (Interview 2004. Panevezys, 11 Dec).

It is fair to conclude that Soviet authorities were successful in weakening the church to the extent that the church hierarchical structure was severely broken as it immerged from communism. Yet as an institution, with the capacity to serve its adherents and provide temporal and spiritual care exclusive of state intervention, the church quickly became functional and efficient after 1991 (Interview 2004. Father Ribandov, Assistant to Bishop of Vilnius, Vilnius, 26 Oct). The assistance of Rome undoubtedly quickened this bounce-back. After 1991, there was an enormous infusion of new priests as well as the opening of seminaries throughout Lithuania stocking parishes with theologically trained, well-educated, and well-travelled students (Interview 2004. Gintaras Cernius, priest of Palaimintojo Basilica, Vilnius, 30 Nov). The caliber of these students appears to be very high with many speaking three or four languages (Interview 2004. Father Petr, senior official in Charge of Seminary Training, Vilnius, 2 Nov).

The combination of church resistance to a Soviet administrative takeover, the post-1991 purge of subservient priests with the assistance of Plumpa, and the steadying hand of the Roman Catholic Church resulted in the church feeling little constraint on its ability to operate and distribute religious resources in the transition.

In contrast to the defensive posture of many within the Georgian Church, the Lithuanian Catholic clergy feel that they were in a favorable position to operate after 1991, both in terms of reputation and in providing for the spiritual care of the populace (Interview 2004. Father Ramunas, head priest of St. Anne's Church, Vilnius, 30 Oct). One priest boldly asserted, "The [communists] attempt to destroy the church failed" (Interview 2004. head priest of St. Raphael the Archangel's Church, 20 Nov). While Georgian Orthodox clergy note Soviet oppression to justify their inability to compete thus necessitating restriction of new religious entrants, Catholic clergy rarely mention Soviet-era constraints when discussing their church's transitional problems. Catholic clergy do not believe that communist oppression crippled them competitively after 1991. Their optimism is not simply residual defiantism from the Soviet-era or loyalist enthusiasm. Many clergy have genuine concern about a diminished religiosity among Lithuanians. However, they are much more likely to ascribe this to present-day trends and western influences than to the atheistic indoctrination of Lenin-Marxism or a competitive disadvantage because of Soviet-era oppression.

Legitimacy and Organization Unity

Apart from strengthening the institutional integrity of the church, the post-1991 church reformation and the transparency of Petras Plumpa's work allowed the church to retain its legitimacy in the eyes of the people. Perhaps more than any other Soviet-era constraint on a religious firm, credibility seems to be the most influential determinant of a church's transitional success. The link between legitimacy and competitiveness is inseparable to a religious organization. Since religious commodities are intangible, the reputation of the supplier stands proxy for the product. In contrast to the Soviet-era behavior of the Georgian Orthodox Church, the

Lithuanian Church's struggle against communism enhanced the organization's social credibility. In Lithuania, the church's continued positive position in society has directly contributed to its competitiveness *vis-à-vis* other churches. Bishop Sabutis of the Lutheran Church opined, "The position of the Catholic Church in society is extremely strong and was hardly weakened by communism" (Interview 2004. Bishop of Lutheran Church in Lithuania, Vilnius, 3 Nov). It is interesting to note that even early Soviet-era clergy were not oblivious to the relationship between resisting Marxist atheism and keeping the trust of the people. An underground, religious dissident wrote as early as 1972:

> "No one in Lithuania believes that dialogue is possible with the Soviet government. The atheistic authorities need it only in order to get into a better position to destroy the Church the more successfully from within. In Lithuania it is plain to all that the church will not be destroyed if the priests are imprisoned, or if school children are forced to speak and act against their beliefs, or if there is no Catholic press and no officially published prayer books or catechisms; but the Catholic Church in Lithuania will lose the people if it should lose their confidence because of bootlicking the Soviet government. Something similar to this has already happened to the Russian Orthodox Church" (*Chronicle* 1989, 149)

Church resistance coupled with Plumpa's internal cleansing allowed the church, at least as a respected social institution, to be robust after 1991. In this way, the struggle with communism has helped the church to, "stay close to the people, identify with the population's spiritual, social and national needs" (Vardys and Sedaitis 1997, 116-117). Consequently, the church "came out of the ordeal of almost half a century of suppression strong enough to command attention" (ibid.). Opinion polls verify this idea by ranking the church as one of the most trusted institutions in the country. A survey found that three-fourths of Lithuanians "feel that the Church can contribute significantly to solving the moral, family, spiritual and social problems of society", opposed to 38.5 percent in Estonia and 55.1 percent in Russia (Bogomilova 2004, 5-6). Bishop Kauneskas notes, "More than any other Catholic nation, the Church in Lithuania is very well respected in the eyes of its citizens. It was so during the Soviet times and so it is now" (Interview 2004. Panevezys, 11 Dec).

The lack of discontentment both inside and outside the church contributed to the absence of schismatic groups or even internal dissensions among clergy. The opinions and orientation of Catholic clergy are surprisingly uniform. It is important to note that Catholic clergy, on the whole, seem to have misinterpreted the foundation of public support for the church under communism. Many assumed that the church's resistance would "increase spirituality among Lithuanians" (Interview 2004. Bishop Emeritus Zemaitis, Marijampole, 14 Dec). Such an assessment has proven to be misguided. Jeffery Haynes suggested that the church became a resistant beacon not entirely for religious reasons, but for more practical reason, "In communist societies there were no alternative social spaces where opposition could organize; everything else was dominated by the Party-State. However, church buildings sometimes offered a physical space, if their clergy were sympathetic to pro-democracy demands" (2001, 48). While the Soviet-era struggle did strengthen the church's social legitimacy, transitional trends suggest that it did not strengthen the faith of Catholic adherents.

Church Political Culture

The inability of Soviet authorities to fully co-opt the church and to alter church leaders' perception of their own power has also had a profound influence on the orientation of clergy. Prior to the annexation of Lithuania by the Soviets, the Lithuanian Catholic Church was a key actor on the political scene as a supporter of independence, democracy and reform. Stanley Vardys and Judith Sedaitis described how "the church supported the establishment of a democratic system and almost belligerently opposed the rise of authoritarian rule in the 1930s. The bishops denounced censorship and closure of political parties, fought for freedom of Catholic organizations, and helped to contain the extremism of the nationalist regime" (1997, 33). That same progressive tendency toward reform and opposition to totalitarianism continued in the communist era and was not diminished by the bitter persecutions suffered as a result of Bolshevik repression.

The battle against communism and the struggle for religious and individual freedom is still in the forefront of most clergy thinking. The values of democracy, freedom, and human rights, which the church fought so long to safeguard, are still possessed and practiced to a large degree by its leaders. Bishop Zemaitis notes that the church "learned democratic values during non-democratic times" (Interview 2004. Bishop Emeritus, Marijampole, 14 Dec). Far from adopting the authoritarian Soviet political culture, the years of Soviet religious policy only strengthened the church's pre-existing values. When asked to define the church's primary transitional task, Catholic clergy are more apt to respond with a positive statement, such as to "spiritually feed the Lithuanian people", while Georgian clergy are more likely to respond defensively such as to "defend the soul of the nation."

Evidence of the clergy's progressive ideology is found in their abhorrence of many of Putin's non-democratic reforms and in their acceptance of religious freedoms (Interview 2004. Monk Miroslav, Franciscan Official of the Blessed Virgin Mary Assumption Church, Vilnius, 27 Oct). Concerning the latter, Bishop Tunaitis commented on the appearance of new religious groups, "They are everywhere now and we rejoice that they have the freedoms we were once denied for so long" (Interview 2004. Auxiliary Bishop of Vilnius, Vilnius, 6 Dec). Bishop Kauneskas more reluctantly opined, "There should, of course, be freedoms, but I don't always joy in it" (Interview 2004. Panevezys, 11 Dec). Opinion patterns of Lithuanian Clergy and Georgian leaders reveal the former being much more supportive of religious freedoms than the latter. Sixty-nine percent of Catholic leaders interviewed support the right of non-traditional religious groups to own property. Furthermore, three-fourth of respondents maintain that the plurality of denominations is good for society. Catholic clergy—hierarchical or parish level—lack the culture of inefficiency, authoritarianism and anti-democracy, which permeates many former Soviet institutions.

In summary, when the critical juncture choice between Soviet collaboration and recalcitrance confronted the church, the latter was clearly chosen. The Lithuanian Catholic Church, more than any other religious organization within the former Soviet Union, defied Soviet religious policy.

On an institutional basis, they successfully fought against a Soviet style transformation. Soviet religious policy failed to transform the church into an inefficient politicized organization. Consequently, the church's Soviet past has not had significant influence on its activities or behavior post-independence. This is evidenced by 83 percent of Catholic leaders interviewed maintaining that the Soviet repression has not amounted to a serious constraint on their church's transitional activities. A post-Soviet analysis of the Lithuanian Catholic Church reveals that:

1. The leadership of the church is not excessively politically-minded or pre-occupied with engaging in the political process.
2. The church's administrative structure, while severely weakened by communist oppression, has been quickly rebuilt, largely with the assistance of the Roman Catholic Church.
3. No significant internal strife has arisen and the church has kept and enhanced its positive public image in Lithuania.
4. The church's leaders continue to possess the progressive values held by the pro-democratic hierarchs of the early 20th Century.

The Immediate Context: Transitional Marketplace

Legal Framework

Religious tolerance and the abundance of religious liberties have never been under serious threat in Lithuania since independence and "government policy continues to contribute to the generally free practice of religion" (Freedom Report 2004a). Although Roman Catholicism is by far the dominant religious organization in the country, legislation does not recognize a state religion. Differentiation between traditional religions, state-recognized religions, and registered groups does exist. For instance, nine religious communities are classified as traditional by the Lithuanian state. They are: Latin Rite Catholics, Greek Rite Catholics, Evangelical Lutherans, Evangelical Reformed Church, Orthodox Christians (Moscow Patriarchate), Old Believers, Jews, Sunni Muslims, and Karaites. Traditional religions are entitled to certain privileges; however, the number of religions classified as traditional is large while the extent of their privileges is not substantial enough to qualify as a competition-distorting non-tariff barrier (ibid.). John Anderson concluded that of all traditionally dominant churches in the former USSR, "Lithuania's national church is amongst the least formally privileged 'national' church, whilst its minorities have experienced very little in the way of legal and institutional constraints" (2003, 141).

Church Structure and Policy Making Processes

Institutional and policy legacies from the Soviet past have had minimal impact on the post-independent institutional design process in Lithuania. Bishop Kauneskas asserts that the Soviet religious structure was "completely opposite from the system the Lithuanian people desired" (Interview 2004. Panevezys, 11 Dec). Shortly after the demise of the Soviet Union, a constitution was passed which provided religious rights to both individuals and organizations. Membership in the European Union contributed to this religious liberalization. The June 1993 Copenhagen European Council outlined the following European Union accession criteria for Central and Eastern European nations: "Membership requires that the candidate country has achieved stability of institutions guaranteeing democracy, the rule of law, human rights and respect for and protection of minorities" (European Council 1993).

In such a *laissez-faire* religious market structure, the Lithuanian Catholic Church quickly regained its prominent role as the national church and overall church activity increased after 1991. This church restoration coincided with the infusion of an abundance of religious firms. The absences of the legacies of Sovietism, however, meant that the Lithuanian Catholic Church entered the transition comparatively unfettered. Consequently, it has faced few transitional constraints and, therefore, experienced a vastly dissimilar transitional context compared to its Georgian counterpart.

Church-state interactions in Lithuania are straightforward and transparent, for the most part. The church restricts contact with the state by all clergy outside of the twelve-member Bishops' Conference. Members of that Conference consist of diocesan bishops, titular bishops and currently three retired bishops. The three-member Permanent Council has frequent contact with government officials during which church positions on societal issues are presented. Several bishops place little emphasis on these governmental meetings and express doubts that the church's positions carry much weight in government decision making.

Market Dynamics

The present religious institutional design in Lithuania theoretically should provide for a vibrant religious marketplace. Market access is liberal; state favoritism is minimal; and religious firms are plentiful. Yet despite a legislative framework that provides for a free and competitive religious market, religious activity has not flourished in the nation, particularly among non-traditional entities. By 2004, only 16 percent of religious associations and communities registered by the Ministry of Justice were non-traditional religious groups; and only 0.23 percent of the population were affiliated with such groups (Freedom Report 2004a). According to the 2011 census, less than 1 percent of the population belongs to other religious groups such Jehovah's Witnesses, members of the Full Gospel Word of Faith Movement, Pentecostals/Charismatics, Old Baltic faith communities, Baptists, Seventh-day Adventists, Methodists, members of the New Apostolic Church, and The Church of Jesus Christ of Latter-day Saints (Freedom Report 2017). In many cases, supply has outstripped weak demand to such an extent that religious firms that entered the market after the 1991 liberalization have abandoned their activities in the country.

Religious activity in Lithuania is largely unregulated, but is neither competitive nor pluralistic. This fact would seem to contradict the supply-side rational choice assumption that state regulation and favoritism are negatively correlated with religious pluralism. The Lithuanian state does not provide the church with a comparative advantage, yet non-traditional religious groups do not thrive in the country. To understand why this is the case, it is essential to distinguish between government-granted monopolies and monopolies created by market features. Unlike the Georgian Orthodox Church, which, at least in part, owes its hegemonic position to the state, the Lithuanian Catholic Church has monopolized the religious market due to historical and competitive factors. Anthony Gill has described such a church as a "religious organization, which commands hegemonic loyalty among the population, and is not tied to any secular political actor" (2005, 8). Paul Froese writes:

> "Majority religions grow most substantially in regions where minority religious groups are more highly regulated. The Lithuanian Roman Catholic [Church] is a clear exception to this trend; it was able to recruit a high percent of the population without any substantial restrictions on religious competitors" (2004a, 70).

The Catholic Church's predominance in society is not attributable to state interventionism but due primarily to the church's dominating historical and social influence and, more particularly, to the strength of the church as it emerged from communism. As one Catholic priest stated, "Lithuanian believers are not dissatisfied with our product" (Interview 2004. Head priest of Church of Saints' Peter and Paul, Vilnius, 26 Nov). Both Georgia and Lithuania lack vibrant religious pluralism but for entirely different reasons.

The religious market structure in Lithuania consists of a competitive dominant church which lacks the inefficient monopolistic characteristics possessed by the Georgian Orthodox Church and maintains its market share dominance. However, all has not been entirely favorable to the Catholic Church. Although the relative quality of the church's religious commodity appears not to have lessened over time, religious participation has ebbed away from the church during the transition. While the percentage of the population affiliated with the church is not in decline, clergy stress that the activity of those adherents is becoming passive. John Anderson writes:

> "Despite the existence of a Christian Democratic Party few politicians looked to clerics for advice on policy-making, whilst the church itself has turned inward to some extent as it faces a reality where the initial religious enthusiasm of the early 1990s had ebbed. Though over 70 percent of Lithuanians still consider themselves to be Catholic most reports suggest that only 10–15 percent of the population regularly attend church" (Anderson 2003, 140).

The outflow of parishioners is not to other churches but to passivity due to westernization and secularization.[4] Jeff Haynes explains that "despite continuing adherence to religious beliefs at the level of the individual, the aggregate trend in Eastern Europe is that, under conditions of democratic pluralism, secular materialism turns attention away from traditional forms of religiosity" (1998, 88). Catholic clergy keenly perceive this trend towards religious inactivity today. This phenomenon corroborates a central tenet of religious rational choice theory: religious monopolies diminish overall levels of religious participation and belief (Gill 2005, 3).

An additional characteristic of the marketplace is the absence of religious tension in Lithuania. Most clergy, regardless of denomination, perceive very little religious hostility in their country. Two-thirds of Catholic leaders interviewed do not believe that the infusion of sectarian groups after 1991 resulted in societal tensions. One of the few early points of contention between the Catholic Church and other denominations revolved around the ownership of Soviet acquisitioned church property. But the courts dealt with these cases with a great degree of equity. Conversations with leaders of all the major Christian churches in the country reveal an environment in which churches are concerned more with internal consolidation and improvements than a preoccupation with the activities of other churches. This can partially be explained by the lack of mobility among religious believers and the minimal proselytizing efforts by most churches. Instead, most are concentrating solely on the retention of members. This non-hostility between denominations as well as the dearth of

---

4 These findings counter an assertion of Steve Bruce, that of the three Baltic nations, "Lithuania is markedly more religious than the other two and it is the one with the most homogeneous religious culture." He uses the situation in Lithuanian as evidence to discredit the link between religious pluralism and religious participation. This assessment may have been accurate directly after the fall of communism, but as the transitional institutional design played out, religious participation sharply decreased. The Catholic Church has maintained its market share in spite of decreased religious participation. Steve Bruce, 'Modernisation, religious diversity and rational choice in Eastern Europe', Religion, State and Society, 27 (1999), 265-275 at 272.

success of new entrants is reflected in the words of a leader of The Church of Jesus Christ of Latter-day Saints:

> "The influence of the Lithuanian Catholic Church and westernization is very strong here. Per capita we seem to have more success among the Russians. For instance, our Vilnius branch is half Russian and Lithuanian with meetings being conducted in both languages... Apart from occasional derogatory comments on TV directed towards us, we are largely left alone to operate freely. Links between our church and the Catholic Church do not exist. They basically don't pay us any attention and we like it that way" (Anonymous 2004. Interview with author. Senior official of The Church of Jesus Christ of Latter-day Saints, Vilnius, Nov).

While Catholic clergy are generally dissatisfied with their own church attendance, there is little sense of a competitive atmosphere. Former Bishop Zemaitis cares little about new religious entrants: "They are of no real concern to us; they are few in number and are not growing" (Interview 2004. Bishop Emeritus, Marijampole, 14 Dec). The Bishop of Panevezys has no knowledge of sectarian groups working within his diocese (Interview 2004. Bishop Jonas Kauneskas, Panevezys, 11 Dec). The Church of Jesus Christ of Latter-day Saints did, in fact, station missionaries in Panevezys shortly after 1991 but withdrew them due to a lack of success (Interview 2004. Anonymous, senior non-Orthodox leader, Vilnius, 10 Nov). This type of indifference is reflected in interview responses. Seventy-nine percent of respondents assert that the activities of sectarian groups had little or no relevance to their church's health. A further indication of this is their opinions on what poses the greatest danger to the spiritual health of society in post-Soviet Lithuania. Few mention the appearance and proliferation of non-traditional religious groups. Instead, social vices and spiritual weakness such as materialism, individualism, and hedonism were referred to as reasons for low church attendance (Interview 2004. Father Aurelijus, Director of Kaunas Seminary, Kaunas, 16 Nov).

Notwithstanding secularization trends in society, the post-Soviet years have been remarkably favorable to the Catholic Church. Apart from the rebuilding of churches and the re-opening of seminaries, the church has had no difficulty in regaining its pastoral effectiveness. While the Georgian Orthodox Church can be characterized as an organization that considers itself under siege from non-orthodox activity and has primarily taken a defensive posture through political activism, Lithuanian Catholic clergy feel confident in their church's societal position and optimistic about the future. The differing orientations have understandably influenced each church's respective policy formation on legislation concerning religious liberties. Against this transitional backdrop, as well as the Soviet past that has shaped it, hierarchs within the Lithuanian Catholic Church have had several opportunities since 1991 to articulate a position on the continuation of liberties for religious suppliers. On all occasions, they have sided with openness and hospitality.

Power Perception and Rational Decision

While the creation of the religious institutional design in Georgia was shrouded in secrecy and nationalism, the political and religious situation in Lithuania allowed the bargaining and policy making process on religious liberties and pluralism to be carried-out in a transparent manner, largely free of ulterior agendas or Soviet-era continuity. The political stability in Lithuania and the nation's Western orientation meant that the state sought much less legitimization from traditional religion than did the Georgian state.

The Catholic Church's role in creating the post-Soviet religious institutional design has been primarily advisory. Yet, even that advisory role has not been hostile to pluralism. The absence of Soviet baggage and the relatively favorable position the church had in society post 1991 were key factors in Bishops Tamkevius, Backis, Kauneskas, and Tunaitis in the late 1990s and early 2000s having little appetite for religious protectionism. These leaders had no need to cling to or find reference points from the past. The church's culture and organization stayed largely separate from the Soviet system. While the Georgian Orthodox Church played a significant role in creating the institutional design of Soviet-era religious activities in Georgia, the Lithuanian Catholic Church's defiance resulted in the church playing no role in creating the institutional design. These leaders had, in a sense, no seat at the political bargaining table that decided Soviet-era religious arrangements and, therefore, made no investment in the political decision-making process related to religious affairs. Their only influence came from opposing religious policies and the spreading of Catholic ideology. This emphasis on religious channels of influence over political avenues of power continued into the transition. Father Vitaytas characterizes this by saying, "Of course from 1940 to 1990 we had no influence, and now our political power is not much greater" (Interview 2004. Catholic priest, Vilnius, 12 Nov). The clergy do not seem overly pre-occupied with reversing this trend.

In addition to a disinterest in gaining political stature, extensive interviewing of religious hierarchs reveals that the restricting of religious pluralism and liberties and the pursuit of a political agenda against non-traditional religious groups is not a high priority of the church's leadership. Many church leaders view these groups with neither animosity nor warmth, but largely a sentiment of indifference to their existence, activities, and survival. Others demonstrate severe disdain for non-traditional religious groups such as The Church of Jesus Christ of Latter-day Saints, Jehovah Witnesses and Baptists. But even these leaders concede the right of these groups to exist and freely operate within Lithuania. The opinion of Father Ausuydos, who previously acted as a Chaplain to the Lithuanian police force and as an informal liaison between the church and the Judiciary, illustrates this point. While he has a very negative opinion of many of these new religious entrants into his country and believes that they add nothing to the spiritual vitality of society, he forcefully rejects any attempt to restrict their activity (Interview 2004. St. Theresa's Church and Carmelite Cloister, Vilnius, 6 Nov). The large gatherings that The Church of Jesus Christ of Latter-day Saints and Jehovah Witnesses' found throughout the many nations of the former Soviet Union do not exist in Lithuania. Indeed, most of these churches are expanding very slowly, if at all. The slow growth rate of non-traditional religions in Lithuania, in contrast to Georgia, results in the Lithuanian clergy feeling themselves less embedded in a zero-sum power struggle with other religious groups. The distributional advantages available to the church through state favoritism, therefore, have less appeal among Catholic clergy than Georgian, simply because state intervention would not be as significantly advantageous.

The absence of a competitive risk from other churches is just one reason Catholic leadership is not active in restricting their behavior. Another reason is the widespread acceptance of the concept of freedom of religion. The political culture within the church is supportive of the democratic recognition of the rule of law. Two-thirds of church elites interviewed assert that the government should leave sectarian groups alone. And more than three-fourths express views, which indicate a respect for democratic values and the rule of law. Those few priests who do advocate for the restricting of religious groups, use as justification the breaking of laws by these groups (Interview 2004. Vytantas Bvilivis, head priest of Marian St. Gertrude's Church, Kaunas, 16 Nov). But the anger, resentment, and criminality displayed by segments of the Georgian Orthodox Church are not found within Lithuanian Catholicism.

Another influence at play on church leaders is the diminishing of political importance and social significance of their ideas and positions. Sixty-eight percent of interview respondents believe their church has little or no influence on governmental policies and decisions. Furthermore, the democratic sentiments prevalent in Lithuanian society mean that even if the church was inclined to petition for protectionism, church leaders understand that it is unlikely that such pleas would be enthusiastically embraced by the public. Jeff Haynes's description of the post-Soviet political development in Polish society resembles what is occurring in Lithuania:

> "The paradox is that while many Poles looked to the Church as a nationalist focal point of anti-Communism, once democracy was won most shifted their attentions to conventional—that is, secular—political parties to try to achieve socio-political aspirations and objectives . . . No doubt aware of its declining influence, the Church did not dare sponsor or overtly support one particular political party" (1998, 94).

Since 1991, the church was forced to take a position on restricting the religious liberties of other churches, and on both occasions, church leadership backed the progressive status quo. These examples illustrate the church's political neutrality and non-interference as well as its rational decision to not obstruct the actions of other denominations. The first involves the short political career of Alfonsas Svarinskas. As perhaps the most famous Soviet-era dissident besides Bishop Tamkevicius of Kaunas, Father Svarinskas was elected in the early 1990s to the Lithuanian parliament as a member of the Christian Democratic Party. His harsh rhetoric directed at other churches was, however, not reflective of the church or of its clergy (Interview 2004. Egantas Rydokas, head priest of Saints' Peter and Paul, Vilnius, 26 Nov). Even during the Soviet-era, fellow clergy respected him for his integrity and subversive actions but disagreed with his radical confrontational stance toward other churches. Another religious dissident, who served with him in a Soviet work camp, recalls that while other Catholic priests would befriend and assist imprisoned religious clergy of various denominations, Svarinskas would not (Interview 2004. Petras Plumpa, Soviet-era dissident, Vilnius, 12 Nov). Bishop Sabutis of the Lutheran Church remembered hearing Svarinskas state during a political interview that the "two worst things to happen to Lithuania in 500 years were communism and the reformation" (Interview 2004. Mindaugas Sabutis, Bishop of Lutheran Church in Lithuania, Vilnius, 3 Nov). Most Catholic priests did not appreciate such rhetoric. When he began to encourage the parliament to restrict religious organizations' access to Lithuania, the church decided that it would not only refrain from throwing its weight behind such an initiative, but decided to pressure Svarinskas to resign and abstain from political participation (Interview 2004. Petras Plumpa, Soviet-era dissident, Vilnius, 12 Nov). To his death, he was considered a non-conformist by many senior church officials. In a similar move in 2001, the church did not support proposed legislation by Stanislovas Buskevicius, a nationalist member of parliament, entitled "On Barring the Activities of Sects" (Freedom Report 2004a). Articulating the church's posture on the legislation, Bishop Kauneskas stated that the Catholic Church "is not in need of assistance from politicians to fulfil our religious duties" (Interview 2004. Panevezys, 11 Dec). His remarks reflect the church's belief that the possible benefits of openly seeking institutional privileges or restricting competitors would be minimal compared with the cost that such an endeavor would exact on the church's image.

The differing structural-historical contexts of the Lithuanian and Georgian churches have led to contrasting transitional experiences, which in turn has shaped the churches' policy formation on religious liberties. This is because the variation in past experiences and the path-dependent transitional situation has profoundly affected the churches' "perceptions of the degree and direction of change in the basic parameters of the pre-existing balance of power" (Luong 2002, 103). Empirical evidence confirms that while the Georgian Orthodox hierarchs perceived a downturn in their power and influence after 1991, the Lithuanian Catholic leaders have seen their relative power with regard to other religions stay stable or even increase. The Georgian Church has, therefore, had a vested interest in seeking to design the religious market structure to retain its waning influence. The confluence of past and present contexts of the Lithuanian Church described in this chapter has resulted in three-fourths of church leaders expressing little incentive to seek an alternative to the current market structure. Most leaders perceive their church to be competitive, close to its adherents, and void of serious public relations problems. On Pew Research Center's religious freedom scores for 'limits on religious activity' Lithuania scored a 0.5—one of the lowest scores in the world and well lower than all Western European nations (Pew 2019).

6. The Russian Orthodox Church
Finding Its Voice at the Expense of Others

"The Government recognise[s] that apostasy from the Orthodox faith into another Christian confession or religious teaching is not subject to prosecution and should not involve any consequences that are unfavorable with respect to personal or civil rights; moreover, upon attainment of majority the apostate from Orthodoxy is recognized as belonging to the religious confession or teaching that he or she has chosen" (Tolerance Edict 1905).

Tsar Nicholas delivered this enlightened imperial decree on 17 April, 1905. Much has changed in the past 116 years. Indeed, the freedom of religious expression in Russia has had good and bad days. A little more than a decade removed from that edict, Russia witnessed the start of perhaps the greatest sustained assault on religion perpetrated by a nation-state in modern history. The demise of the Soviet Union ushered in a period from 1991 to 2016 in which ambiguity best defined Russia's regulatory framework for religious activities. In such an ill-defined institutional design, non-traditional churches thrived while only suffering sporadic and uncoordinated adversarial actions from the state. Unfortunately, the tolerance of the 1905 religious emancipation declaration and the vagueness of the 1990s and 2000s have given way to a more definitive policy by the state on religious pluralism. Religious policy is still not uniformly enforced from region to region, and in some cases, from town to town; however, the Yarovaya Law has provided a structure and purpose to crackdowns not seen before. The Russian government no longer reluctantly legislates and applies religious restrictive measures. To understand why it took so long for the present restrictive design to solidify in Russia, an examination of Soviet antecedents and post-Soviet market features is imperative.

The two previous chapters described how legacy and present-day market structure combined to mold church hierarchical activities and decisions in two churches. The decisiveness of the critical juncture choice, as well as the clarity of the structural and institutional legacies that materialized from that decision, afforded an orderly and analytical interpretation of the two churches' orientation as they emerged from the ashes of communism. An evaluation of the respective post-Soviet marketplace dynamics provides further insight into the interests, motivations, and reasons behind policies on religious liberties, in general, and agendas toward non-traditional religious groups, in particular. The Lithuanian Catholic Church agenda is characterized by an openness and general tolerance for non-traditional religious entities. In Georgia, the antithesis of the Lithuanian experience produced an opposite agenda, namely a resistance and hostility towards other religious groups. Legacy and market structure played a determinative role in shaping these churches' utility function on religious liberties.

In Russia, church decision making on religious liberties since 1991 has been much more muddled. This is because the intersection of the structural-historical context and the immediate-strategic context, which determines shifts in power perception, were largely ill-defined. This less coherent situation stems from the fact that the Russian Orthodox Church did not experience a definitive critical juncture. Russian Orthodox clergy both resisted and conformed to Soviet pressure. The most singular ramification of this inexact critical juncture on post-Soviet circumstances is the absence of an ideological-homogenous clergy within the Russian Orthodox Church.

Conversations with Orthodox clergy in Russia reveal a church that is much more multifarious than most Western academics depict—a church with a prominent, although often latent, moderate wing. In 1996, Jane Ellis was one of a handful of scholars to recognize two ideological persuasions in the church vying for the future of the institution (See Ellis 1996). Later, Stephen Shenfield commented that "the main division [in the ROC] is between a liberal or modernizing wing that draws inspiration from the philosopher-theologians of the Silver Age, and a fundamentalist or reactionary wing that looks back to a golden age of true Orthodoxy under the Tsars" (Shenfield 2001, 64). Only in the free market environment of the 1990s did these cleavages become apparent. I maintain that the roots of this divide between a small group of reformists and a larger segment of conservatives or traditionalists lie in the Soviets' failure to subjugate the entire church. The impact of this phenomenon—a type of halfway critical juncture between the extremes described in the two previous chapters—on current clergy demographics and church policy is significant. It is precisely this divided church, placed in the context of transitional marketplace conditions, that contributed to the fluidity of institutional design in Russia prior to 2016.

The Critical Juncture

Much scholarship has been dedicated to describing the wholesale destruction by Soviet authorities of the Russian Orthodox Church in the 1920s and 1930s. In its infancy, the Bolshevik regime sought every opportunity to destroy an institution it considered its antithesis. To this end, the regime purposely supported other religions and schismatic-Orthodox groups, or at least ignored minority religious groups while directing full attention to the disestablishment of Orthodoxy.[5] At the same time, the state unleashed a sustained anti-religious propaganda campaign and commenced an intense effort to promote socialism. The line between political repression and religious genocide became blurred as churches were destroyed, laity imprisoned, and thousands of clergy executed without trial. The clergy's response to the revolution in general, and the subsequent persecution in particular, varied. Both revolutionary and counter-revolutionary elements flourished within the church establishment. Resistance by the church, while sparsely investigated in academia, was widespread within the church; and clergy-led acts of civil disobedience were commonplace (See Husband 1998). The hierarchs in particular had hostile feelings toward the new regime and its Marxist-Leninist policies. In addition to the defiant anti-revolutionary rhetoric of the Moscow Council of 1917-18, in January of 1918, Patriarch Tikhon denounced the ruling regime in his anathema. He condemned what he called the "horrible and beastly massacres," and "satanic deeds," of the new regime and called upon "the faithful children of the Orthodox Church to have nothing to do with such monsters of the human race" (Message from Patriarch Tikhon in Struve 1967, 345-45). The Bolshevik response was overwhelming. From 1917 to 1939, approximately 80,000 Orthodox priests, monks, and nuns were murdered by the Soviet system. Of the 50,000 pre-

---

5 The history of the Renovationist Church illustrates the state's attempt to disestablish the Orthodox Church. The Renovationist Church, originally a genuine Orthodox splinter entity, was transformed by Soviet authorities into a movement designed to be a Soviet-favored alternative to Tikhon's church (See Pospielovsky 1997).

revolutionary churches, a mere 200 to 300 were operational in 1939 (Davis 2003, 11-14, 22-27).

After this initial period of severe persecution, Soviet religious strategy transformed from one directed at disestablishing the church to a policy of discrediting the institution and forcing its incorporation into the structural control of the Soviet system. Boris Talantov explained why Marxist hardliners were willing to accept this policy change:

> "Contemporary influential atheists regard[ed] adaptation as a modernization of religion which is politically useful for the CPSU and harmless for the materialistic ideology. This (Adaptation—our addition) is one of the paths to the dying out of religion" (1982, 78).

The process of church subjugation was brought about essentially by means of force, directed primarily at church leadership. A parish priest explained, "The government did not try to buy or force our loyalty, they concentrated on controlling senior church leaders" (Interview 2005. Mikhail Khclenov, parish priest of Tobolsk, 15 Aug). The example of Patriarch Tikhon serves as an illustrative case in point. Fiercely defiant of Soviet policy, he recanted and reluctantly agreed to support the ruling regime only after numerous arrests and multiple interrogations (See Kolesnikova 1997). Other hierarchs chose death as martyrs over submission. Against such repressive tactics, the church leadership structure was given the option of resisting the authorities and trying to preserve the Orthodoxy subculture and ideological integrity or of compromising with the Soviets and keeping some level of structural integrity.[6]

It is imperative to not underestimate the terms and conditions of the Bolshevik offer. At the time, Orthodox church leaders almost certainly understood how dissimilar Soviet demands were from Tsarist arrangements. The Russian Orthodox Church had long been a state religion closely tied to the political realm, but the restrictions the Soviet authorities placed upon the church differed drastically in their severity and destructive intention from the Petrine model of church-state existence. Counter-

---

6 Russian academics have named this phenomenon Sergianstvo or in the English version Sergianism which "refers to a purported doctrine of craven submission to the communist and atheistic government of the former Soviet Union on the part of the Hierarchy of the Orthodox Church of Russia, led by the Patriarchate of Moscow and All Russia" (Sergianism, 1992)

revolutionary clergy understood this distinction since they experienced first-hand the church closures and arrests that did not occur under Tsarist rule. A full capitulation to an atheistic entity was uncharted ground and was not universally accepted within the church. Over time, however, Soviet religious policy instigated a sedimentary process within the church in which accommodating clergy ascended in position and all other clergy, of whatever political orientation, settled into a compulsory ecclesiastical lethargy. Internal debate and the airing of grievances were prohibited by the church and persecuted by the CRA.

The beginning of this sedimentary process and the collaboration between the two entities has generally been regarded as starting with Tikhon's successor, Metropolitan Sergius. In his "Declaration of Loyalty", he pledged church support to the state "whose joys and successes are our joys and successes, and whose setbacks are our setbacks" (Cited in Walters 1993, 12). After Sergius' declaration, resentment began to grow among believers and clergy alike. Unease among the clergy regarding the church's proximity to the state resulted in a rift leading to the formation of the Russian Orthodox Church Abroad and the True Orthodox Church (Andreyev 1950). Both were comprised of hierarchy and clergy disenchanted with the mother church's subservience to the Soviets. As a result, both were condemned and persecuted by the Russian Orthodox Church. The example of Bishop Basil of Kineshma was typical. He was a highly respected hierarch, who refused to give in to Bolshevik oppression. His rejection of Sergius' declaration gave the authorities grounds to imprison and exile him. His sense of alienation from the mother church led him to accuse Sergius of not being Orthodox and resulted in his association with the Nomadic Council of the Catacomb Church (Saint Basil 2004).

The 1929 compromise started a process that was not totally cemented within the church establishment until Stalin's rapprochement with the church during World War II. As previously noted, the most probable single event that acted as the critical juncture occurred on 4 September 1943 when Stalin met with three metropolitans (Chumachenko 2002, 189). The precise motives and feelings of Soviet-era subservient clergy are impossible to discern. But it can reasonably be deduced from historiography of Soviet-era actions and statements of church leaders, that from Tikhon to Aleksii, an accommodation process occurred in which hierarchical attitudes towards the regime gradually evolved from one of defiant opposition, to bitterly reluctant cooperation at gun point, to eventual comfortable collaboration. Nonetheless, the entire church did not blindly follow their leaders and, as a consequence, ideological stratification arose among the clergy.

In this covenant of compromise, the state loosely agreed to give the traditionally dominant church privileged status and its hierarchy a type of elite rank in exchange for support in suppressing religious dissidents, backing the regime's domestic agenda in the international arena, and remaining silent about the destruction of churches. Domestically, the task of the hierarchs was to ensure compliance while internationally, they were to portray a country with religious freedom in which all churches unanimously backed Soviet policies.[7] Sabrina Ramet summarized:

> "The Russian Orthodox Church was subordinate and controlled by the Soviet State. Its chief newspaper was proofed by the KGB before publication. Its clergy were promoted, demoted and assigned according to the preferences of state authorities. Its curriculum and admission at its seminaries were subject to the veto of authorities. Some clergymen and Bishops turned KGB informants. As for the patriarch, he was obliged to make "positive propaganda" for the Soviet Union abroad" (1998, 229).

Soviet church representatives, which included Patriarch Aleksii, as well as Patriarch Ilya who served as a president of the World Council of Churches, not only prevented those ecumenical bodies from criticizing Soviet foreign policy, but used them as forums to preach the virtues of Marxist-Leninism and to deflect attention from dissident groups (Arnold 1993, 251-256). Despite such behavior on the part of leaders, the destruction of the church continued unabated by a regime that sought every opportunity to dismember the church, erode devotion, and minimize the effectiveness of the clergy.

---

7 Further examples of church support for the regime include: supporting the repression of the Hungarian uprising of 1956; the building of the Berlin Wall and the invasion of Czechoslovakia and Afghanistan in 1968 and 1979 respectively. An example of the church's role can be found in Metropolitan Sergius' assurance to Western journalists that priests and believers were not persecuted, "declaring there was no illegality in the way they were treated" (Ramet 1998, 230).

It is significant to note that the church hierarchy did not immediately transform into the institution described by Ramet. Furthermore, many low to middle level Orthodox officials were never fully in agreement with the actions of their ecclesiastical seniors. Even today, internal church disagreement over Soviet-era hierarchical policy remains palpable. Many priests and leaders with counter-revolutionary and anti-Soviet tendencies, who remained with the church, believe that the church's submissive posture toward the state was not absolutely necessary. One particular priest opined, "Our leaders probably could have kept more autonomy from the state despite the repression" (Interview 2005. Anonymous, priest of Orthodox Church of Resurrection, Moscow, 6 Jan). Douglas Perkins points out that many in the church believed that the decision to compromise was not essential for church survival. He states, "While persecuted, especially at the top levels—the church on the ground had weathered the storms fairly well, and in many areas, bishops had, of their own initiative, begun to create organizational trenches" (2001). However, once the compromise was completed, the church lost its ability to support such endeavors at religious preservation, and indeed, was turned into an instrument of the state to repress them. Bishops and priests who refused to swear allegiance to Stalin and Soviet values were routinely excommunicated from the Church. Many from the laity and the clergy felt betrayed by their leaders' decision to subordinate the church. Jane Ellis has written regarding these religious dissidents in Russia, who "felt themselves to be struggling not only against the Soviet state and communist party, but also against the hierarchies of their own church, who, willingly or otherwise, had become the captives of the state and, in part, its instrument for holding the church in thrall" (Ellis 1990, 307).

Resistance by elements within the Russian Orthodox Church, while less visible than in Lithuania, was nevertheless present throughout communist rule, particularly in rural Russian areas and within the republics. Jane Ellis' landmark 1986 book, *The Russian Orthodox Church: A Contemporary History*, details Russian Orthodox dissent from the 1950s till the mid-1980s. Hers is one of the only academic volumes that attempts to incorporate Russian Orthodox resistance under Soviet rule in an analysis of present-day church behavior. She cites the actions of Archbishop Khrizostom of Vilnius and Father Aleksandr Men as evidence of a reform movement in the church. This resistance was a sort of residual defiance inspired by the overt opposition of many heroic hierarchs and parish-level martyrs during the 1920s, 30s and 40s. Although much less dramatic than Catholic behavior, there were numerous examples of covert acts of rebellion by Orthodox clergy. Father Constatin commented, "Many of our priests were put in prison; others were more pragmatic in the earthly church. We had underground bishops baptizing in secret. It all depends on where you look" (Interview 2004. Anonymous, head priest of Church of Peter and Paul, Moscow, 26 Dec). The opinions of Catholic, Lutheran and even Old Believers' clergy authenticate this assertion (Perkins 2001). In Lithuania for example, many non-orthodox clergy have expressed deferential feelings towards their Soviet-era Russian Orthodox contemporaries. In particular, Catholic priests insist that there was a kind of comrade bond between the two churches in combating communism (Interview 2004. Arynac Tyashkaytec, senior priest of St. Anne's Church, Vilnius, 20 Oct). The head of the Old Believers' Church in Lithuania said that while some of the persecution of his church from Moscow were essentially undersigned by the patriarch, Russian Orthodox clergy in Lithuania never persecuted his church and even, at times, came to its aid (Interview 2004. Grigori Boyarov, leader of the Old Believers' Church in Lithuania, Vilnius, 23 Nov). Bishop Jonas Kauneskas of Panevezys stated:

> "We worked with many Russian Orthodox dissidents and priests, but not with the hierarchy. The Russian Orthodox hierarchy was totally in the hands of the Soviet power. But local priests, while less pro-active in subversive activities than our church, were resisting the authorities' policies" (Interview 2004. Panevezys, 11 Dec).

In a similar manner, the Lutheran Bishop of Lithuania, Mindaugas Sabutis, acknowledged that despite the subservient nature of the Russian Orthodox Church in Moscow, in the Baltic countries there were friendly relations between the two churches. He mentioned that, "The building in which our large congregation met in Klaipeda was completely demolished by the authorities, so the Russian Orthodox Church was kind enough to allow us to meet in one of their churches" (Interview 2004. Vilnius, 3 Nov). This is in contrast to frequent occurrences in Russia where church officials would take advantage of state persecutions of other churches to increase property and position.

One reason for the uneven or incomplete Soviet take-over of the church was the fact that the Soviet authorities purposely disrupted the church's command structure, thus causing organizational paralysis. This was accomplished by means of surveillance and the appointment of subservient church leaders. The former discouraged communications between ecclesiastical echelons (parish-diocese–synod) due to threat of persecution. The latter accomplished the same by fostering mistrust in the line of command. Parish priests were hesitant to discuss and operate with leaders they could not trust. An unintended consequence of this action was that it allowed for pockets of resistance, particularly those removed from Moscow. A 1957 KGB report listed only four out of 52 Orthodox priests in Lithuania has having been recruited (Streikus 2006). In addition, the church's position as a minority church within many of the republics fostered a mentality of cooperation with other denominations. The incompleteness of the Sovietization of the church is evident from clergy interviews where a statistically significant cohort expressed objective historical interpretations and moderate inclinations.

While the majority of Russian Orthodox clergy appear to be apologists for Soviet-era church behavior, there is much variation in how far they go in justifying their church's actions. Opinions range from blanket denials of any Soviet-era subservience or misconduct to an acknowledgment that some leaders, albeit a minority, did cooperate with the KGB. Within these two opinions is the position that "A certain degree of cooperation was required for survival" (Interview 2004. Head priest of the Orthodox Temple of Apostles Timothy and Elijah, ROC, Moscow, 20 Dec). Statements of senior church officials whose offices were very close to the Kremlin's walls are revealing. A pattern becomes apparent when their opinions and attitudes are compared and contrasted with church priests and leaders further afield in the provinces and in the former Soviet republics. This pattern appears, not according to age or even church experience or position, but geography. As one travels away from the Kremlin, attitudes toward Soviet-era church behavior appear increasingly objective.

The statements of three members of the clergy illustrate this phenomenon. Elder Priest Yaroslav is of the opinion that the church acted admirably under Soviet rule. He is much more interested in recounting tales of heroism by priests during the siege of Leningrad than he is in Soviet-era religious repression. This aged priest, working in a church adjacent to Red Square, maintains that reports of KGB-informant priests were "invented" (Interview 2004. Senior ROC official, Moscow, 26 Dec). His attitude is in contrast to that of a provincial priest who was transferred to Moscow in the 90s. He recalled that "leaders did not always act honestly; people would work in a formal manner with the KGB, but most did not sell their souls, although there were some Judases, of course" (Interview 2004. Anonymous, Catholic priest, Vilnius, 10 Nov). He was not ready to condemn the church's hierarchy, of which he is a member, but was willing to concede that many decisions and policies were questionable. On the other hand, Father Alexander of Trakai, a village in Eastern Lithuania, readily admits that compromise did take place and he went so far as to state that "Yes, after 1991 public opinion of the church was such that there was a shadow, or layer of dirt, on the Orthodox church because of compromise with the KGB by bad priests" (Interview 2004. Head Priest of the Orthodox Church of the Birth of the Holy Mother of God, ROC, Trakai, 25 Nov).

The comments of these three are mirrored by a number of other priests with the common element in each cluster of opinions being the geographic distance, both figuratively and literally, from their church's seat of power and the Soviet state. In contrast to their Lithuanian Catholic and Georgian Orthodox counterparts, there is a clear lack of homogeneity of opinion among Russian Orthodox clergy on the church's Soviet past. This suggest that many in the church were, in a sense, disingenuous servants of the Soviet state. The top echelon leaders in the church were undeniably supporting Soviet policies and were effective puppets of the state from the 1960s to the early 1980s. However, many others resisted in a passive way and were able to do so because of their circumstances.

The reality of a somewhat segmented church emerging in 1991 from Soviet repression is understandable in view of how Soviet religious policy was administered in Russia. The process of co-opting the church was done top to bottom. It was also administered in an inconsistent and incoherent manner, depending on the political climate and the whims of communist leaders. Consequently, Soviet religious indoctrination and policy were by no means universally administered. A further explanation for the incomplete nature of the takeover of the church by the state is the fact that authorities were not excessively concerned with the possibility of a Russian Orthodox-supported separatist movement because there was little chance of such activity occurring. In each of the Republics and the Eastern bloc states, the repression of churches was motivated, not so much by atheistic ideals, but rather to thwart any separatist movement, nationalism, or church-based political resistance. This was not necessary with the Russian Orthodox Church. Therefore, after the initial religious purges and the acquisition of the hierarchy, the KGB was much less intrusive in parish level affairs in the Soviet satellites compared to non-Orthodox churches. Since the likelihood of a separatist movement originating among the implanted Russians against the Russian-dominated Soviet state was highly unlikely, the KGB's efforts against the Russian Orthodox Church in such areas were relatively minimal. Father Alexander admits, "[His] situation in Lithuania shielded [him] from many persecutions" (Interview 2004. Head Priest of the Orthodox Church of the Birth of the Holy Mother of God, ROC, Trakai, 25 Nov). As a consequence, the Russian Orthodox Church in peripheral regions was less subservient in action and in ideology than church leaders in Moscow. This phenomenon in the republics is illustrated in post-1991 meetings regarding the issue of separating from the mother church, which will be discussed later in the chapter.

The reformist-traditionalist divide that I found should not be entirely a surprise as many have written on the phenomenon predating the 1917 revolution. Andrew Phillips noted that:

> "Long before the Revolution of 1917 different tendencies had appeared in the Russian Orthodox Church. Some of them were 'high', nationalist and ritualist, they stressed the links of the Church with the State; others were 'broad', they were political and leaned to the fashions of uprooted liberalising intellectuals and modernists; yet others were 'low', more linked to a fundamentalist peasant culture and, close to Old Ritualism, verged on sectarianism" (1999).

Scholarship on pre-revolutionary Orthodox clergy holding moderate to reformist sentiments is abundant (See Freeze 1983 and 1996, Meyendorff 1978, Valliere 1976). Several clergymen from the Russian Orthodox Church Outside of Russia acknowledge a 'faithful' element with the mother church. Father Paul said, "I am sure that faithful priests kept going in Russia throughout the period 1917—1991 and did their best to preserve the faith in the face of what ROCOR calls Sergianism" (Electronic correspondence 2005. Priest of Birkenhead Parish UK and rector of Stonyhurst College, Aug).

As the critical juncture decision in Russia was less defined, the trickle-down effects of subservient leadership took longer to reach the parish or provincial level, if in fact it ever did. The Sovietization of the church was not complete by 1991 and pre-revolution cleavages and orientations were not entirely erased. Soviet authorities had not reached the desired goal of controlling the entire church, physically or ideologically. As a result, the church that emerged was a mixture of formerly subservient KGB-appointed priests, pragmatic compromisers, passive resistors, and everything in between. Rather than finding a church with a collective identity and common views on issues ranging from religious pluralism to the church's post-Soviet mission, I found in my interviews a church with myriad views and a plethora of orientations.

The Historical Context: Soviet Legacy

The disagreement over Sergius' declaration and collaboration appeared to permeate the Soviet-era church on a subterranean level. The repressive tactics of the state coupled with the hierarchy's prohibition on internal discord meant that discussion and debate within the church were nearly non-existent. For the most part, disenfranchised clerics were purged by the system, driven to schismatic groups, or remained silent. Soviet religious policy eased somewhat in the 1980s, allowing for some Orthodox clergy to find their voice. However, it was not until after 1991 that clergy began to feel comfortable opining on church doctrine, history, and direction. Examples of outspoken figures during this timeframe included Gleb Yakunin, Father Dimitri Dudko, and Alexander Ogorodinikov.

Within the confines of the four legacies of Sovietism, the following section will depict the 21st Century Russian Orthodox Church as having inherited two distinct ideological camps from the Soviet era. The predominant group, made up of conservative clergy, possess neither democratic nor liberal characteristics. The other less visible wing of the clergy consists of members whose views range from moderate to reformist. Once this division is highlighted, an analysis of transitional circumstances will be presented describing how this clergy stratification produced, perhaps not the "creative tension" asserted by Jane Ellis, but an institutional drag on the antiquated religious agenda the traditionalists wished to pursue from 1991 to 2016.

Church Politicization

Much has been written about the Russian Orthodox Church's gradual transformation "into something resembling a classic Soviet institution" (Polyakov 1997, 148). Occasionally called Sergianism, the process of adapting "to atheism represented a maniacal union of Christian dogmas and rites with the socio-political views of the official ideology of the CPSU (Communist Party of the Soviet Union)" (Talantov 1982, 463). Victor Sheymos, former KGB agent, described the establishment of "The Fifth Directorate, responsible for suppressing ideological dissent, running the Soviet Orthodox Church, and laying the groundwork for the subversive promotion of favorable opinion about the country's position and policy" (Sheymov 1993, 418). Utilizing similar incentive packages as described in the previous chapters, state organs and security forces largely succeeded in paralyzing church activity and in both shaping and transforming the hierarchy's conduct. Myriad techniques were employed to transform religious elites into political players. After Sergianism was fully ossified within the church hierarchy, a reciprocal relationship developed between the Kremlin and the patriarch's office. One means by which the latter supported the former was in defending Soviet policies in international religious bodies. As Michael Bourdeaux describes:

> "Soviet propaganda launched a worldwide effort to conceal this outrage (the closure of churches) and that its efforts were largely successful was due primarily to the willingness of the hierarchy to abet the cover-up. Perhaps the key moment, in retrospect almost outrageous in its boldness, was the permission the Kremlin gave to the Russian Orthodox Church to join the World Council of Churches at its New Delhi assembly in 1961. This inaugurated a campaign of misinformation which continued for a quarter of a century. . . Clearly, Aleksii did not speak out about any of the problems of the church in the Soviet Union to the hundreds of western church leaders he was to meet over the next few years" (1993, 233).

Rewards for such acts of obedience included retention of one's position, promotion, and the receiving of material support. One priest described how "the KGB would repay priests for giving them information on disobedient clergy . . . and limiting religious participation" (Interview 2004. Anonymous, ROC priest, Moscow, 23 Nov). A common rationale for the church's questionable behavior under Soviet rule and present-day activities in the political arena rests in the distinction between what is called the "heavenly" and the "earthly" churches (Interview 2004. Anonymous, senior ROC, Vilnius, 7 Dec). A Moscow-based priest explains this dual nature of the church:

> "The church is perfect but it is located in a foreign environment, which is corrupt. The church is found among people and politics. The conditions of the earthly church have political limitations and require a certain amount of political manoeuvring for the church's survival. It was harder for people to attend church [under communism] but these same people could have the heavenly church in their hearts" (Interview 2004. Anonymous 2004, ROC priest, Moscow, 23 Dec).

This idea of a heavenly or inward church, which is pure, and an earthly church, which works in the sectarian world and often has to dirty itself in politics in order to survive and thrive, is a common refrain running throughout the rhetoric of church leaders.

> "The earthly church did rationally compromise with the Soviet power; it was necessary for the safety of the church and its legal existence. Without normal relations with the government there was no possibility to have normal religious life" (Interview 2004. Anonymous, head priest of the Church of the Assumption, Moscow, 25 Dec).

A senior Russian Orthodox official in Lithuania explained that most compromised leaders were forced to spend all of their time sustaining the earthly church and were unable or unwilling to give attention to the heavenly church under communism. He opined that church elite's understanding of institutional success slowly "changed from using the earthly church to sustain the health of the heavenly church, to a view of providing only for the earthly church" (Interview 2004. Anonymous, Vilnius, 24 Oct). In the mid-1990s, John Dunlop observed the relevance of this process on the modern church:

"The overwhelming majority of the current one hundred and nineteen bishops of the Moscow Patriarchate were ordained to the episcopacy prior to August of 1991 [the date of the effective end of Communist rule in Russia]. This suggests that each of these bishops was carefully screened and vetted by both the ideological apparatus of the Communist Party and by the KGB" (1995, endnote 2).

He continued by observing that at the time, four of the six permanent members of the Holy Synod were former KGB agents: Former Patriarch Aleksii II (agent code-name "Drozdov"), Metropolitan Iuvenalii of Krutitsy ("Adament"), Metropolitan Kirill of Smolensk ("Mikhailov"), and Metropolitan Filaret of Minsk ("Ostrovskii") (ibid., endnote 72). Of course, Metropolitan Kirill is now Patriarch Kirill. The extent to which hierarchs were willing to cooperate with authorities has become clear from recently released archival records. The former Patriarch Aleksii II, for instance, was described in 1974 by the vice-president of the Council for Religious Affairs "as one of the most loyal bishops of the Russian church, who understands the church's lack of interest in the strengthening of religion" (Alimov and Charodeyev 1992, 243).

Not all of the Russian leaders decided to cooperate with the authorities. The examples of Archbishop Yermogen, Father Aleksandr Men[8], Dimitri Dudko, Aleksander Ogorodinikov and Gleb Yakunin are just a few examples of prominent church officials who refused to submit to the state and follow the patriarch's compromised positions. Harshly punished for defiant religious behavior and anti-atheistic views in the 1970s, Dudko suffered psychiatric abuse at the hands of the authorities. Indeed, Michael Bourdeaux has called upon the Russian church to make amends and come to a reconciliation with many of these Orthodox human rights campaigners such as Gleb Yakunin who was imprisoned in 1979, "who truly did bear the burden of the heat of the day in Soviet prisons while the likes of Aleksii were staying in Luxury hotels abroad" (1993, 234). Yakunin, along with Nikolai Eshliman and Archbishop Yermogen of Kaluga, sent letters of rebuke in 1965 to the church and government in which

---

8 Father Aleksandr Men (1935 -1990) was a proponent of ecumenical activities. A skilled writer, Men was persecuted severally for his encouragement of religious participation in his parishes and was eventually murdered a year before the fall of communism.

mistreatments of the church were listed in the context of Soviet law and church canonical law. For these and other actions, the three were removed from their posts (Church History 2020).

In contrast to the reaction of the Georgian Orthodox Church, there was clearly resistance to politicization in the Russian Orthodox Church. Explanatory factors for the divergent outcome are hard to pinpoint. What is apparent, however, is that the majority of present-day top leaders were groomed by the Soviets. In fact, conservatives seem to be overrepresented in the top echelon of leaders. Yet, opinion patterns of second tier leaders indicate that the forces of clergy stratification preserved a non-politicized segment of the church. A similar historiography of the Soviet era suggests that such a non-politicized segment does not exist within the Georgian Orthodox Church. A representative of the Russian Orthodox Church Outside of Russia (ROCOR) opined before the 2007 Act of Canonical Communion with the Moscow Patriarchate that:

> "Many clergy in Russia are not satisfied with some of their hierarchs. They are waiting for the 'dinosaurs' to die. They have a different understanding of Sergianism than we in the West. They deplore the idea as much as those in ROCOR, but think there are mitigating circumstances. This is understandable; they were in the middle of it" (Electronic Correspondence 2005. Anonymous, Aug).

One-third of the Orthodox officials interviewed agreed that the church should not back political candidates, while two-thirds disagreed.[9] The same third emphasized the church's political neutrality, while the two-thirds asserted that the church should be the only religious voice in the political realm. They further declared that the church should be recognized and rewarded for its "historical contributions to the Russian soul" (Interview 2004. Priest Vladimir, head priest of ROC, Vilnius, 29 Nov). The third, which expressed misgivings about the actions of church hierarchs under Soviet rule, also cited transitional goals and ambitions for the church, which revolved around the spiritual not the political sphere. Their responses mirrored that of Father Vladimir who thinks "strengthening believers' respect for deity" should be the church's primary mission (ibid.).

---

9 Political neutrality is plainly mandated in the Holy Synod's "The Basis of the Social Concept of the Russian Orthodox Church" and routinely referenced by reformist clergy.

The conservative two-thirds agreed with Soviet-era church behavior and expressed a desire to improve the church's position in Russia by means of political or national-level public methods. Father Constantine stated, "Our most important task today is to help the government control the religious sphere in order to establish a system appropriate for Russia" (Interview 2004. ROC priest, Moscow, 26 Dec).

Opinions on the church's political role in society differ according to location. Outside of Moscow and St. Petersburg, Orthodox clergy on the whole are not nearly as politically oriented as a survey of purely Moscow-based or bishop-level hierarchs would reveal. Responses to questions that measure one's political nature suggest that the entire church did not undergo this transformation of incentives. Two opinion patterns are evident in today's Russian Orthodox Church. The suggestion here is not that the conservatives are any less devoted to the church or its cause, but simply that their interpretation of how to further the church's agenda differs drastically from reformists. Their Soviet behavior facilitated a tendency to view church success through the prism of politics and not spirituality or parishioner activity (see Roslof 2002).

Soviet Administrative Structure

All religious institutions, regardless of their stance toward the repressive regime, suffered greatly in a temporal manner under Soviet rule. Monasteries were closed and churches were either abandoned or turned into museums of atheism. The majority of churches also experienced a downsizing of personnel. Whether through clergy execution, forced exile, or draconian Soviet entry requirements for seminaries, the number of priests decreased across denominations. For the Russian Orthodox Church, Peter Scorer described just how restrictive church administration was under Soviet rule:

> "The Patriarch, the members of the Holy Synod and the hierarchy were all carefully watched, any decisions and any pronouncements were scrupulously vetted. Appointments could only be made with the prior approval of the state through the Council of Religious Affairs. The activity of local diocesan bishops was equally supervised. Clergy were little more than 'servitors of the cult', their work restricted exclusively to taking services. Church life had effectively been reduced to no more than attendance and services, the observation of church

ritual. Religious education, outside the very limited number of theological schools was virtually non-existent, and publishing was restricted to an extremely small number of service books, a few very limited editions of the Bible, a calendar and a couple of small circulation journals" (1996, 36).

The church was at once supported and deliberately and systematically hobbled by the state. The situation resembled, in a way, a state-protected business monopoly, but to the extreme. Steve Bruce explains the process of atrophy that occurs with monopolistic churches:

"Central to the supply-side model is the belief that, for a wide variety of reasons, hegemonic religion, especially when it is state-provided, depresses take-up. Because it derives its power from something other than popularity (land taxes, for example) hegemonic religion is unresponsive to needs. For example, it is slow to move its resources as population shifts. And it is slow to change its products as the wishes or needs of its people change. Because there are no popular checks on its costs, it is inefficiently expensive (building big cathedrals, instead of small wooden churches, for example) its officials have little incentive to become or remain popular. In an open market those defects would be remedied by the formation of dynamic, cheap, and ambitious religions, keen to serve unmet demands. But hegemonic religion, especially when it is supported by the state, prevents the emergence of competing and potentially more popular brands of religion" (2008, 84).

But the system the Russian Orthodox Church endured was even more detrimental to church health and competitiveness than what Bruce had in mind. Monopolistic characteristics had time and space to be engrained deep in the church as the state aggressively attacked the church's mode of operation. It wasn't just atrophy, but deliberate disintegration of the church's competitiveness. With the lack of incentives and the abundance of untrained priests, the church became accustomed to selling a lower quality of religious goods. In the post-Soviet era, churches had to re-acquire property, rebuild churches, and re-staff clergy. In reference to the Russian Orthodox Church, Professor Andrei Osipov, a respected theologian commented in the mid-1990s:

"We have not had time to train our priests properly. Monasteries are reopened, but we lack sufficient numbers of well-trained priests to serve in them. We have made priests of people who are poorly prepared, and this shortcoming is seriously affecting the internal life of the Church. It is crucial that the people in such

RUSSIAN ORTHODOX CHURCH 163

positions have both an excellent education and a deep spiritual life" (Quoted in Wallace 1996, 375).

In the competitive market of the 1990s, this Soviet legacy amounted to a significant constraint on competitiveness. Anthony Gill comments:

"In Russia, the Orthodox Church is on the defensive. Given its highly bureaucratic structure and over seventy years of laws repressing the free exercise of religion, the Orthodox Church is at a competitive disadvantage against the myriad of decentralized Protestant churches that have been flooding the country" (1998, 189).

Confirming Gill's assertion, a Bishop of the former Russian Orthodox Church Outside of Russia believes as late as the 2000s that the Moscow Patriarchate church was woefully unprepared to compete for souls (Electronic correspondence 2005. Bishop Agafangel of Crimea, Aug). His sentiments are repeated by numerous other former clergy previously affiliated with the break-away church outside of Russia. In addition, moderate priests within the church believe the transformation of the church under communism has fettered its ability to operate successfully as a distributor of religious goods. Father Moborodkov described the difficulty the church has had in "adapting to a new time" (Interview 2004. head priest of Michael Constantine Orthodox Church, ROC, Vilnius, 7 Dec). Conservatives and hierarchs alike argue that they are at a comparative disadvantage with other religious groups in the transition. While many clergy note material and personnel constraints, others point to an inability to adjust to a purely competitive market structure.

Legitimacy and Organization Unity

There is no clearer symptom of internal discord than the appearance of schismatic groups. The Russian Orthodox Church Outside of Russia, the Russian Orthodox Autonomous Church, the True Orthodox Church, the Russian Orthodox Free Church, the Latvian Orthodox Church and the Ukrainian Orthodox Church—Kiev Patriarchate serve as evidence of earlier disagreement and dissension within the church. The creation of the latter two partially revolved around political nationalism in their respective countries post 1991. The former churches were formed directly as a product of discontent over what were considered Soviet-era church misdeeds.

A 1985 declaration by the Russian Orthodox Church Outside of Russia clearly presents that organization's rationale for separation:

> "The Church Abroad does not recognize as lawful the hierarchical leadership of the contemporary official Russian Church, headed now by Patriarch Pimen, and before him by Patriarchs Sergius and Alexii, considering them enslaved by the God-battling forces and entering into impermissible agreements and compromises with the forces of evil" (Nathaniel 1985).

Disagreements with these splinter groups, fighting over property rights and ecumenical dialogue occupied much of the Synod's attention and resources until reunification occurred with the Russian Orthodox Church Outside Russia in 2007. The suspicious absence of splinter groups from the Georgian Orthodox Church demonstrates that schismatic elements and organizational disunity are not a legacy of complete church subservience, but rather a symptom of a church that possessed disharmonious elements. These elements originated from discontent over church subservience and, therefore, serve as further evidence of the divergent course of the Georgian and Russian Churches under communism.

Compromise by the church hierarchical establishment brought deep divisions during communist rule and demands for the hierarchy to account for its misdeeds. While the Catholic Church made a concerted effort to cleanse the post-1991 church of KGB informants, a similar program was never undertaken within the Russian Orthodox Church. Indeed, many Moscow-based Orthodox officials maintain that such an inquisition was unnecessary. Those that do admit to the presence of a compromised clergy, state that "it is a personal problem for the priest and his conscience. Remember Jesus never kicked Judas out of the last supper" (Anonymous 2004. Interview with Russian Orthodox priest in Moscow, 23 Dec). However, in the provinces and republics, many seriously considered breaking from the church after the collapse of the Soviet Union. In 1992, Priest Alexander co-chaired a congress of 300 Lithuanian-based priests and officials in Vilnius. The reason for the meeting was to consider separating the church in Lithuania from Moscow. Soviet-era corruption was one rationale among many for breaking communion with the Moscow Patriarchate (Interview 2004. Head Priest of the Orthodox Church of the Birth of the Holy Mother of God, ROC, Trakai, 25 Nov). A church hierarch went so far as to assert that the patriarchs were nothing more than "hand puppets for communist propagandists" (Interview 2004. Head priest of Michael Constantine Orthodox Church, ROC, Vilnius, 7 Dec). Although they eventually decided to stay with the Russian Orthodox Church, the meeting itself was indicative of dissatisfaction and disagreement by the church's periphery with Moscow-based leadership decisions made under communism. In Latvia, a segment of the church did, in fact, decide to separate from the Russia Orthodox Church, while the Free Russian Orthodox Church (FROC) movement saw several parishes (such as St. Constantine the Great, in Suzdal, Vladimir province) break with the Moscow Patriarchate. The so-called "Suzdal Schism" is little more than a historical footnote now, but its existence attested to the internal turmoil arising from the critical juncture.

Internal schism and conflict are symptoms of institutional confusion and organizational disunity. In Lithuania, as well as in Georgia, this confusion does not exist since the institutional arrangements are more defined due to the critical juncture having been more definitive. This fact, coupled with the incomplete Soviet takeover of the church described previously, has enormous implications for the legacies of Sovietism on the Church today and, by extension, for the church's posture on issues of religious pluralism.

The credibility of the Russian Orthodox Church in the fifteen former Soviet republics also came under considerable scrutiny after 1991. Mark Elliott explains, "Evangelicalism appears at the moment to be the only route to faith for some Russians who will never trust an Orthodox hierarchy they see as compromised by its past ties with the Soviet state" (1997, 238). This disillusionment was partially due to the actions of Patriarch Aleksii, who in December of 1990 was the only religious leader to sign a document urging Gorbachev to fight separation and "avoid the break-up of the USSR" (Pozdnyayev 1993, 350). The corrupt and compromised position of top clergy in the republics mirrored that of the hierarchs in Russia. The head of the Russian Orthodox Church in Lithuania, Archbishop Khrizostrom, who admitted to cooperating with the KGB, faced questions of integrity after 1991. Mikhail Pozdnyayev's interview with him, which was printed in *Religion, State and Society*, reveals a member of the church hierarchy on the defensive and struggling to justify his association with the KGB (1993, 49). The incremental opening of KGB archives during the 1990s caused the question of the 'red clergy' to resurface repeatedly, with members of the church leadership dodging questions, eluding interviews, and attempting to justify past actions. Parliamentary commissions have revealed evidence of the KGB hiring bishops and other clergy as agents. The names of leading members of the current hierarchy have surfaced in KGB files under code names. Ramet concludes that such evidence validates Father Popov's charge that "the Russian Orthodox Church became thoroughly entangled in the evil policies of the state, and has consciously associated itself with them" (Quoted in 1998, 241).

This legacy has directly affected the church's competitiveness. Two-thirds of the converts to The Church of Jesus Christ of Latter-day Saints attributed, at least partially, their abandonment of Orthodoxy to the subservient nature of the Russian Orthodox Church under Communism. Sister Larisa, a convert to the Church of Jesus Christ of Latter-day Saints, stated that many of her acquaintances "lost faith in the clergy because of their actions under communism, and now they are joined to other churches" (Anonymous 2004). Nine-tenths of respondents thought that the church's relationship with society weakened under communism. Three-fifths described Orthodox behavior as contrary to what one would expect of a religious figure. Even a sizable minority of clergy within the church questioned their church's legitimacy. Father Alexander stated, "As long as we continue to dirty ourselves in politics, the average Russian won't accept us as a religious authority" (Interview 2004. Head Priest of the Orthodox Church of the Birth of the Holy Mother of God, ROC, Trakai, 25 Nov).

Church Political Culture

Two comments by Russian Orthodox leaders illustrate the range of democratic values possessed by Orthodox clergy:

> "Ideas like democracy and freedom of speech can in actual fact be useless and harmful when they allow for the spread of spiritual terrorism in Russia" (Interview 2004. Father Leonid, head priest of Kazanskii Cathedral on Red Square, ROC, Moscow, 22 Dec).

"I don't wish them success, but I agree and support the government in that they permit these sects freedom of existence and the right to spread" (Interview 2004. Priest Vladimir, Church of the Assumption, ROC, Moscow, 25 Dec).

The first comment by a priest working close to the Kremlin confirms represents a large body of the clergy which have no qualms about discrediting the importance of minority rights and egalitarianism. Examples are myriad. Father Vladimir Zaitsev of the Yekaterinburg diocese was a particularly outspoken advocate of restricting liberties. In the early 2000s, he led an intense campaign in the media to prohibit a sizeable Jehovah's Witnesses' gathering. In addition to falsely linking the group to Hitler, he asserted that the group is a "destructive religious organization, totalitarian sect and destructive cult" (Fagan 2005a). His appeal fell on sympathetic ears and the government agency responsible for licensing the gathering agreed to prohibit it. Another example of anti-democratic tendencies among the clergy can be found in the Union of Orthodox Brotherhood, established by Aleksii in 1990. Despite the original intentions behind its formation, Stella Rock notes:

"Movement has been plagued by xenophobia, anti-Semitism, intolerance and political conservatism visible in many areas of the Russian Orthodox Church, and the Union of Orthodox Brotherhoods has arguably become a symbol of the worst aspects of post-Communist Orthodoxy" (2002, 1-2).

The auxiliary Catholic Bishop of Vilnius believes:

"The Russian Church is 'in bed' with the Russian government, and is active in restricting non-traditional religious organizations. . . I strongly believe that they reject religious pluralism and freedom and I condemn their accusations of Catholic proselytising of the Russian population. Their church is fearful of our actions in Russia" (Interview 2004. Juozas Tunaitis, Vilnius, 6 Dec).

The Bishop's words ring true when considering the earlier actions of Elder Priest Alexander Rebtsev. Rebtsev was one of a handfull of Orthodox officials in Moscow that petitioned the government unsuccessfully in the 1990s to restrict the activities of groups, which he labeled as a plague on society. He believed that the state has a responsibility to protect people from the ills of the transitional society (Interview 2004. senior ROC official, Church of St. Simon, Moscow, 29 Dec). The aforementioned examples illustrate that the political culture of the Soviet system found fertile ground in the minds of many church leaders. But until 2016, such voices, while numerous, were not sufficiently loud or authoritative enough to elicit change.

However, among another segment of the clergy, attitudes vary from being progressive to a belief that the freedoms of speech and democratic rights are less important than social stability, which should nonetheless be respected (Interview 2004. Anonymous, senior ROC, Vilnius, 24 Oct). Here again, two opposing camps emerge. One camp pays some deference to concepts such as freedom of speech, the democratic process, human rights, and the rights of minorities, while another segment of the clergy is hostile to such principles. Of those officials interviewed, less than half respected such principles, while slightly more than half did not. Three-fifths of priests agreed with the assertion that non-traditional "foreign cults should be prevented from buying land or constructing buildings" (Interview 2004. Anonymous, ROC priest, Moscow, 23 Dec). The democratically-inclined priests, on the other hand, were less interested in securing a prohibition on non-traditional religious activities post-1991 than they were in regaining the trust of the people and achieving growth in their pews. They were also less biased in their interpretation of Soviet history. One-third of respondents believed that religious pluralism is good for society. A Moscow-based priest asserted:

> "The government has a historical responsibility to help the Russian Orthodox Church. Groups such as the Mormons, and Jehovah Witnesses, which refuse to serve in the military, have a terrible, negative effect on Russians. The government should assist the traditional church and not help others, but they should also not punish or harm or prevent these churches from their activities" (Interview 2004. ROC parish priest, Moscow, 22 Dec).

A close advisor to the Orthodox Archbishop of Vilnius expressed similar sentiments:

> "There should be religious pluralism and freedoms. Churches should be allowed to operate in Russia. However, the government needs to be careful with the harmful sects that break laws. I don't like the aggressive stance of western churches; however, I respect the freedom of choice because I lived when it was not allowed" (Interview 2004. head priest of the Orthodox Church of the Holy Mother of God, ROC, Vilnius, 26 Oct).

These opinions, while not representative of the entire church, do reflect the tolerant attitudes of a distinct, small wing of the clergy. I was only successful in identifying such moderately-minded clergy at the parish-level. In 1995, Nicolai Petro optimistically opined that Russian Orthodoxy could actually serve as a tool in favor of democratization in Russia (1995). This was clearly wishful thinking as the overwhelming majority of Russian Orthodox Clergy, even those with more objective and modern views, hold an unfavorable opinion of non-traditional religions. More than nine out of ten questioned, support the view that The Church of Jesus Christ of Latter-day Saints, Jehovah Witnesses and other Western protestant denominations are "apostates from the original apostate church in Rome" (Interview 2005. Father Vasili, Uspenskii Cathedral, Moscow Patriarchate, Kiev, 20 Aug). Ecumenism is not a priority for most Orthodox clergy.

The legacies of Sovietism appear to be weaker in the Russian variant of Orthodoxy than in the Georgian. Even the most adamant anti-democratic Russian priests refuse to advocate violence as a means of halting sectarian activities. Said one priest, "We have no need to act violently against them. Rather we pray for them. They are a sickness on our sociсty. The Orthodox prayer is that this sickness will be healed" (Interview 2004. Alexander Rebtsev, senior ROC official, Church of St. Simon, Moscow, 29 Dec). Furthermore, although they are angry at any proselytizing of their members, many Russian Orthodox leaders have a broader definition of traditional churches than their Georgian counterparts. In addition to Catholicism, Judaism, and Islam, the often more polarizing groups such as Baptists and Methodists are routinely mentioned as traditional churches that, without qualification, should be allowed to operate in Russia.

The legacy of Sovietism on the Russian Orthodox Church, therefore, appears to be one of ideological stratification—an amalgamation of the divergent legacies of the Georgian and Lithuanian churches. The origin, or at least the continuation of this divide, can be traced to the contentious critical juncture. Indeed, a clear-cut, path-dependent trajectory, with Sergianism at the intersection, did not materialize in Russia. Imperial-age trends and pre-Soviet disagreements certainly played a role in the lack of homogeneity within the church. Whether or not the Soviet experience created this phenomenon or simply acted as a means of continuity, is uncertain. But the Soviet experience did function as a catalyst to expose and intensify this division. The composition of the church upon obtaining autonomy from communism included the following:

1. Two loosely-defined wings of the clergy existed, one that placed emphasis on political means to achieve institutional success and another that underscored the need to re-energize and reform the church's modes of distributing religious goods. The conservatives were in the majority and had a subjective view of church-state relations under communism. The more open segment was in the minority and questioned, to varying degrees, previous church behavior.
2. The same division between conservatives and reformists is revealed in their attitudes towards democracy, liberalism, and rights of minority religious groups.
3. The church's image was tarnished by hierarchical behavior under Soviet rule, which led to the development of schismatic groups.
4. Monopolistic features acquired as a result of the church's Soviet-era experience damaged its capacity to provide competitive services following 1991.

The Immediate Context: Transitional Marketplace

Legal Framework to 2012

After the breakup of the Soviet Union, Russia's new government initially swung the pendulum of control over religious activity drastically in the opposite direction from the Soviet system. The 1990 Law on Freedom of Conscience effectively opened the religious marketplace and provided the basis for the proliferation of religious organizations and the free expression of individual religiosity. Notwithstanding some isolated cases of local and regional authorities restricting certain rights, from 1991 to 1997, the religious marketplace in Russia was as capitalistic and as open as anywhere in the world. It was not until the 1997 Law on Freedom of Conscience and Religious Associations that a swing back in the direction of more state control began. While its wording is both vague and perplexing, the 1997 law called for restrictive requirements for registration, pointed out the singular status of Orthodoxy in Russia's development, and segregated religious groups into varying categories with corresponding legal privileges. The legislation's vague provisions increased local and federal organs' ability to subjectively discriminate. However, intense international criticism and a general indifference on the part of the ruling elite concerning democratic promises compelled the state to water down the legislation from overtly restricting non-traditional groups. In its place was an ambiguity that allowed for local authorities to act according to their own instincts.

From 1997 to 2012, this state of legal limbo hung over the activity of non-traditional religious groups. There were no clear prohibitions, but one always had to be on guard for the wrath of local authorities. The 2006 law on nongovernmental organizations followed this same pattern. At that time, the US government warned that "given the use of vague criteria, there is a real risk that the law could be applied selectively for political purposes" (Finley 2006). No matter how one interpreted the Kremlin's motives in the creation of these religious laws, the reality in the market was that the application was unpredictable and inconsistent to a degree that "fluctuation in religious freedom policy [was] its distinguishing feature in Russia" (Fagan 2005).

Russian Orthodox Church Market Position

The Russian Orthodox Church's transition from communism to 'managed' democracy has been characterized as a journey "from captivity into the desert" (Kiskovsky 1996). The constraints and opportunities encountered by the Russian Patriarchate post-1991 have been considerable. Fetters were removed such as the Council on Religious Affairs, intrusive surveillance, and state control over internal decision-making. At the same time, the church successfully capitalized on growing Russian nationalism which afforded it a prominent standing on the national stage. The success on the national level, however, was not immediately mirrored by achievement in the parishes. As has been said of the political sphere, in the realm of worship and worshippers, all religion is local. The national-level publicity, media presentations, and political endorsements that characterized the church in the post-Soviet World have not translated into conversion or retention of the citizenry. The disconnect between national and local-level success is primarily due to the transitional constraints facing the church and the opposing approaches to remedy those constraints by various segments of the clergy.

The structure of the Russian Orthodox Church in the 1990s also added to this diffusion of decision-making from the center to the region, which inhibited the congealing of a nation-wide posture on religious pluralism. Similar to the Georgian church, the Russian Orthodox structure consists of a Holy Synod made up of bishops and led by a patriarch. Perhaps as a consequence of geography and post-independence confusion, authority within the Russian church was more dispersed in the 1990s than in Georgia. Indeed, the church experienced, to some extent, a decentralization of power to the dioceses mirroring the transfer of political power from Moscow to the regions during the Yeltsin years of the 1990s. From 1991 to the mid-2000s, the church was more federalized than in Georgia with bishops given leeway to set policy in their ecclesiastical jurisdiction and interact with local officials on matters pertaining to religious regulation. For instance, Michael Bourdeaux details how then-Metropolitan Kirill worked directly with civic authorities to enable him to rebuild his diocese quicker than others. Bourdeaux, at the time, labelled Kirill the second most powerful individual in the church and a bishop that largely dictates policy in his region (2001, 3). This political savvy and business acumen have been put to good use as patriarch.

The church emerged from communist control battered and discredited, only to find itself in a dynamic religiously pluralistic environment, which it neither anticipated nor in which it was prepared to compete. The infusion of new and specialized religious entrants required the church to restructure its mode of operation and transform itself, much like old Soviet enterprises, from the command economy to a market orientation. This, however, was a difficult proposition for an organization which even its own leaders describe as ill-equipped for the new marketplace. As previously noted, anti-religious policy and mandatory institutional stagnation under Soviet control had weakened the church's ability to distribute religious commodities. In addition, many of its leaders were exposed as tools of Soviet oppression. The church had atrophied under communism and taken on monopolistic characteristics not conducive to success in the liberated market. Consequently, the transitional constraints encountered by the church were products of both Soviet legacies and the emergence of competitors.

Market Dynamics

The single most significant consequence of the advent of religious liberties in Russia was the appearance and spread of Western proselytizers. Russia, more than any other nation in the world, has for decades been seen as the forbidden 'Promised Land' by Western evangelists. Many groups labelled as outside invaders by members of the media and the Orthodox community had actually been firmly established in the country for some time. For instance, the Methodists, Baptists, and Jehovah's Witnesses had a long history of operation in Russia prior to 1991. During the Cold War, many other missionary-oriented Western evangelical groups were anxiously awaiting access to Russia, with some actually working clandestinely in the region.[10] When religious pluralism was conclusively established, these groups swarmed into the country, with literature already translated into Russian, missionaries trained specifically for work in the region, and strategic plans and tactical assignments drawn up in advance. These groups were adept at turning converts into proselytes, localizing church structure quickly, and morphing to the needs of members and the desires of potential converts. Their efforts were highly successful early on, with sizable congregations and a firm foothold in the country. Mark Elliot and Sharyl Corrado explain these groups' comparative advantages:

> "Quickest to take advantage of new opportunities were parachurch ministries (more flexible than church bureaucracies), ministries headed by Slavic immigrants from the region (whose leaders understood the region's languages and cultures firsthand), and missionaries with worldwide programmes (which could rapidly redeploy substantial resources and personnel to former Soviet-bloc states)" (1997, 238).

---

10 These groups were also active in western politics exerting pressure on Western governments to punish the USSR for human rights violations in the religious sphere. They were smuggling Bibles into the country and providing covert assistance to religious dissidents.

In contrast to these groups, the Russian Orthodox Church lacked a clearly defined post-Soviet strategy. A Moscow-based official stated that "the other churches were organized while we were disorganized when these laws were enacted" (Anonymous 2005. Interview with priest of Orthodox Church of Resurrection, Moscow, 6 Jan). The sudden changes in institutional arrangements caused the church to search for new points of reference. At the same time, tremendous opportunities presented themselves. Freed from the fetters of Soviet control, the church gained decision-making autonomy and was able to determine its own agenda. Confiscated lands were returned and abandoned churches and monasteries repaired and reopened. The removal of anti-God propaganda and a slight uptake in Orthodox-tinged nationalism contributed to many switching affiliations from atheism to Orthodoxy. The church has increasingly and successfully cast itself as the bearer of Russian culture, nation and soul. Indeed, church-state relations prior to 2014 resembled, in some respects, the pre-revolution Imperial relationship in which the church was used as a "pillar of political legitimacy" to "re-sacralize and re-legitimize autocracy" (Freeze 1996a, 309-311). Orthodoxy has become for many politicians a "badge of ethnic identity" (Uzzell 2000). The benefits of this political trend have helped the church in myriad ways. Preferential treatment from the state takes many forms, such as access to the military and ceremonial roles at national events. Nonetheless, such measures were not a dramatic advantage in competing for converts. This fact is reflected in the large non-Orthodox religious congregations, the Orthodox clergy's disquiet regarding their organization's stunted growth, and the fact that most Orthodox priests feel threatened by non-traditional groups.

In comparison with the Lithuanian Catholic Church, the existence and actions of non-traditional religious groups are much more in the forefront of the Russian Orthodox political agenda. Many clergy, whom I interviewed, consider such groups as the most destructive threat to their society's welfare. They are labelled as spiritual terrorists and are accused of committing "terrible crimes against the spiritual life of Holy Rus" (Anonymous 2004. Interview with Russian Orthodox priest in Moscow, 23 Dec). While Catholic priests were not congenial in their comments regarding non-traditional groups, they did not give the impression of being threatened by their existence. Many Orthodox clergy, particularly in Russia, believe that the increase in membership of non-traditional religious groups is directly correlated to their own church's decreased attendance. A zero-sum playing field is described (Anonymous 2004. Interview with senior Russian Orthodox official in Moscow, 21 Dec). The terminology used by Russian Orthodox leaders to describe such groups reflects the competitive nature of the religious environment in which they find themselves. Many are referred to as "pick pocketers", "poachers" and "spiritual thieves" (Anonymous 2004. Interview with senior Russian Orthodox official in Moscow, 21 Dec). One indication of the competitive threat perceived by Russian Orthodox Church leaders is their strong support for the Catholic promise to abstain from proselytizing. They are insistent that such an agreement should be had with all foreign religious organizations. A leading Orthodox official in Moscow expressed this competitive atmosphere by stating, "These sects are working here on their American money; they are rich and can be nice to Russians because they have pockets full of money. They are taking advantage of our weakness to steal people from us" (Anonymous 2004. Interview with Russian Orthodox priest in Moscow, 23 Dec).

The vitality of the market in the 1990s and early 2000s is also evidence of the inability of one firm to dominate. The infusion and success of these groups, as well as the expansion of indigenous minority religions, has produced a religious environment in Russia which was much more vibrant and diverse than in either Lithuania or Georgia.[11] In Lithuania, the Catholic Church acts as a religious monopoly due to its high standing in society. In Georgia for most of the post-Soviet era there was a suppressed competitive market and a *de facto* law-enforced religious monopoly. In Russia, however, a weakened monopolistic church existed among an overabundance of denominations competing for a limited number of adherents in a dynamic religious marketplace. The situation in Russia

---

11 Here I am referring to the number and actions of religious firms in operation in Russia. With regard to the demand-side, the religious revival in Russia appears to be limited to a small percentage of the entire population. Religious firms are competing for a limited number of customers. Indeed this is true of all post-Soviet countries. Paul Froese wrote "On average, around 20 percent of the population of each Soviet state have taken up some form of religious affiliation since 1970" (Froese 2004a, 58). However, the percentage of active religious adherents as opposed to titular members is well below twenty percent.

confirmed many supply-side assumptions and presented the Russian Orthodox Church with a disheartening predicament. The market became more pluralistic as it became increasingly unregulated. At the same time, new firms became highly specialized. Most consequential to Orthodoxy, market growth, in real terms was concentrated among non-traditional firms.

Orthodox Revival Fallacy

To properly grasp church leaders' changing perception of power, it is imperative to move beyond the headline slogans of an 'Orthodox resurgences' and delve deeper into demand side factors. In particular, the role of human religious capital and religious mobility must be appreciated. Many Western scholars in the 1990s and beyond supported the narrative that Orthodoxy was re-emerging in the region and that "monopoly religions across the former Soviet Union are currently reaping the benefits of state support" (Froese 2004). In Russia prior to 2016, the church unquestionably benefited from a privileged status with the current government. However, an extrapolation of this support to explain a blossoming of religious participation has little connection with reality. Discussions with Orthodox and non-Orthodox clergy contradict the assertion that there is a significant upsurge in Orthodox religious participation and that state favoritism has contributed to competitiveness. Even in the wake of the 1997 law 'On Freedom of Conscience and Religious Association', state support never reached the point where the Russian Orthodox Church had a significant comparative advantage over other churches in respect to competing for converts and retention of members. Speaking about the pre-2014 environment, Mark Elliott asserts that "ambiguities in the law and delays in its implementation have minimized its impact for Russia's minority faiths" (cited in Newsroom 2000).

Surprisingly, among the former Orthodoxy members who are now affiliated with The Church of Jesus Christ of Latter-day Saints, two-thirds felt in the early 2000s that other than rhetorical abasing on television, their former faith did little to obstruct their activities. Furthermore, from 1998 to 2006, only 52 religious workers were denied visas to Russia, and several of these were later granted (Fagan 2005b). Non-Orthodox churches' attempts at obtaining property, while cumbersome, time-consuming, and bureaucratic, were largely successful. Said one religious administrator, "We have struggled for three years to receive permission from the government to build chapels throughout Siberia . . . it has been difficult but we now have property and buildings in Novosibirsk, Krasnoyarsk, Vladivostok, and many other cities" (Anonymous 2004. Interview with senior official of The Church of Jesus Christ of Latter-day Saints in Siberia, Krasnoyarsk, Feb). Attempts by either local or central Orthodox officials to alter the balance of power among religious firms through governmental subsidies to their church or restrictions on competitors have for the most part failed prior to 2012.

Academics who assert the occurrence of an Orthodox revival often base their analysis on decade-old statistics on the change in religious affiliation from the 1970s to the mid-1990s (see Froese 2004). They use, as a base-line, the time when the church was the most subservient and when distrust of the church and atheistic affiliation among the populace was highest. From that time to 1995, 23 percent of the adherents lost from 1900 to 1970 were regained (ibid.). A similar phenomenon occurred in other dominant churches. The revival interpretation is based largely on this data, which can easily be explained by the gradual receding influence of popular atheism and increased nationalism, and not by a colossal Orthodox revival (Freedom Report 2003). By the same token, the notion that favoritism decreased the growth of non-Orthodox groups in the 1990s stems partially from the mistake of taking into account only registered religious groups. As the U.S government noted in 2003:

> "The number of registered religious organizations does not reflect the entire demography of religious believers. . . An estimated 500 (official estimate) to more than 9,000 (Council of Mufti estimate) Muslim organizations remain unregistered. The registration figures probably also underestimate the number of Pentecostal believers. New Pentecostal organizations are forming rapidly, and unofficial estimates suggest that there are between 1,500 and 2,000 Pentecostal congregations nationwide, many of which remain unregistered despite their efforts" (Religious Freedom Report 2003).

Affiliation with the Russian Orthodox Church may be large, but actual church attendance is not much higher than in Western Europe—and in some cases lower. It was recently estimated that a mere one to three percent of Russians attended Christmas church services in 2018, a number lower than in secular France (Interview 2020. Senior Ukrainian Orthodox Church official, London, Jan). Detlef Pollack states:

> "The extremely high degree of trust in the Church, thus, does not go hand-in-hand with a high level of religious or church practice. If the Russians turn to the church, they do not do so because of individual needs in the realm of religion or church. Their attachment to the church is based far more on the wish the church may be of use to society . . .to work as an integrating factor, to impact societal values, to fulfil social tasks, and to convey a normative foundation to society at large" (2010, 137).

The important ingredient here is the calibre of members explained by the demand-side assumptions, specifically the role of religious human capital. Mark Elliott and Sharyl Corrado explain:

> "While a recent poll indicates a substantial increase in the percentage of Russians claiming affiliation with the Orthodox Church (from 30 per cent in 1991 to 50 per cent on 1996), the percentage of these respondents who have taken Orthodoxy to heart and who practice their faith is another matter. The June 1996 survey indicated that believers (50 per cent of respondents) were far more often non-observant (37.3 per cent) than observant (12.7), and even among self-described observant believers corporate worship proved to be strikingly erratic. When asked how often they had attended church in the past twelve months, only ten per cent answered once a month, while 55 per cent answered, on religious holidays and on family occasions" (1997, 342).

The limited number of religious seekers with human religious capital is reflected in a United States' government analysis of the religious marketplace in Russia:

> "In practice, only a small minority of citizens identify strongly with any religion. Many who identify themselves as members of a faith participate in religious life only rarely or not at all. For example, while an estimated 64 percent of respondents to a 2000 Public Opinion Foundation poll identified themselves as members of a particular faith, only 19 percent said that they visited a place of worship more than once or twice a year (many Orthodox believers attend church only on Christmas or Easter). An estimated 11 percent of respondents said that they observed Lent or other fasts. Only 4 percent of respondents stated that they took communion more than once or twice a year (in the Orthodox tradition, taking communion requires personal preparation by fasting, confession, and prayer)" (Freedom Report 2003).

The religious awakening among Russians, while relatively large compared to other nations, is concentrated among a minute percentage of the total populace. John Burgess notes that "very few Russians are actually in-churched. Although honoring the Church in principle, they keep their distance from it in everyday life" (Burgess 2017, 207). While religious affiliation numbers have increased in Russia since 1991, the percent change among Russians who attend church from 1990 to 1996 was a mere three-tenths of one percent (Froese and Pfaff 2001, 484). The market dynamics are reflected in polling data. Those identifying as Orthodox Christian rose from 31 percent in 1991 to 72 percent in 2008. Yet among the same group regular church attendance was 2 percent in 1991, 9 percent in 1998 and 7 percent in 2008. Those claiming affiliation with a non-Orthodox church rose from 1 percent in 1991 to nearly 10 percent by the end of the decade only to steady out at 6 percent by 2008—where it hovers currently (Pew 2014). Demand-side assumptions correctly predict that this small segment of the population is highly mobile, has a high degree of human religious capital, and contributes disproportionally to the health of a church. Of the religious leaders and parish-level priests in Russia I interviewed prior to 2006, the comments of the majority of clergy suggest that overall market share, to a large degree, is insignificant. The market share of devoted adherents, not titular affiliates, is what is vital to a church's health and success. Although statistically the Church has only lost members in the margins, many of these defectors were anything but marginal Orthodox members. In fact, research findings indicate that most defectors from Orthodoxy come from the small segment of the church that possess the highest levels of human religious capital. Priests understand that the exodus is proportionally larger than statistics indicate since active adherents, not passive affiliates, began abandoning the church after 1991.

My conversations with both Russian Orthodox parish priests and numerous Russians, who have been converted to The Church of Jesus Christ of Latter-day Saints in Riga, Vilnius, Moscow, St. Petersburg, and Siberia reveal precisely this trend of religious capital fleeing the Orthodox Church. Seven out of ten Mormon converts surveyed were formerly active Orthodox believers before embracing the new faith (Survey data collected 2004-2005). Ninety-seven percent now attend their new church three or more times a week and more than half support their new faith through significant financial contributions. The demand-side assumptions of chapter Two describe theoretically the situation currently being played out in Russia. Demand flow is directed away from Orthodoxy. While this trend is also true to a lesser degree in the Lithuanian Catholic Church, leaders there rightly ascribe it to Westernization and secularization. The small congregations of other denominations support this assumption. In Russia, however, overall religious participation did not decrease, but became more mobile, which affected the Russian Orthodox Church negatively. Most Orthodox officials do not deny that this phenomenon occurred in the 1990s. The reasons for this exodus from the church are difficult to ascertain from interviews with Orthodox clergy. Reliable insights in this regard again come from former members who have, since 1991, joined other churches. Most people surveyed in such a category cited two reasons for abandoning Orthodoxy. First was disenchantment with the ritualistic repetition found in church liturgies. Second was dissatisfaction with the spirituality or 'heavenly legitimacy' of clergy. These sentiments align with demand assumption 3—"For consumers searching for goods, the character of the producer stands as proxy to the quality of the product." They also corroborate distinctions between ritual congregational and highly collective churches and the movements of members with religious human capital from the former to the latter. Additionally, survey data validates the contention that there were highly specialized religious groups equipped at eroding market share from Orthodoxy.

Many former Orthodox members refer to Soviet-era corruption or present-day drunkenness as reasons for losing confidence in Orthodox spiritual leadership.[12] A female leader in The Church of Jesus Christ of Latter-day Saints in Siberia believes that due to the effects of communism, "The Orthodox Church stopped knowing people personally. For

---

[12] It is important to note that the diminishment of the church's credibility took place pre- and post-1991 regardless of the resistance of some clergy discussed earlier. Legitimacy is an easy commodity to lose in the religious realm. While resistance was present in the church, it was much less public than the overt displays of subservience by the Moscow-based hierarchs. The other three legacies of Sovietism were shaped by the mingling of subservient and resistant elements. Unfortunately for the church, its post-Soviet legitimacy among a cohort of believers was largely influenced by the Soviet-era behavior of corrupt officials.

priests there are no individual persons, just the crowd" (Interview 2004. President of local women's chapter of The Church of Jesus Christ of Latter-day Saints in Krasnoyarsk, Russia, Apr). Several Orthodox officials admit that their struggles in the transition stem from a tendency on the part of the population to not take the church seriously. Father Michael Kynarev agrees with many of my respondents that the church's bond with society was significantly weakened under communism (Interview 2004. Mid-level parish priest of Naujoji Vilnia, ROC, Vilnius, 7 Dec).

An examination of the intricacies of market dynamics from 1991 to 2012 reveals the following market characteristics:

- The increase in Russian Orthodox affiliation during the past three decades has largely come from non-observant believers.
- There exist high degrees of religious mobility among the small percentage of the populace that are religious seekers.
- A small, but very significant, segment of Orthodox parishioners with an advanced level of human religious capital are the most susceptible to non-traditional proselytizing efforts.
- Apart from draconian restrictions on property in some regions, federal and provincial legislation prior to the Yarovaya laws did not seriously handicap the activities of non-Orthodox religious firms.

Division of Remedial Course

Orthodox clergy were keenly aware of these market features and the necessity for a church response to reverse the success of Western evangelism in Russia. Priests and hierarchs alike were cognizant of their presence and success as well as the Orthodox Church's weaknesses. Yet, throughout the 1990s and well into the 2000s, a division was clearly apparent within the church over how best to deal with post-Soviet challenges. The divide between the conservatives and the moderate/reformist segments of the clergy is manifested in the course they want the church to take in light of transitional constraints and opportunities. Zoe Knox explains this division under the leadership of previous Patriarch Aleksii:

> "There has been opposition to the patriarchate as reformists and religious activists have taken directly opposing stances on key challenges the church faces in the post-Soviet period. These forces have been pushing for perestroika

within the church since the first revelations of the extent of the leadership's collaboration with the KGB. Within church structures, traditionalists have condemned all attempts to update church practice; they viewed these initiatives as heretical and as attempts to destroy church unity. Reformists view the church as for the people, and argue that its clergy should be accessible in order to fulfil a meaningful social role. The latter regard the primary task of the church as the recovery of tradition, including the restoration of a privileged position in a secular state. Patriarch Aleksii is forced to negotiate between the two conflicting currents in church life, and concessions to one inevitably lead to criticism from the other" (2003).

Traditionalists desired to use Orthodoxy to fill the ideological void left by the quick departure of Marxism, linking Russianness and national identity with the church. They believed that an intimate church-state relationship could shield them from competition. They saw nationalism as a means to achieve dominance, rather than doing the work to change into an innovative market-savvy producer of religious commodities. The reformists, while not averse to a privileged status for the traditional church, sought to recover from Soviet oppression, not only materially through the rebuilding of destroyed churches and monasteries, but also spiritually. Rather than seeking to advantageously modify institutional arrangements, these priests wished to return to the Imperial Age when the church was in the forefront as a religious distributor and authority on social issues. They viewed the presence of foreign evangelism as motivation to change and innovate, much as the Reformation prompted the Roman Catholic Counter-Reformation. They believed the competitive threat should serve as a "catalyst, reenergising Orthodoxy out of a complacency born of tradition and nominal predominance" (Elliot and Corrado 1997, 338). Reformists placed emphasis on parish level innovation and success. They cited Father Men and his attempts to make the church more responsive to the parishioner, as a model for which to strive. Zoe Knox notes that Men's initiatives included "making fasting voluntary, replacing Old Church Slavonic (not necessarily with Russian; the language is determined by the language of the congregation), and making traditionally long services shorter" (Knox 2003, 36). A senior Russian Orthodox official in Lithuania stated, "All people here are Orthodox at heart; they simply need the pure, undefiled Orthodoxy to be presented to them"

RUSSIAN ORTHODOX CHURCH 183

(Anonymous 2004. Interview, 24 Oct). A Western academic noted this debate within Russian Orthodoxy:

"Largely for its xenophobic, anti-Semitic and nationalist stand, an ultranationalist wing of the clergy has dominated the headlines. It alone has largely given shape to the currently dominant view of the Russian Church as a proponent, ally or pawn of broader conservative and nationalist forces. In contrast, other internal church currents go largely unnoticed or have gotten short-shift. Moreover, 'in house' debates, especially those which on the surface seem to deal strictly with 'religious matters', go for the most part unreported—in the erroneous belief that quarrels over doctrine and practice have little relationship or bearing on society as a whole" (Della Cava 1997, 388).

The debate concerning the church's support for the 1997 law On Freedom of Conscience and Religious Associations also spotlights the division between those within the church who support ecumenism and a progressive response to Western proselytism, on the one hand, and those who seek restrictions and protection on the other. Several clergy were dismissed for their opposition to a law the church fully supported. Veniamin Novik was forced to resign from St Petersburg Theological Academy for criticizing the law and other church policies and doctrine (Knox 2003, 41). He wrote:

"The new law in spirit not only eliminates the possibility of ecumenism and religious reconciliation in Russia, but also further forces apart and separates a multi-confessional society. Only a rather low level of religiosity in society, and the social marginalisation of religion, can assuage the social consequences of this law" (Novik 1999, 361).

These remarks and numerous statements by clergy in support of the law illustrate the extent of division within the church. The division aligns with historical interpretation of Soviet-era church actions, and clergy disagreement on the church's post-Soviet direction. Contrasting interpretations of Soviet and post-Soviet contexts produce dissimilar assessments of relative power. Slightly fewer than half of those interviewed in Russia believe that the main goal of the church in the 21st Century should be to increase the religiosity of Russians. Their answers reflect their belief that the success of the church is determined and rooted in the spirituality of its adherents and of all Russians. This reformist segment of the church, if one can label them as such, fought against Soviet sources of continuity, consequently they consider the church's relative power to be rooted in the religious sphere.

The other half of those interviewed cite nationalistic and political goals, such as defending the Russian soul and protecting Russianness and tradition from foreign influence as is their church's primary goals. Some go so far as to state that increased cooperation in church-state relations is their organization's paramount goal. The source of institutional success, for these clerics, lies largely in the political realm and the audience of mass public opinion and not in individual spiritual enhancement. Findings suggests that while most clergy interviewed feel their church's standing in society is threatened, there exists a disagreement, on the nature and source of that threat on the church's competitiveness and need for reform.

There appears to be a division among the leadership as well as the clergy between a segment that reflects the politicized and totalitarian inclinations of Georgian clergy and another, albeit much smaller segment, that approximates the moderate mentalities of Lithuanian Catholic clergy. My findings on a split church correspond with other scholars. Irina Papkova divides the church into three major groups—traditionalists, liberals and fundamentalists (2011, 47-69). As recently as 2017, John Burgess makes a cogent case for a liberal strain with a "progressive vision of Church and Society" (2017, 203). For his part, Burgess somewhat optimistically argued in 2014 that "contemporary Russian Orthodoxy has strands of social thought that can be developed in other directions" than anti-democratic (2014, 177). He goes so far as to proport a "significant democratizing potential" which at present "seems more latent than manifest, [and] cannot be wholly repressed" (2014, 178).

The ideological division stemming from the ill-defined critical juncture and the incomplete Sovietization of the church produced a disharmonious organization emerging from communism without a clear strategy. An organization's efficiency in settling upon institutional direction from among several alternatives and then successfully pursuing that course, depends in large measure on its ability to consolidate and mobilize its members. Despite any consensus among upper echelon leaders, an organization, be it a political party or a church, can make little significant progress in an initiative when not fully supported by its base. Internal disharmony creates friction that slows down or halts organizational initiative. To be sure, outspoken critics of restrictive policies in the Russian Orthodox Church, such as Novik, were in the 1990s and undeniably even more so now, in the minority in the church on issues of religious liberties and pluralism. Yet this wing of the clergy likely acted for many years as a partial check on the ability of the church to implement restrictive policy.

Conversations with clergy post-1991 reveal a church threatened by the competitive religious marketplace and torn between two opposing approaches on how to remedy the situation. Both the legacy of division within the Russian Orthodox Church during Soviet rule and the present-day marketplace have combined to account for this policy confusion. A comprehensive understanding of the church's utility function, therefore, is tricky because the conception of the organization's power and influence is evaluated differently by various segments of the clergy. The stratified wings have drastically dissimilar frames of reference. The fact that the two orientations exist in the church, and that dual interpretations of the sources of institutional success are present, prevents organizational consolidation on issues. As mentioned previously, organizations naturally have diminished power in the political arena if they lack a clear mandate from their employees and constituents. Additionally, the process of bargaining for political power is not confined to just the federal level. Regional initiatives serve to buttress a church's federal agenda. The situation in Georgia is an example. In the 1990s, protectionist initiatives by parish and regional-based Georgian Orthodox officials laid the groundwork and provided the momentum for Tbilisi-based hierarchs to petition the government and to gain a seat at the bargaining table. In this way, an organization's power, i.e., the ability to influence the institutional design of religious activity in a particular country is partially determined by the organization's unity and mandate on the issue. As such, the implementation of the traditionalists' restrictive agenda in Russia and their success in interfacing with local officials to curtail the free market has been sporadic and ineffective for much of the post-Soviet era.

Power Perception and Rational Decision

In the absence of internal agreement within the dominant religion, irresoluteness of institutional design dominated the religious scene in Russia for 15 years. That was the case until the start of Putin's third presidential term in 2012. In fact, in 2012, Jerry Pankhurst, at the time professor of sociology at Wittenburg University, acknowledged that even after more than two decades the Russian Orthodox Church had yet to formalized a clear path on religious pluralism. Pankhurst posed the following questions:

> "Experience in other countries suggests that, if general religious freedom persists, Russia is likely to become a great deal more diverse in its religious culture. While Orthodoxy recoups its strengths, other "religious entrepreneurs" will win a significant share of the religious market in Russia. Still, the daunting question persists: will the Orthodox Church continue to stress the form, encourage nativistic elements in the government, and deny the newer groups access to the population? Stated differently, will the Church put nationalistic goals and church-state unity above service to the spiritual needs of the population?" (Pankhurst 2012, 28)

Irina Papkova noted in 2011 that following the 1997 Law of Freedom of Conscience and Religious Organization, "the ROC leadership failed to translate any of its substantive political preferences into actual federal policy" (2011, 93). From 2011 to 2016, some of the church's political preferences were achieved such as restoring property, introducing military chaplains, integrating Orthodox culture courses into public schools, and reincorporating splinter groups. But on the issue of restricting religious pluralism, Papkova's diagnosis remained largely valid until the Yarovaya laws in 2016.

From 2008 to around 2012, the ambiguity of religious pluralism, as well as church-state relations, turned more into what Harley Balzar, discussing civil society more broadly, called managed pluralism (2003, 189). Antecedents to the restrictive measures became apparent with such events as the change of patriarchs. Aleksii II was not eager to sacrifice church autonomy for the sake of closer church-state relations. Although he had little reservation about appearing ceremonially with politicians or endorsing the military campaign in Chechnya, Aleksii had consistently opposed any type of church-state structural ossification. The political bargaining and policy making between church and state took place largely on a local level, where neither the state nor the church had a unified ideological approach to the application of religious pluralism and liberties. This, coupled with the ambiguities of federal laws, resulted in religious law and enforcement being unpredictable and fluid. The divide in the church continued to influence the ambiguity of the religious policy in the 1990s. Since becoming primate of the Russian Orthodox Church in 2009, Kirill has had much less inhibition on engaging with the state.

Three developments, post Kirill's ascension, should have alerted scholars to the church's more exalted position in Russia's religious scene. First was the 2010 policy that enforced the church's claim on lands seized during Soviet times and expedited their return with government coercion if required (Kishkovsky 2010). Second was the 2009 directive that overturned a 1992 law allowing for religious education in public schools. Although dubbed non-evangelizing, the church has in fact employed these religious courses to strengthen its position in Russian Society and propagate the ideal of a Russian national identity that coincides well with that advocated by the Kremlin (Kollner 2016, 366-386). The church's ambitions in the education realm were recently illustrated by the proposal made by the head of the Department for External Church Relations of the Moscow patriarchate, Metropolitan of Volokolamsk to replace the reading of "Gulag Archipelago" by Alexander Solzhenitsyn in Russian school curriculum with the study of the Bible. The plan was readily endorsed by the first deputy chairman of the Russian State Duma's Committee on Education and Science, Oleg Smolin (Credo 2019a). Third, financial benefits offered to the church in the form of tax breaks, partial ownership of energy firms, and government subsidies on utilities (Solodovnik 2014, 58-59).

Further signs of coming restrictions to the religious sphere were seen in state laws passed from 2012 to 2015 in response to the 2011-2012 mass protests against Putin's return to the presidency. The first such law that essentially ushered in the most significant post-Soviet campaign against individual freedoms was the Foreign Agents Law of 2012 targeting media outlets and civil society groups. That law has been expanded many times, including as recently as 30 December 2020 when individual journalists and bloggers were added. The 'undesirable organizations' law of 2015 likewise used the cover of anti-extremist measures to target and inhibit the activity of any entity with foreign funding. Many of these laws have potentially debilitating implications for religious providers, but few direr predictions materialized before 2016.

Another disconcerting portent was the growing ideological pull on the patriarchate from the right. Interestingly, the COVID-19 situation has highlighted the predominance of the conservative segment of the clergy. Indeed, Sergey Chaplin makes the point that the COVID-19 pandemic provided a space for fundamentalism to grow (2020). The 2020 standoff with Priest Shigumen Sergey in the Urals was particularly insightful in showing the strengh of fundamentalist clergy. The white bearded old priest called on Putin and Kirill to abandon their posts as he refused to surrender his monastery to COVID-19 measures. The renegade priest was defrocked, but remains defiant. His monastery of 500-plus inhabitants has acted as an independent hotbed of ultraconservatism in the region since 2005. His case is not singular. In fact, anti-ecumenical hardliners are common and have had to be discipled often since 2006 (Goble, 2020).

Notwithstanding this severe tilt to state favoritism for the church, or state restrictive laws passed from 2012 to 2015, religious freedoms and pluralism remained largely unscathed until the 2016 measures. While the final chapter of this book delves deeper into post-Yarovaya restrictions, it is important to note here the contrast in operating environments for non-traditional church pre- and post-2016. As already noted, the Supreme Court banned the Jehovah's Witness in 2017 and labelled all its communities as "extremist organizations. Raids against the religious group have taken place in nearly half of Russia's regions with over 200 members charged" (Arnold 2019). Recent interviews with members of The Church of Jesus Christ of Latter-day Saints in Russia highlight the debilitating impact of the measures on church operations. Since entering Russia in 1992, missionaries from that church have used free English language classes to meet locals and introduce them to church teachings. That practice is now banned across Russia. The missionaries are also discouraged from wearing their easily recognizable black name tags. The church, which is perhaps the greatest global example today of a proselytizing church, is prohibited from any type of gospel discussion outside of meeting houses. Finally, The Church of Jesus Christ of Latter-day Saints places great emphasis on genealogical work, yet the church's main family history church website is banned in Russia (Anonymous 2019. Interview with senior official of The Church of Jesus Christ of Latter-day Saints in Russia, Aug).

All this state-supported oppression has come as a result of state-Orthodox cooperation that has no historical parallels. Collaboration certainly occurred in the past. For instance, during World War II when priests supported partisan movements and financial collections for the war effort, and the Soviet government supported church initiatives, including printing church leaflets (Chumachenko 2002, 4). Even so, the level of church-state interaction seen since 2014 surpasses such arrangements of convenience. For one, decades of communist rule either created or reinforced historical tendencies towards authoritarianism in many of these societies and institutions (Gibson *et al.* 1992, 332). Furthermore, recent decisions appear more rooted in zero-sum calculations motivated by "maximizing members, net resources, government support, or some other basic determinant of institutional success" (Iannacconne 1997, 27).

Church-state cooperation has deepened so much that even conservative elements within the church are taking note. A group of orthodox believers organized the Meeting of Orthodox Laity in Moscow in late October 2020 to criticize state interference with church actions during the COVID-10 pandemic. The laity group called upon Vladimir Putin to stop Rospotrebnadzor and other government entities from interfering in the internal affairs and liturgical practice of the Russian Orthodox Church. They held their strongest condemnation for the Council of Bishops of the Russian Orthodox Church:

> "Recent events clearly testify that an unusually difficult moment has come in the life of our Church. Recognizing this fact with a broken heart, our Orthodox conscience testifies to us that in the actions of a number of higher representatives of the hierarchy of our Church, for which we all continue to pray tirelessly, purely religious motivation, unfortunately, is clearly inferior to obedience to the

powers that be, in turn, in the opinion of many authoritative people, broadcasting in this case the will of the behind-the-scenes world power" (Rogaleva 2020).

The very recent denunciation letter by a grouping that has espoused anti-ecumenical views reveals the extent of church-state interface. The aforementioned factors lead most senior Russian Orthodox leaders to have believed by 2016 in the utility and the right to restrict the freedom of operation of other groups.

All three churches examined in this book seek an institutional design for the religious sphere that is optimized for church operations and success. For the Lithuanian Catholic Church, that means a continuation of existing religious liberties and pluralism. The Georgian Orthodox Church, on the other end of the spectrum, believes prohibitions on activities of foreign producers of religious goods best serve its cause. Both churches' clergy appear to be supportive of the respective agendas. The perception and trajectory of the organizations' respective power is clear and the path for retaining or enhancing it is evident. In Russia, the situation is less straightforward as research reveals that the degree of subservient-induced Soviet legacies on clergy attitude varies considerably among Russian Orthodox clergy. The perception of the source of power and the definition of institutional success was divided for most of the Soviet era. But as we will see in the final chapter of this book, certain powerful forces, trends, and events converged in 2016 to allow for a more unified and obstructive posture on religious pluralism. Events of recent years suggest that the question posed by Jerry Pankhurst back in 2012—"Will the Church put nationalistic goals and church-state unity above service to the spiritual needs of the population?"—will continue to be answered in the affirmative for the foreseeable future (2012, 28).

7. Regional Findings and Methodological Implications

A definitive answer as to why religious liberalization in the former Soviet Union has not taken root, as many had hoped, is not easily ascertained. The social, political, and cultural characteristics of the fifteen states grow more unique with each passing year. Disparate post-Soviet experiences translate into region-wide generalizations losing explanatory value. It is becoming increasingly arduous to group nations as dissimilar as Estonia and Turkmenistan under the guise of a shared history. Even so, certain organizations and institutions, particularly those as insular and resistant to change as traditional churches, continue to manifest shared traits acquired under Soviet rule. After all, those entities most transformed under the communist structure would be expected to be the last freed from the bonds of their Soviet legacy. Furthermore, the uniformity of Soviet religious policy across the region and the cultural imprinting of Soviet norms on the clergy suggest a shared historical experience with considerable shelf life. Interviews with religious leaders in the region attest to this, revealing the lingering influence of Sovietism on the political culture of religious elites.

For many churches, the past remains relevant not only in the form of lost religious buildings, less than efficient ministry, and various levels of spiritual lethargy among the populace, but also through subconscious manifestations of a Soviet-like *modus operandi* by church leaders. Prior to the creation of the Soviet Union, churches in the region existed in circumstances that were largely unrelated. The institutional designs for religious activity in pre-Bolshevik Eurasia varied drastically across time and location for national churches. For these traditionally dominant churches, the Soviet period acted very much like a bottle-neck highway, paved with standard constraints, persecution, and state regulations. In figurative terms, Soviet occupation forced churches, particularly those that interacted extensively with the state, to run the same gauntlet. Therefore, while the academic practice of clustering national institutions together under the flag of a shared Soviet historical experience is becoming ever more impractical, when the subject matter is narrowed to encompass just the actions of traditionally dominant churches, cross-national comparative analysis remains useful.

Indeed, the findings of several years of research suggest that Soviet-era factors are highly determinative in shaping church posture on religious institutional design, and that, as a result, religious suppliers in the region hold a very distributional mentality to church operations. Although the present-day challenges of churches such as the Lithuanian Catholic Church and the Orthodox churches in Russia and Georgia can be diverse, the processes by which their leaders devise agendas to address these concerns have commonality. The paramount common denominator is a rational approach to policy-making which emphasizes the protection and enhancement of church success. As a concomitant to this phenomenon, when considering the institutional design process, one would expect to find the nature of church participation largely determined by the religious elites' perception of current or potential shifts in their organization's relative success and influence in society. For example, if a church perceives its success to be negatively correlated with the course of institutional change, then one would expect the religious leadership of that church to enact strategies to manipulate that course in its favor. These reactionary strategies can be of a political nature, such as seeking state favors, protection and a restricted market. Or a non-political agenda could be pursued such as internal attempts at restructuring or recasting the church in society to enhance competitiveness. Conversely, if church leaders perceive the course of institutional change to be beneficial to their organization, then an interventionist posture would be unwarranted.

The first two case study churches presented in this book offer clear examples of this means-ends, policy-making calculation. Many Georgian Orthodox Church clergy believe that their church would be detrimentally affected if the religious marketplace were liberalized. Therefore, they have advocated, with varying degrees of success over the past thirty years, political strategies to prevent such liberalization. By contrast, the Lithuanian Catholic Church believes that the existing institutional structure is advantageous or, at the very least, irrelevant to church success. Because of this, church hierarchs have largely refrained from enacting political strategies.

The findings outlined in chapter Six, however, suggest that not all churches have such an easily defined calculation, and indeed, even the first two case study chapters reveal that the policy formulation processes for the Georgian and Lithuanian Churches' are much more intricate than they appear on the surface. Religions do not have the advantage of commercial businesses where the meaning of success and the means of achieving it are obvious—profit, increased productivity, and competitiveness. Church leaders may have vastly different interpretations of what defines church success. For example, Lithuanian clergy place significance on increasing adherents' faithfulness, while Georgian priests interpret improvements in broader church-state and church-societal consciousness as a more consequential barometer of success. For much of the post-Soviet period, Russian Orthodox clergy lacked consensus on the meaning of success.

Furthermore, a leader's perception of the direction of church power, and by extension the preference of remedial options, depends upon his individual interpretation of market developments. Once an institutional design course correction is deemed necessary, internal and external constraints on the church may limit the extent of a non-political corrective agenda. For instance, one could argue that the inability of the Georgian Church to deliver a credible and competitive religious product immediately after 1991 meant that a non-political response to the challenges presented by a free-market (for example increasing product attractiveness) was not seen as a viable option by hierarchs. The product they were selling was unappealing after 1991 compared to what was on sale by foreign entrants who had sharpened their products in the competitive markets of the West. Put more bluntly, Orthodox priests had forgotten how to minister effectively. On the other hand, an aversion to the political scheming of church officials on the part of the government or public might preclude a political alternative. In the case of the Lithuanian Orthodox Church, adopting an anti-democratic posture to religious liberties and pluralism may not have gone over particularly well with the state or society in that Baltic nation in the 1990s. Other factors, such as a politicized leadership, may contribute to the narrowing of options available to policy-makers. Because of these dynamics, if one is to fully appreciate policy-formulation on religious liberties and pluralism within traditional church hierarchies, a thorough consideration of contextual variables is required.

I have attempted to accomplish this task through a utility framework which incorporates the myriad variables playing upon church leaders when they analyze their churches' success, interpret current and potential shifts in that success, and consider the option of political recourse. These interrelated factors have been divided into historical and transitional categories with the former marked by a defining event that has carried path-dependent repercussions through to the present day. The historical context revolves around the political identities, structural composition and level of competitiveness, which were either altered negatively by a subservient response to the critical juncture decision or remained largely unchanged due to a resistant response. These two paths, one fraught with Georgian Orthodox-type baggage, the other mostly free of Soviet legacies, arrived at the same time at the exogenous shock that was the transitional marketplace. As historical institutionalism accurately predicts, religious leaders that operated within Soviet-created institutions became more adept and knowledgeable of those institutions approaching the point of dependence (Deeg 2001, 4). The conceptual framework of the model becomes more convoluted with the uncertain peculiarities and changing contours of the post-Soviet marketplace. Nevertheless, indicators of Soviet-historical trajectories from the critical juncture are still as discernible, as they are influential, on church elites' points of reference and their perceptions of power shifts.

It might be argued that this path-dependent modelling turns too much on a critical juncture which in all likelihood did not occur in a vacuum and which was heavily influenced by antecedent variables not common among the churches. While this argument is not without merit, it is important to remember that it is the path after the critical juncture, not before, that is of interest in determining a church's current position on religious liberties. The critical juncture helped illuminate the tendencies already found within churches and cement those tendencies into a Soviet-era trajectory. While the choice was undoubtedly influenced by antecedents, the consequences of the choice were the ultimate deciding factors in predicting final outcomes (Mahoney 2001, 7). Because of this, I did not feel the need to perform an exhaustive pre-Soviet analytical exercise, but instead focused on the critical juncture and the ensuing multi-dimensionality of the policy process taken by church elites. The findings of that investigation suggest that after the fall of communism, church policy-makers engaged in a rational process in which they appraised the degree and direction of changes in their relative power against the backdrop of both the communist-era setting (structural-historical context) and the present institutional circumstances (immediate-strategic context) (Luong 2002, 14). After such an assessment, they then "develop strategies of action based on what they expect their influence over the outcome to be *vis-à-vis* other actors" (Luong 2002, 14). Therefore, an appreciation of religious elites' perception of power change assists in comprehending "both the process and outcome of institutional design" (Luong 2002, 29).

The conceptual framework of the two contexts merging to shape elites' power perception has proven remarkably robust when applied to the experiences of the Georgian, Lithuanian and Russian national churches. Church leaders' views on religious liberties strongly correspond to their opinions on church-Soviet state interaction. Regardless of church affiliation, clergy who personally defied Soviet religious policy or wished that their church hierarchy had resisted, generally have a progressive attitude towards religious freedoms. Conversely, those church officials that displayed subservient behavior or had no misgivings about their church having a close relationship with the Soviet state, possess a very restrictive interpretation of religious freedoms. This link between Soviet-era behavior and present attitudes on religious freedoms among church leaders is a key empirical finding of this book. It underlines that the critical juncture choice is step-wise correlated to a church's policy on institutional design in general, and religious liberties for non-traditional churches in particular. And the steps that make up the subservient path leading from the juncture are lined with the historical and transitional constraints described in this book. In both Georgia and Lithuania, research has drawn out that the divergent independent variable (Soviet-era subservient choice) has resulted in a clear dependent variable contrast (current policy on religious liberties). Interviews conducted among Russian Orthodox clergy indicate that the church faces the two divergent paths within its own makeup due to a protracted critical juncture. And this mixed ideological composition and the friction that it generates account for initial weak internal consolidation and exterior progression on protectionist measures emanating from the Russian Orthodox Church. It took over twenty years for the church to break firmly toward the conservative course.

Empirical findings have substantiated many of the assumptions put forward in chapter One relevant to church behavior in the aftermath of a state-controlled institutional design for religious affairs.

Those church leaders who were trained, appointed, and worked for a heavily Soviet-infiltrated church tend to be more authoritarian in their views towards the activities of other religious groups.

The close association with the Soviet apparatus produced a unique set of ideologically derived values within church leadership. This historically derived political culture is manifest in the attitudes of many senior church officials toward religious pluralism and freedoms. Opinion samples from religious elites of the Georgian Orthodox and Lithuanian Catholic churches plainly demonstrate that the clergy of the former are comfortable with restricting the rights of religious minorities, while the latter are not. The Russian Orthodox Church is an amalgamation of both churches. Even though it was impossible to precisely determine if an interviewee had willingly cooperated with the state, a pattern is discernible if one substitutes a religious elite's interpretation of church behavior under Soviet rule as the independent variable. Russian leaders who maintain, without reservation, that the church acted admirably, also hold their Georgian counterparts' posture towards religious liberties. On the other hand, those clergy that possess a more objective interpretation of Soviet history tend to advance a more moderate position on religious minorities, similar to the Lithuanian Catholic clergy. Every Georgian Orthodox official interviewed expressed support for restrictions on non-traditional churches in contrast to only one-fourth of Lithuanian Catholic clergy. The two-thirds of Russian Orthodox Church leaders that agreed with the church's cooperation with the Soviet state are the same two-thirds that disapprove of religious sects' right to own land and support other limitations on non-traditional groups. The remaining third that objected to their church's Soviet-era conduct are not concerned with restricting land ownership rights of sects and are not pre-occupied with protectionism. The divide between the two ideological groupings within the Russian Orthodox Church was clear in my research and substantiated by the findings of others.

Heavily Soviet-infiltrated churches were less competitive in the post-1991 marketplace than those churches that were not subservient to the Soviet state. Sectarian churches were more successful in formerly co-opted church territory than in areas where the dominant church resisted the Soviet State.

A church's competitiveness has been assessed by: (1) measuring the success of other religious organizations in the nation with the assistance of available statistical information and conversations with non-traditional church officials; (2) questioning church elites on their perception of church competitiveness; (3) considering any non-competitive attributes which were developed under Soviet rule and perpetuated in the transition (examples are high average clergy age and priest shortage); (4) and finally, discussions with and surveys of former adherents of traditionally dominant churches who have in the transition switched denominational affiliation. The combination of these methods reveals a correlation between past subservience and present non-competitiveness within churches. The peculiarities of market features make this correlation less observable than it might otherwise have been. For instance, in Georgia many indicators point toward the Orthodox Church losing ground upon liberalization, but any clear manifestation of the church's woes is largely hidden by the partially close market. In Lithuania, Catholics and non-Catholics clergy alike recognize the church's competence and prominence. Four-fifths of Catholic leaders interviewed state that Soviet repression has little or no impact on the church's transitional competitiveness. But the Catholic Church's gradual downturn in parishioner activity due to secularization factors conceal its market share competitiveness *vis-à-vis* other religious organizations. The situation in Lithuania does, however, clearly validate the second premise of this conclusion—non-Catholic denominations have found it extremely difficult to establish a firm foothold in a nation where the dominant religious organization fought against Soviet rule. This is contrasted with Russia, where many non-Orthodox churches, prior to the 2016 measures, experienced significant success and leaders of such churches feel that "the field [was] still ripe for more harvesting" (Anonymous 2004. Interview with senior official of The Church of Jesus Christ of Latter-day Saints in Siberia, Krasnoyarsk, Feb).

Ecclesiastic leaders that previously worked closely with authorities are more willing to engage in political machinations than are leaders that resisted Soviet policy.

All religious officials who agreed to be interviewed from the three case study churches were asked if they thought that churches should abstain from direct participation in the political process. Their responses support the assertion that the Soviet "state structure and policies create[d] and reinforce[d] an individual's desire and capacity to consciously invest in certain identities rather than others, particularly in his/her political life" (Luong 2002, 62). Indeed, their answers mirror almost perfectly the interpretation of their church's Soviet history and their attitude on religious liberties. All but one Georgian Orthodox official interviewed favor political activism on the part of the church. On the other hand, a vast majority of Lithuanian leaders disagree with church intervention in the political process. Russian officials, again, broke along the same stratification, with two-thirds for and one-third against, church political involvement. Admittedly, seventy-four may not be a totally reliable sample size for firm statistical inference. But the pattern does imply both that a relationship exists between proximity to the Soviet apparatus and politicization. This conforms to what Luong described as the "the persistence of the political identities that [were] adopted under the previous regime" (2002, 276).

Clergy from churches that were subservient to Soviet power feel more threatened by foreign and domestic sectarian groups after 1991 than do officials from churches that resisted Soviet polices.

Further indication of the grouping along the two paths becomes evident when clergy are asked to express their opinions on religious sects operating in their canonical territory. The majority of Lithuanian Catholic clergy are not threatened by the presence of non-traditional religious groups, whereas the majority of Georgian Orthodox officials and a significant share of Russian church leaders are anxious regarding the appearance of competitors. The degree of anxiety differs between the two

FINDINGS AND IMPLICATIONS   199

Orthodox establishments. Most conservative Russian Orthodox priests interviewed are opposed to sectarian activity, yet they are not averse to a discussion on the subject and rarely consider violence a legitimate method of curtailing sectarian actions. Georgian leaders are much more uncompromising on the topic. The hostile rhetoric emanating from Georgian Orthodoxy between 1991 to 2007 exposed the perceived threat presented by highly specialized sects to existing institutional design.

There is a deductive correlation between the degree to which a church cooperated with Soviet authorities and its willingness to pursue a policy of religious protectionism through political interventionism.

I have endeavored to connect the seven-decade old critical juncture with current church policy positions on religious liberties by merging structure and agency. Discussions with church leaders reveal that even though they have space in which to exercise agency, structural-historical factors shape and limit the boundaries in which that agency can be exercised. And the more subservient a church, in general, and a leader, in particular, was to the Soviet state, the more history and structure restrict present-day agency. Because the Lithuanian Catholic Church was not politicized, did not lose competitiveness, and did not allow its culture to be altered during Soviet occupation, structural factors stemming from Soviet oppression have not profoundly influenced transitional agency. Georgian Orthodox Church decision-making, on the other hand, has been conducted amidst substantial conscious and subconscious structural constraints. Thus, protectionism, which is routinely preached by dominant churches today, demonstrates the interplay between structure and agency—between structural-historical and immediate-strategic contexts. Both contexts are intertwined to shape elites' perception of shifts in their relative power. While many factors manipulate that perception, the effects of the critical juncture are the most discernible threads influencing both contexts and, ultimately, the final outcome.

Orthodox-Authoritarian Fallacy

Often research streams lead to unexpected discoveries. Years of in-country investigation of the attitudes of post-Soviet Russian Orthodox clergy revealed surprising findings that relate to the centuries-old debate concerning Orthodox theology and authoritarianism. While not an academic consensus, there have been times, particularly in the aftermath of the fall of communism, that scholars viewed the wider Eastern Orthodox tradition as "an antidemocratic force reinforcing authoritarianism" (Pollis 1993, 356). Yet my research found a statistically significant division within the church between those holding liberal views and those holding more totalitarian views. Orthodoxy and authoritarianism may not be synonymous after all. The diversity of Orthodox opinion on religious pluralism, not just in Russia but across the region, points to the strength of the critical juncture on current orientation. It undercuts the argument that antecedents hold greater sway—specifically that Orthodoxy is more prone to totalitarian tendencies than Catholicism. I have previously stated historical and scholarly arguments that undermine such a generalization. My research adds a more contemporary data point to those arguments.

Another data point against the argument that present-day attitudes within the Russian Patriarchate can be explained by an appeal to Eastern Orthodox tradition is found in the Ukrainian Orthodox Church. That church gained its self-governing status through an act of autocephaly by the Patriarchate of Constantinople in January of 2019. Thereafter, it quickly became apparent that the new church would forge a significantly different course than its former overseer on several key issues from church-state interactions to interfaith dialogue. That course was first articulated post autocephaly by a group of like-minded laypersons and junior clergy in the Ten Theses for the Orthodox Church of Ukraine which is essentially the Bill of Rights for the newly independent church. They read as a refutation of the Russian Orthodox Church. In addition to a call for more laity involvement, the document explicitly states a need to withdraw "from church-state relations paradigms, and symphonies of the Byzantine or Western types, and disavowal of the Church's political engagement" (RISU, 2019). Most remarkably is the final thesis which supports the embracing of other Christian and non-Christian religions. This tenet is not simply aspirational, but already well-engrained in Ukrainian Orthodoxy. The newly autocephalous Ukrainian Orthodox Church has continued to support an ecumenical council made up of seventeen religious communities in Ukraine. The body, with a rotating chairmanship and a motto of equality for all members, has among its members Baptists, Adventists, and Pentecostals in addition to more traditional denominations and religions. According to a senior Orthodox church member, the council's aim has long been to find "common ground for cooperation" (Interview 2020. Senior Ukrainian Orthodox Church official, London, Jan). An analogous grouping in Russia is unimaginable in Putin's Russia today.

The Ukrainian example underscores that the intellectual tradition of Eastern Orthodoxy is multifaceted and not deducible to generalization. Any set of beliefs developed over two millennium among dozens of diverse and geographically separate nations would undoubtedly display individuality. The doctrine may be canonically consistent, but approaches on church and societal interaction vary. Indeed, the new Ukrainian Church offers empirical support to recent scholarship highlighting that Orthodoxy is not anchored to a theological aversion to modernity and democracy as some have purported. Recent Western scholars, including Kristina Stoeckl, refute previous assertions that while the West's religious-cultural development is defined by individuality and agency, Orthodoxy is defined by totalitarianism and collectivism (2009, 16). If there is nothing inherently authoritarian in Eastern Orthodoxy theology, then the diversity of approaches on religious pluralism and church-state relations among Orthodox churches must be a result of unique historical and -cultural elements.

Implications of Findings on Rational Choice Assumptions

Rational choice theorists claim to be working towards a general theory of religious activity, complete with a catalogue of propositions, which have universal application. Laurence Iannaccone asserted back in 1998 that the approach, which he has championed, has "set off a small revolution within the sociology of religion" (1998, 1489-90). Critics counter that religiosity cannot be analyzed by a methodology based upon rationality. They maintain that predictions are too simplistic, do not hold up against case studies, and that the approach has found success only when examining religious activity in the United States. A tangential aim of the research supporting this book was to be the first to use empirical research, not merely secondary census or survey data, to evaluate rational choice assumptions against religious reality in the former Soviet Union. Extensive interviewing with traditional and non-traditional church leaders, in which questions were intentionally geared towards testing rational choice assumptions, produce noteworthy results. The findings from these interviews suggest that the approach has much to offer in certain aspects of the scientific study of religious producers. In other areas, however, generalizations appear overly simplistic for sociological arrangements governed so much by structure and culture.

Where the theory seems most promising is in the cost-benefit model of supply-side behavior and in market structure assumptions. Karl Barth stated, "The Christian congregation does not live in heaven, but on earth, therefore a change in the form of the state may not be indifferent to her" (cited in Kodacsy 2004, 35). Sentiments expressed by religious officials of many churches in the region reveal that the profit maximization principle is highly applicable to religious suppliers. Some clergy maintain that the goal of religion is to assist individuals in the attainment of spiritual fulfilment. However, most officials interviewed evaluated success more tangibly by measuring increases in parishioners, monetary contributions, public exposure, and societal influence. In fact, interviews with traditional church leaders reveal that business analogous terminology is not only useful but essential in understanding the self-interested behavior of suppliers of religious commodities. As a consequence of operation in a distributional arrangement with competitors and with the possibility of political interference and bottom-line budgetary calculations, in order to "survive and grow, religious organizations must be rationalized and bureaucratized" (Riis 1999, 25). While Lithuanian Catholic clergy exhibit a material, rational approach to church existence in general and church-state relations in particular, it is manifested even more profoundly by churches that worked closely with the Soviet state. This is precisely because the Soviet experience served as a mechanism for extracting any irrationality out of religious leaders' actions. The politicization process made church leadership cost-benefit analysis less obscure and more measurable. The rationalistic principles have been proven to be extremely resilient when describing supply-side behavior in the former Soviet Union.

In addition to demonstrating that religious leaders in the region are rational optimizers, conversations with religious elites in the former Soviet Union suggest that economic theory relative to markets, competition, and regulations are suitable to the religious environment. Leaders from the three churches examined are keenly aware of marketplace developments and market share trends. For instance, formerly subservient churches, such as the Russian Orthodox Church, are conscious of the "burdens of monopoly" (Iannacconne 1997, 40). State-sponsored monopoly churches understand that free religious trade produces power shifts between churches. Hence, as traditional producers, they seek a limit on goods produced abroad and sold domestically. The way in which most Georgian Orthodox and many Russian Orthodox clergy frame their organizational priorities attest to the assumption that government regulation on religious activity changes the incentives and strategies of churches. Likewise, the political vacuum and economic depression that has typified Georgian society has enabled the church to gain a prominent position in the political processes and thereby guard against undesirable market adjustments. The lobbying efforts of traditional churches manifest that their leaders are sensitive to what market structure change means. At least among those churches scrutinized in this book, Anthony Gill's assumption is validated that "religious market structure has an important impact on church political strategy" (1998, 189).

Despite the fact that many of the supply-side assumptions have been supported by findings in the region, others of the more contested assumptions remain unsubstantiated. For instance, a central assumption of rational choice proponents is that religiosity is a function of competition and that where regulation is lower, overall levels of religiousness will tend to be greater. This is not demonstrated across the board in the religious environments scrutinized. The sluggish Lithuanian religious market shows that a decrease in religious regulation does not automatically result in an upsurge in religiosity. While there are few countries in the region with a more liberal set of religious laws than Lithuania, clergy from a broad range of churches feel religiosity is on the wane. Many firms appeared after 1991 only to scale back operations because of a lack of profits.

Furthermore, among those clergy interviewed, most admit that displays of religiosity in Georgia increased throughout the 1990s, as regulations remained draconian for all but the Orthodox Church. The continued high level of religious activity in Georgia appears to demonstrate that an increase in regulation does not automatically translate into decreased religious participation. In Russia, religious plurality was indeed impressive before 2016 with hundreds of new market entrants. However, the religious revival in the country only encompassed a small portion of the overall population. Yet in 2020, Tymofil Brik and Stanislav Korolkov examined the surprisingly vibrant and diverse religious marketplace in Ukraine. They linked the religious revival in that country to religious competition, particularly among the three Orthodox churches vying for influence before 2019 (2020). The Ukraine example appears to support the assumptions that religious vitality in a society is a result of structural features, specifically the competitiveness of a religious market.

The circumstances in the former Soviet Union also illustrates that no two church monopolies are the same and that oversimplification can lead to skewed results. A government-protected monopoly is dissimilar in characteristics to a church that monopolizes without state sponsorship. The Lithuanian Catholic Church is an example of the latter—a church which receives little practical competitive advantage on the ground for its titular role. It has essentially monopolized the market on its own. Contrary to conventional wisdom, the Russian Orthodox Church prior to 2012 found itself in a similar situation. The state provided relatively few market-distorting advantages to the church directly, notwithstanding laws such as those passed in 1997. Only in the extensive state-favoritism found in the 1990s in Georgia and after 2016 in Russia do we find churches "reaping the benefit of state support" (Froese 2004a, 72).

In a like manner, in order to protect against skewed results, rational choice proponents and opponents should take into fuller account the distinction between titular members and high religious human capital members. For example, survey data among converts of The Church of Jesus Christ of Latter-day Saints and discussions with clergy of all three case-study churches demonstrate the importance of human religious capital on demand-side mobility and supply-side interpretation of success.

Information obtained from former Orthodox believers indicates that while the flight away from traditional churches may be small, those that are abandoning the churches for other organizations have a disproportional amount of religious human capital. Sentiments from religious leaders, especially in the Russian Orthodox Church, suggest that they are keenly aware of the significance of this exodus and the disproportional advantage to churches that adherents with high levels of religious human capital provide.

While rational choice sociologists have studied human capital's impact on household production, the role on supply-side phenomenon needs to be better measured. Clergy in Russia and Lithuania underscore that market share movement among adherents with high levels of religious capital is paramount. While tracking this market share movement might be problematic, a failure to account for it can compromise the accuracy of conclusions. A case in point exposed by my research is the conclusion that the Russian Orthodox Church increased its hegemonic position among believers in the 1990s and early 2000s. This presumption is based on the fact that the exodus from the church to new religious sects, post 1991, was insignificant and that religious affiliation with Orthodoxy among the public nearly doubled in the past half century. While both these trends were not disproved by my research, conversations with religious believers and leaders in Russia indicate that the impact of these trends on the health of the church has been exaggerated—mainly due to the role of human religious capital. The large numbers added to Orthodoxy during the past five decades has largely been discernible only statistically, while those lost to other churches, particularly during the 1990s, were discernable from the pews. A small percent loss in market share could be significant if it involves individuals with a large percent of high religious capital. In all three case-study churches, religious elites seem keenly aware that affiliation numbers are relative and, while advantageous to public and political prominence, they are less significant than service-attending, tithe-paying adherents.

Scholarship investigating religious behavior through the lens of rational choice theory was abundant in 1990s and early 2000s, but has abated in recent years. Even so, the theory has merit. My research provides field-testing of this approach, which has largely been confined to assumptions and predictions based on historical data. This book does not purport to be a definitive report card on the theory, but rather a measured assessment of the economic theory's applicability to religious studies. The manner in which the approach was applied against my research puzzle exhibits its usefulness as one instrument among an assortment of tools that have utility in the study of religious activity. As demonstrated in the experiences of churches that were subservient to the Soviet state, historical and structural contexts influence religious supply-side activity to such a degree that a pure agency-based methodology has little extrapolative worth if used in isolation. This is precisely the reason why, when proponents of the approach present a general assumption, it must be accompanied by certain caveats.

All this is not to say that the approach does not have merit, or that methodological individualism is not valuable in the study of religious suppliers. Indeed, to the contrary, my research validates the assertion that religious leaders act purposively, weighting costs and profits prior to a decision. Also, the collective micro-agency actions of suppliers can account for macro-level phenomenon such as religious protectionism. The manner in which Orthodox churches seek limitations on their competitors substantiates many religious-economies suppositions. The case studies have demonstrated the interpretative value of applying strict rationality to church leaders. However, more often than not, that agency is bound by structural social-cultural factors not common among all religions. The utility model of church elites involves a combination of structural and agential explanatory variables. Soviet history does not predetermine post-Soviet choices, but it does define the assortment of strategies available to religious actors. For these reasons, rational choice theory likely lacks the breadth of understanding to ever be a stand-alone methodology for examining religious behavior, particularly in terms of supply-side operations and agendas.

Critical junctures and profound structurally-significant histories are not an exclusive feature of former Soviet churches. Consequential historical contexts are more the rule than the exception among traditional churches worldwide. Because of this, the study of religion requires a recursive interpretation of behavior in which the relations between structures and agents are addressed. In support of their Strategic-Relational approach, Bob Jessop and Colin Hay argued for the need to fuse structure and agency in social scientific analysis. My research reveals that nowhere is that synthesis needed more than in the study of religious suppliers. Rational choice can play an important part in interpreting the agency of religious elites. But a comprehensive understanding is impossible without historical and structural context. Unfortunately for ambitious rational choice theorists, this conclusion debunks the notion of a general theory, but it does validate the approach as a useful framework for the social scientific study of religious organizations.

8. Collusion That Matters
Church-State Symbiosis After Crimea

Regardless the disposition of the dominant church, any sustained suppression of religious freedoms in a particular nation requires state participation. As stated in chapter 3: *The capacity of a single religious firm to monopolize a religious economy depends upon the degree to which the state uses coercive force to regulate the religious economy.* A church can petition and posture all it wants for restrictions on religious competitors, but secular authorities typically have the final word. In Russia, that word was unequivocally uttered in 2016. But what explains that abrupt U-turn to religious protectionism from such a longstanding stance of indifference? The answer is undoubtedly multifaceted and almost certainly related, at least in part, to broader trends in de-democratization and the refutation of Western norms in Russia during Putin's third presidential term. But the answer also lies, perhaps to a greater extent, in the evolution of church-state relations. Developments in that domain since 2014 have surpassed even the high threshold of historically close ties between the Kremlin and the patriarchate. A mutually-beneficial relationship has been a staple of religious life in Russia for centuries. Yet, recent historic church-state cooperation in Russia has transformed into outright collusion.

It is true that there have been many instances prior to 2014 when little daylight was discernable between the two entities. But this scope and depth of interaction and assistance is historically unprecedented. Indeed, the benefits of collusion have become more integral to the successes of both entities than ever before. At the heart of the collusion is a rather simple quid pro quo: the church receives diminished religious competition and the state receives assistance in securing regime survival and objectives. The first part of the equation—the motives and backstory to the church's willingness to enter into a covenant with authorities—is the central subject of this book. The second part of the equation—understanding the Kremlin's 'ask'—is the topic of this concluding chapter.

Church-state relations in Russia, and more specifically, the political utility of the Russian Orthodox Church for the Kremlin has changed drastically over the years, but can be categorized into three broad phases:

Phase I (1991-2007): As noted earlier, in the Soviet-era the church preached the virtues of communism in global ecumenical gatherings, but church assimilation into Soviet Active Measures was modest. Notwithstanding much scholarship on the issue, at the end of the day, the ultimate Soviet goal was to make the church irrelevant, not to transform it into an element of state power. After 1991, state control and minimal accords of cooperation faded away into the chaotic and sporadic church-state dealings of the 1990s. The church provided little to the state apart from symbolically buttressing the regime with legitimacy and odd statements of support. These occurred primarily around election cycles and had little sustaining impact on society or on either entities' institutional power. The change from Yeltsin to Putin did not change this dynamic in any meaningful way. By 2007, John Anderson noted that "issues of religion and politics have rarely been of central importance during the Putin years, and the Russian Orthodox Church, though broadly in sympathy with the president's aims and political style, has not enjoyed the political influence that liberal critics feared" (2007, 200). For the church's part, Gregory Freeze noted that "Patriarch Aleksii II (1990–2008) focused mainly on brick-and-mortar rechurching, reacquiring and rebuilding physical churches, with minimal engagement in secular issues" (2017). For the state, the supply-side opportunity costs associated with a restrictive deterred action. As noted by Anthony Gill, "To the extent that political survival, revenue collection and economic growth are hindered by restrictions on religious freedom, or subsidies to a dominant church, religious regulation will be liberalized or left un-enforced (de facto liberalization)" (2005, 7). Because Russia was more engaged in the world community than for instance reclusive Belarus, the Russian government had more to lose in the enforcement of draconian religious legislation. This explains why the strict religious laws passed before 2014 usually were not enforced comprehensively or with vigor. This first stage of church-state interaction from 1991 to 2008 was, by and large, unremarkable as the church and the state were otherwise occupied.

Phase 2 (2008-2013): The second stage of church-state interaction, or interwar period, witnessed a gradual strengthening of the bond between church and state as a result of Putin's nationalistic resurgence following his 2007 Munich speech and Patriarch Kirill's ascendency a mere six months after the Georgian conflict. As previously noted, Kirill was, from the start, more politically-minded than his predecessor. As such, the church quickly became involved in counter-color revolutionary campaigns during his tenure, such as the soft-power Russkiy Mir project which sought to spread Russian culture across the former Soviet space. In return, as mentioned in chapter 6, the state, among other gratuities, expedited the process for reclaiming lost Orthodox properties, providing additional tax breaks and allowing for Orthodox-led religious education courses. At the same time, coordination mechanisms became quite overt and formalized between the Church's Department of External Church Relations and Russia's Ministry of Foreign Affairs (Blitt 2011, 383).

The quid pro quo association intensified even more before the Ukraine crisis. The Kremlin mediated the re-incorporation of Soviet-era schismatic elements into the Moscow Patriarchate. This was a particularly remarkable gift for the Russian Orthodox Church and likely ingratiated its leaders to state authorities. For its part, the church's support of the regime deepened and became a bit more socially delicate. Clergy overtly attempted to delegitimize the regime's political opponents. The church backed the controversial ban on foreign adoptions (Tolstaya 2014), and suppressed the 2011-2012 public protests (Solodovnik 2014, 74-75). The latter was a particularly pivotal point for the church and illustrative of the disconcerting trend of church submission. Kirill may be more politically savvy than his predecessor, but early on in his tenure he appeared to cherish church autonomy. At first, he showed an initial hesitancy to support the regime and even hinted at backing the street protests against Putin's re-election to the presidency. This neutrality was undoubtedly motivated by a desire to retain or regain a connection with the population. Yet this independent streak was quickly extinguished after Kremlin-backed media began highlighting the ostentatious style of the patriarchate's living (Coyer 2015, Carbonnel 2012). With the prospect of a sustained state-supported smear campaign against his leadership, Kirill changed course and fell squarely behind the regime, going so far as calling Putin "a miracle from God" (Bryanski 2012).

Phase 3 (2014-present): The war in Ukraine became the defining moment in post-Soviet church-state relations in Russia. While the Russian Orthodox Church and the Kremlin appeared to be marching in lockstep prior to 2014, the annexation of Crimea and de facto annexation of part of the Donbas region, compelled the regime to operationalize the church to an unprecedented degree (Flake and Lamoreaux 2018). The Maidan protests and the prospect of losing Ukraine to the West presented the greatest existential threat to the central tenets of Putin's resurgent narrative. Russian strategists correctly surmised that Moscow's Near Abroad ambitions, including the viability of economic and security pacts, as well as pan-Slavic initiatives, would be rendered null and void without Kyiv. As such, all available means were deployed to prevent the loss of Ukraine from Russia's orbit. The presence of significant social, cultural and religious factors in the Ukrainian dynamic at the time made the Russian Orthodox Church an obvious choice to lead the vanguard of this campaign.

Not unlike his misgivings with condemning the 2011-2012 protests, Patriarch Kirill initially opposed the annexation of Crimea and the media's attempt to use Orthodoxy to legitimize opposition forces in the Donbass (Ziegler 2016, 561-562; Suslov 2016). He undoubtedly foresaw the direr consequences for Orthodox unity and his own church's reach if Ukraine ended up partitioned. Yet, as in 2012, his streak of independence was soon extinguished and the church began participating, from the parish to the patriarchate, in Russia's hybrid warfare in Ukraine (Flake and Lamoreaux 2018). As several scholars have pointed out, the Russian Orthodox Church was rather quickly transformed as a non-military element in the Ukraine War (Simons 2016; Leustean 2017).

From the Ukraine crisis, the church has become a constituent part in the Kremlin's evolving approach to warfare. In order to properly understand the church's precise role in the overall state apparatus, one must peal back several layers of Russian strategy. It is possible to break down Russian strategy into four levels, moving from strategic to tactical: (1) Russia's whole-of-government strategy for succeeding in modern conflicts; (2) the information warfare component of that strategy; (3) the socio-cultural influencers to achieve information dominance; and (4) the religious lever in the socio-cultural toolkit.

1. Whole-of-Government Level

The coordinated use of non-military methods to enact change favorable to Russia is not novel to Vladimir Putin. The practice stretches back at least as far as the Active Measures of the Soviet Union. There are many names for this coordinate approach—hybrid warfare, indirect action, whole-of-government approach, non-linear warfare, and full-spectrum conflict. Whatever the label and whenever the origin, the essence of the strategy is to employ asymmetric tactics across social, political, economic, and other non-kinetic domains, often in tandem with military force, to achieve desired end-states. The approach is founded on the belief that war begins long before the first shots are fired and that goals can be obtained through malign activities that are non-attributable, asymmetric, and fall just below an enemy's threshold for an escalatory response.

This approach was not particularly evident during Putin's first two presidential terms. Those eight years were more about consolidation of power at home than asserting control in the Near Abroad or globally. When the time came, Putin's first foray into war beyond Russia's borders was a heavily qualified success. The Georgian breakaway regions were seized, but not without exposing Russia's military shortcomings, or its inability to dominate the information domain. A failure of coordination between military services and among government agencies was perhaps the greatest lesson learned from the conflict. Several scholars argued that the failure to win the narrative at home, within the targeted audience in Georgia, as well as internationally during and after the 2008 war almost certainly galvanized Russian efforts toward a more coordinated methodology (Snegovaya 2015, 10). Whatever the catalyst, six years after that war, Russia displayed remarkable improvements in the annexation of Crimea and the establishment of the Donbass 'Frozen Conflict'.

Advancements in the interwar period and from the Syria intervention to the present-day do not simply represent a return to a Soviet-era level of integration. Indeed, drawing too distinct a line between Soviet practices and Russia's present-day approach would be ill-advised. First, Soviet Active Measures were largely confined in their scope to pro-regime propaganda and support to anti-capitalist elements abroad. Today, measures are more expansive and "designed to exploit national vulnerabilities across the political, military, economic, social, informational and infrastructure (PMESII) spectrum" (Cullen and Reichborn-Kjennerud 2017, 4). Second, Soviet authorities never had particularly fertile ground for Active Measures to germinate and grow. They were either employed against somewhat inhospitable Western populaces, or against the occupied territories of the USSR and Warsaw Pact, where they were largely unresisted state policies, and not influence tools in a competitive space. In the post-Soviet world, the fourteen former Soviet republics afford the ideal operating environment for Russian influence efforts with their numerous social, historical, economic, political and religious ties with Russia. Third, Soviet-era actions suffered from the spotlight of the Cold War. International attention on malign Soviet actions made them too transparent and predictable, and thus relatively easy to counter in competitive spaces outside the Soviet Union and beyond the Iron Curtain. In contrast, for much of the post-Soviet period, the West has paid meager attention to Russian meddling in the Near Abroad. Even to this day, Russian destabilization activities in the region occur largely unnoticed by Western audiences. Finally, and perhaps most significantly, modernity has brought with it tools that were unimaginable 40 years ago, including cyber and social media exploitation that allows for scalable interference in a targeted country.

The doctrine is also much more defined and openly acknowledged by authorities today. In 2013, military strategist and current Chief of General Staff of the Russian Armed Forces, General Valery Gerasimov delineated the tenets and structure of Russia's new approach to warfare (Gerasimov 2013, 23). A year later, Russia's new military doctrine stated that "characteristic features and specifics of current military conflicts [include] an integrated employment of military force and political, economic, informational or other non-military measures implemented with a wide use of the protest potential of the population and of special operations" (Military Doctrine 2014). Several scholars have questioned how new or novel the strategy actually is, but there can be little doubt of the renewed emphasis behind the approach since 2013. Figure 3 depicts Gerasimov's understanding of how to engage successfully in modern warfare. The escalation stages of military confrontation are on the y-axis and government responses on the x-axis. Beneath are military and non-military tools to escalate or deescalate across the conflict spectrum. As a conflict intensifies, moving from left to right, Russian planners seek to first prepare the battlespace and strengthen deterrence. As tensions rise, activities move to kinetic action and finally attempts to return to stability on Russia's terms by means of dominating escalation of hostilities.

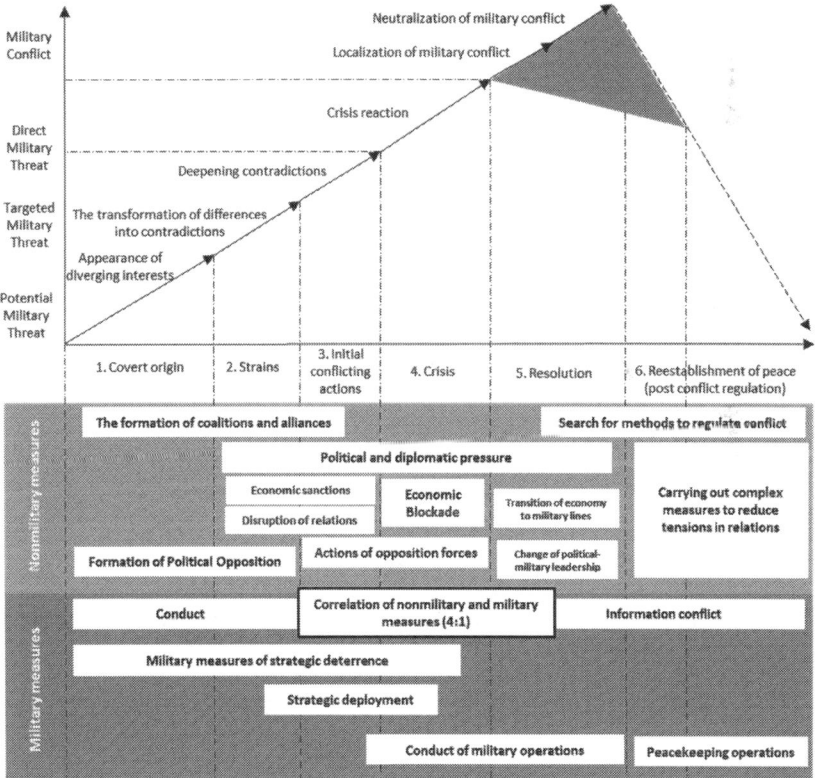

Figure 3. Recreation of graphic by General Valery Gerasimov (2013).

The ultimate aim is to subvert an enemy's social, political, and military competencies to achieve a desired end state without ever having to resort to conventional warfare. This is realized through the synchronized actions of diverse state and state-supported entities to address a particular problem in times of prevailing peace or in the early stages of conflict. If these measures are unsuccessful, then many of the same tools can be refocused, often with more hostile intent, to affect change in times of escalating tension to open hostilities. Most tools, such as actions in the cyber domain, are scalable and able to be employed lightly and surgically in early stages of tension and, if needed, more heavy-handedly in later phases of warfare. As we will see, the breadth of this strategy, particularly in the non-military domains, may be even greater than many appreciate. Recent developments in Russia suggest a more expansive approach— one that incorporates historically benign non-government institutions to establish narrative, undermine the social and political stability of targeted nations, and affect the decision calculus of adversaries.

2. Informational Warfare Level

A crucial element of success in Russian strategy is the early control of the information domain. The importance of the domain is underscored by it being the only measure that spans the entire conflict spectrum in Gerasimov's visual representation of Russia's war posture. Russian planners have developed significant disinformation capabilities in response to what Russia's last two National Security Strategies called the intensification of "the global information struggle" (National Security Strategy 2009, 2015). In 2010, Russia's military doctrine stated the importance of "the prior implementation of measures of information warfare in order to achieve political objectives without the utilization of military force and, subsequently, in the interest of shaping a favorable response from the world community" (Military Doctrine 2010). In fact, Gerasimov asserted that the efficient execution of hybrid warfare should have a four-to-one ratio of non-kinetic to kinetic operations, with the vast majority of that undoubtedly employed in information warfare. Russian actions in Ukraine in 2014 may very well have approached the 4:1 ratio. Nowhere was Russia's informational warfare more on display than in Ukraine. According to former U.S. General and NATO Supreme Allied Commander, Philip Breedlove, Russia's operation in Ukraine was "the most amazing information warfare blitzkrieg we have ever seen in the history of information warfare" (Vandiver 2014).

Russian disinformation campaigns typically fall within the four Ds of dismissing Russian malign action, distorting truth, distracting attention, and dismaying an adversary with bluster and obfuscation (Emerson 2015). Yet, Russian information warfare is not limited to simple digital disinformation. Several western scholars have recently noted that Russia's perception of information warfare is not as narrowly defined as in the West (Connell and Vogler 2017). For instance, Russia views electronic warfare and psychological operations as integral to information dominance. Perhaps the greatest departure from Western notions of information warfare is that all of Russia's significant cyber activities are seen by Russian military strategists as a constituent part of the information domain (ibid.). Cyber methods such as social media hijacking, denial-of-service attacks, and the hacking and release of damaging material are merely means to an end of controlling the information domain.

Even more importantly, individual acts of disinformation or cyber activity often are not standalone shots at an opponent, but part of a larger effort to influence the thought processes of a targeted audience. The objective is to establish meta-narratives in targeted populations groups in order for them to "order and explain knowledge and experience" (Stephens and McCallum 1998, 6) within a Russian constructed framework. These meta-narratives act as an interpretative backdrop for audiences to contextualize events, thereby authenticating Russia's perspective (Hansen 2017, 38-42). For instance, the Kremlin has long sought to imprint on European consciousness the belief that NATO's primary goal is to encircle and isolate Russia. Years of repeating this assertion in various forums has created a cognitive framework against which individual events, such as a U.S. proposal to increase troop strength in Poland, are placed. The desired result is a type of confirmation bias that persuades populations to oppose such actions as too provocative. These cognitive operations are intended to achieve decision bias in favor of Russia through saturating memory and cognitive processes with external cues (see Van Dijk 2006; Johnson et al., 1981; Leynes et al., 2005). Another meta-narrative behind much of Russian disinformation in West is the belief that the U.S./European democratic system is corrupt and failing. This is partially accomplished by engendering cynicism within Western populations in their political and social institutions (Pomerantsev 2015, 42).

These mind-games are also applied to adversarial leadership through what is called 'reflective control'. The goal is to manipulate enemy perception of the battlespace in such a way as to entice foreign decisionmakers to unknowingly make choices to Russia's advantage. Through a coordinated information manipulation strategy, Moscow crafts points of reference, which at once constrain and funnel opponents' decision space to an outcome favorable to Russia. In the case of Ukraine, a relatively restrained Western response to the annexation of Crimea was likely partially due to the employment of reflective control. Moscow's acumen at setting the narrative with regard to the peninsula's history, links to Russia, and Ukraine's more general dysfunctionality likely affected the decision algorithms (Mateski 2016) of Western leaders. In such a manipulated information environment, they may have quickly accepted the annexation as a *fait accompli*.

3. Socio-Cultural Domain Level

In addition to the aforementioned cyber, media, and electronic warfare tools, a much less examined resource which Russia taps to advance its information warfare is found in the socio-cultural domain. The Kremlin has discovered that success at home and abroad in deploying information manipulation depends largely on the number and trustworthiness of the organs disseminating external cues. The more numerous the voices, and the further removed they are from the state apparatus, the greater chance the disinformation finds resonance. This explains why non-state entities, which were always a part of Soviet disinformation campaigns, are increasingly being assimilated into Putin's whole-of-government action. The assimilation of civil society entities is made possible by two decades of democratization in Russia. Not long after Putin's ascension to power, the Kremlin began systematically attacking, subjugating, and appropriating nearly every element of civil society.

These civil society entities are tasked either formally or through cues to mobilize in defense of Kremlin narratives. To borrow a description from the Soviet-era, these entities "act as 'transmission belts' ensuring the implementation of [regime] directives" (White 1994, 5). They likely do so in a manner that is scalable, allowing amplification of Kremlin messaging when most needed. For instance, an extensive 2018 study of social media behavior surrounding the downing of the Malaysian Airlines Flight MH17 in Ukraine in 2014 indicated the strength of individual citizens and civil society groups to curate disinformation in the service of the Russian State. Civil society groups including NGOs, research centers, volunteer news sites, and citizen journalist groups were all enlisted to obfuscate Russian culpability. The study found that citizen posts were much more likely to be further disseminated than state media (Golovchenko *et al.* 2018, 993).

Figure 4 shows how Gerasimov's 2013 chart has likely evolved in response to lessons learned in Ukraine and Syria. As the intensity of conflict (y-axis) increases so does state attribution (x-axis) in employing measures, with the aim of retaining deniability as long as possible. The object of the initial stage of interstate conflict (first box) is to set the narrative through influencers, that cannot be easily traced back to the state.

As tensions mount, more escalatory steps are taken involving both overt and covert activities to affect desired change. In the Ukraine example, the 'little green men' in Crimea and the Donbass 'insurgency' typified this period. As the conflict reaches critical mass, conventional and nonstrategic weapons are threatened and used to control escalation. If conditions deteriorate to this point, socio-cultural levers lose most of their utility. But in the early stages of tension, and during peacetime conditions, the Kremlin increasingly views an array of civil society and non-state institutions as key influencers to establish narrative and prepare battlespace. These socio-cultural levers are often elements of civil society and have travelled a similar path of persecution, subjugation, and appropriation.

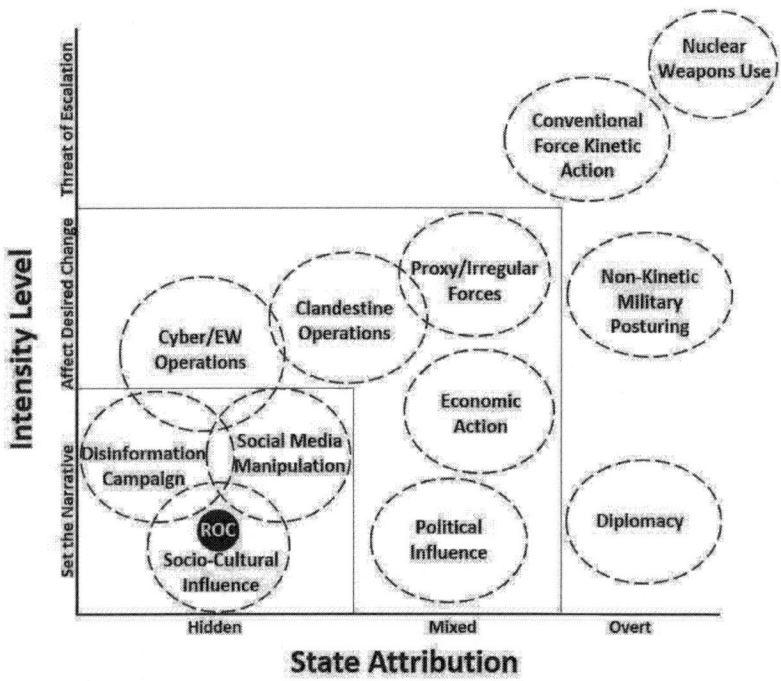

Figure 4. Russian Hybrid Warfare Spectrum and the Russian Orthodox Church (ROC)[13]

The regime's annexation of media to further state aims is the most recognizable example of the assimilation of a non-state entity into Russia's information warfare. Putin's first few years in power witnessed the dismantlement of most opposition and independent media. This was facilitated by state or oligarch take-over of outlets. The result is that the vast majority of TV, print, and online news in Russia today is almost indistinguishable from state messaging. Putin's propaganda tsar, Alexey Gromov, meets weekly with all major media managers to convey talking points, which are in turn filtered down to regional and local outlets (Rubin et al., 2019). Representatives from the Kremlin's foreign media arms, RT

---

13 Dozens of scholars have depicted in graphic form Russia's hybrid warfare framework. This figure represents my understanding. In places it corresponds with those of others including Phillip Karber (2015).

and Sputnik, also attend. After years of practice, this communication is seamless.

Another key civil society entity to fall victim to regime control are Non-governmental Organizations. NGOs were abundant in Russia in the 1990s and were surprisingly non-aligned and constructive to public dialogue. The restrictive 2006 NGO Law purged the country of many independent-minded groups in favor of apolitical or Kremlin-friendly organizations (Gilbert 2016). This filtering intensified after the sizable 2011-2012 protests against Putin's re-election and subsequent 'foreign agents' law in 2012 (Law 2012) and the 'undesirable organizations' law of 2015 (Law 2015). Both were meant to place civil society firmly under the thumb of the Kremlin, with the 'foreign agents' law alone cutting the total number of NGOs by a third (see Snegovaya 2015a; Digges 2015). By the Ukraine crisis, the majority of NGOs that were influential in the political and social spheres were doing the bidding of the state or were outright creations of authorities. Vladimir Putin insinuated this in 2017 when he reported to his Presidential Council for Civil Society that "foreign agent" NGOs in Russia had been halved in two years and were being replaced by NGOs taking a "second path" of receiving funding from the Russian state (Kremlin 2017). Many of these, as Orysia Lutsevych of Chatham House points out, are pseudo-NGOs doing the work of Putin's regime by "undermining the social cohesion of neighboring states" (2016). They can be operationalized at a moment's notice to circulate the Kremlin's perspective.

A particularly useful tactic in the socio-cultural domain has been the historical discreditation of an adversary, often assisted by Russian academia. Russia routinely employs 'fake history', or at the very least, heavily-doctored historical narratives in its information campaigns against its neighbors. A recent example was Vladimir Putin's attempt at recasting in a more favorable light Moscow's motives in the Molotov-Ribbentrop Pact. This particular episode came ahead of the 75th anniversary of the end of World War II and in response to a European Parliament resolution that insinuated that the Soviet Union shared culpability with Germany for instigating the war, and blamed Russia for "whitewashing crimes committed by the Soviet totalitarian regime" (European Parliament 2019). In addition to other counter-informational responses, Putin spent a somewhat awkward 90 minutes at the end of 2019 lecturing several regional heads-of-state on Stalin's commendable behavior in the months prior to the onset of World War II. Russia for years has used history, particularly accusations of collaboration with Nazism, to taint the reputation of its neighbors. In 2014, this 'memory war' tactic was operationalized for more specific purposes to undermine and vilify Ukrainian nationalists as aggressors and accomplices to German atrocities (see Domanska 2019). There has hardly been a conflict, or even elevated tensions, in the region in the last twenty years in which the Kremlin has not deployed this tactic against an adversary (Flake 2020a).

The role of Russia's higher educational institutions in supporting the regime in these 'memory wars' has become increasingly apparent. Government control over universities has strengthened in the past decade, partially as a result of the strongarm tactics of the state accreditation agency, The Federal Service of Supervision in Education and Science (Rosobrnadzor). The European University of St. Petersburg (EUSP) and its relatively liberal curriculum fell afoul of this body and the school's license was pulled in 2017 over a trivial building code violation. While the EUSP regained accreditation in 2019, other non-compliant schools have likewise been bullied into submission or irrelevance. A 2019 study found Russia to be the 119th worst country regarding academic freedoms out of 138 (Kinzelbach et al., 2020, 24). On the level of individual scholars, self-censorship is on the rise as research that counters Kremlin partly line can lead to ostracization. The aforementioned restrictive legislations have probably dissuaded many from collaborating with foreign academics or conducting research that might run counter to Kremlin-approved doctrine (see Dubrovskiy 2018). Several academic-specific moves have also intimated to scholars to color within approved research lines. In 2009 the 'Presidential Commission to Counter Attempts to Falsify History to the Detriment of Russia's Interests' was established in the wake of the Estonia monument removal incident (Interfax 2019). The rationale was to purge Russian academia of views not in harmony with the new nationalist orientation. While it was disbanded a few years later, in 2014 Putin signed a law criminalizing the "rehabilitation of Nazism" (Anishchuk 2014). As with most of these laws, the text is vague and more open to interpretation than the title suggests. In this case, the measure outlaws "the spreading of information on military and memorial commemorative dates related to Russia's defense that is clearly disrespectful of society, and to publicly desecrate symbols of Russia's military glory" (Kurilla 2014). Ever since, academic output has been more aligned with Kremlin-approved dogma. Scholarship in support of state narratives is particularly pronounced in research on Ukrainian history and the origins of World War II.

Finally, and not surprisingly, entertainment is not immune from state manipulation. While less time-responsive to Kremlin needs than the aforementioned elements, Russian-made films more and more resemble Soviet-era propaganda supporting state narratives. Vera Tolz and Yuri Teper assert that since 2016, Russian television coverage has moved from largely de-politicized entertainment to a strategy that "centrally sanctioned communication of ideologized political messages, delivered in accordance with an entertainment logic" (2018, 218).

4. Religious Influence Level

Kremlin strategists hope these socio-cultural levers of influence employed in unison can achieve an effect on the previously mentioned meta-narratives when pushed on targeted populations. As a particularly significant influencer, it was foreseeable that the Russian Orthodox Church would be folded into Putin's information warfare. The aforementioned non-state institutions all had different intake experiences. Journalism was captured and transformed into an information warfare tool rather quickly, comprehensively, and publicly. While academia and entertainment, with more nebulous information warfare utility, were co-opted on an ad hoc basis. The appropriation of the Russian Orthodox Church has been more gradual, deliberate, and in line with the evolution of the regime's expanding view of modern-day conflict. As early as 2004, Tamas Kodacsy asserted that the Kremlin "tries to instrumentalize the church as a cultural-political factor of society" (2004, 35). Yet, at the time, it was clear that the regime had not fully recognized an operational niche for the church. The sociocultural domain within the larger whole-of-society approach to modern warfare had not yet been explored or exploited. Several key events, culminating in the 2014 Ukraine Conflict were needed for authorities to appreciate the benefits of aligning the Russian Orthodox Church seamlessly with state structures.

Considering past behavior, it was not out of character for Vladimir Putin to employ Orthodox imagery to justify the Crimean annexation in 2014:

> "Everything in Crimea speaks of our shared history and pride. This is the location of ancient Khersones, where Prince Vladimir was baptized. His spiritual feat of adopting Orthodoxy predetermined the overall basis of the culture, civilization, and human values that unite the peoples of Russia, Ukraine, and Belarus" (Kremlin 2014).

But the extent of cooperation from the patriarchate to the parish level in justifying and enabling Russia's 2014 land grabs was surprising and new. The cooperation ossified collusion, communication structures, and most of all, church submission so that authorities, at a moment's notice, could tap the church to actualize Kremlin policies. After Crimea, the church moved from being what Irina Papkova called in 2011 a "political lobbyist" (2011, 93) to a full-fledged team player. In addition to acting in support of foreign policy objectives, the church's support to the regime at home moved beyond the mere symbolism of the early Putin years. Domestic support became more systemic and unashamed. For instance, in the fall of 2017, dozens of permanent mega-exhibitions called "Russia— my history" began opening across the country (Ceballos 2018; Kurilla 2018). The exhibitions which substantiate Putin's rule in the context of a shared Orthodox heritage was reportedly pushed by nationalist Bishop Tikhon Shevkunov, a close confidante of Putin. According to Sergey Ivanov, the exhibitions expose the monarchism, clericalism, and all-pervasive conspiracy theory so prevalent in Russian life today (Ivanov 2018).

At the same time, church actions in the broader region and within the Eastern Orthodox community have become synchronized with Kremlin foreign policy goals. Indeed, as with the media, regular coordination meetings occur between church and state officials (Credo 2019). Meetings between senior officials have become more routine and openly described as policy coordination endeavors. In April 2019, Patriarch Kirill met with Foreign Minister Sergei Lavrov where the former expressed the church's desire to be "actively present in the sphere of international relations, for us it is very useful to know your point of view on those problems that disturb us." For his part, Lavrov noted that "we have a joint working group of the Ministry of Foreign Affairs and the Moscow patriarchate....and its members meet regularly and exchange assessments of various situations in one region of the world or another" (Ibid.).

The starkest recent example of church-state collusion and shared interests was the struggle to prevent the Ukrainian Orthodox Church gaining autocephaly. While the Kremlin and the Russian Patriarchate ultimately failed as illustrated by Ecumenical Patriarch Bartholomew's decision to grant autocephaly, or self-government to the Ukrainian Church in January 2019, it was not for want of trying. Prior to 1991, Orthodox believers in Ukraine fell under the jurisdiction of the Russian Patriarchate. Nationalist movements have since divided Orthodox allegiance in Ukraine between three churches—but Russia, at least on paper, retained the right to claim jurisdiction over all Orthodox adherents in Ukraine. Both the church and the Kremlin had vested interest in preventing autocephaly. The ensuing struggle demonstrated the interoperability of the two entities. For instance, at key moments in dialogue between the Russian Patriarchate and Ecumenical Patriarch Bartholomew I over the status of the Ukraine church, the latter's office became the target of numerous cyber-attacks by the Russian hacker group, Fancy Bear. These are the same hackers indicted by Robert Mueller's investigation into Russian interference in the 2016 U.S. election (Satter 2018). Kirill and the Kremlin threw all available assets at dissuading Bartholomew from acting, including painting the Ecumenical Patriarch as a puppet of the US. All these efforts, nevertheless, did not prevent 150,000 people passing through St. Sophia Cathedral in Kiev on 5 January 2019 to view the tomos—a single piece of parchment granting the Ukrainian Church autocephalous status. With that declaration, the Russian Orthodox Church lost 30 percent of all Orthodox Christian believers under its dominion and the Kremlin lost a key cultural mechanism of influence over the Ukrainian populace. The significance for the Kremlin was reflected in Putin holding a special session of his Security Council the day after the Ecumenical Patriarch's decision (Sputnik 2018). The patriarch of the newly formed Ukrainian Orthodox Church understood this when he asserted that "the Russian Orthodox

Church is the last advance post of Vladimir Putin in Ukraine" (Goble 2019).

It is important to remember that the present arrangement is unparalleled, primarily because church-state cooperation in Tsarist times never had the opportunity to affect foreign policy to such a degree. From 1721 to 1971, the patriarchate did not exist, having been abolished by Peter the Great. And while scholars such as Taras Kuzio and Mark Galeotti accurately link present-day information warfare tactics with Soviet and even Tsarist disinformation campaigns, they acknowledge the greater assimilation of non-state entities in actions under Putin (Kuzio 2019; Galeotii 2016). The church's crackdown on dissent further attest to the reality of this dramatic change from 'symponia' to a full assimilation into state apparatus. Post-Crimea, the church moved quickly to squash any criticism of the new arrangement. In 2015, the progressive Sergei Chapnin was fired as a senior editor in the Church's Journal of the Moscow Patriarchate, for pushing back on the church's new-found embrace of state initiatives. Remarkably, a few weeks later, the ultra-conservative nationalist Father Vsevolod Chaplin was relieved of his post as chairman of the Synodal Department for the Cooperation of Church and Society of the Moscow Patriarchate (NPR 2015). The two individuals are on opposite ends of the ideological spectrum and although they share almost nothing in common, they both expressed misgivings with the church's growing closeness with the state. Likely not entirely coincidentally, this purge of non-compliant clergy occurred a year after the Crimea annexation and six months before the Yarovaya laws. Yet at the time there remained little public backlash for the churches' support to the regime. At the same time, apart from heightened scrutiny of the Jehovah's Witnesses, most religious organizations continued to operate largely unfettered by the state.

Church Remunerations

All of this output on the part of the Russian Orthodox Church required renumerations in the form of the Yarovaya Law. Gifts to the church by the state post-1991 have always been commensurate with services rendered. The patriarchate received little for standing on stage with Boris Yeltsin during election rallies in Krasnoyarsk. More tasking during Putin's first two terms, in turn, led to greater rewards. Robert Miller noted in 2007 the appearance of clericalism, in which the state allowed the "church leaders to share in, or even take over, certain policy prerogatives of the state, such as public education, the state of minority religions and the prescription of public morality" (Miller 2007, 73). But full assimilation since 2014 demanded something spectacular in return. In one law, state policy toward non-traditional churches flipped from indifference to open disapproval. There is no proof that this change of heart stemmed from a quid pro quo with the Russian Orthodox Church. But three converging phenomena post-2014 outlined at the start of this book serve as strong inferential evidence. The phenomena include (1) the Kremlin abandoning the charade of feigning deference to Western values; (2) the petitioning of the Russian Orthodox Church for a more restrictive marketplace; and (3) the state recognizing and exploiting a space for the church in its whole-of-government approach. The first is self-evident and is not addressed in this book. The second was the subject of the majority of this book. The third is apparent in the whole-of-society approach just delineated. These three converged and one product of that convergence was the Yarovaya Law and the subsequent drastic curtailment of religious freedoms in Russia.

A mere three years after the law was passed, in a Pew Research Center study on 'limits to religious activity', Russia registered a staggering 7.9 out of ten score. This score is the highest in all of Europe and towers over Lithuania's 0.5, Georgia's 2.1 or even Belarus' 5.7 (Pew 2019). Examples of these limits are everywhere. In late 2019, a German pastor of a small Baptist congregation in Sverdlovsk oblast was deprived of his residence permit after 25 years in Russia for allegedly violating rules on missionary activity. But according to the FSB declaration, the rationale was the pastor "oppos[ing] the Russian Orthodox Church, which creates a threat to the security of the Russian Federation" (Pugachev 2019). In just a matter of a few weeks in 2020, a single Russian region witnessed over 100 police raids against non-traditional religious groups. The Jehovah Witnesses estimate that more than 1,000 home invasions have occurred since the group was outlawed in April 2017. The Russia-backed separatist regions in Ukraine have also not been immune from such restrictions on freedom of religion (RISU 2019a). In many cases, rebels simply seized worship houses and repurposed them for government use, as was the case with four new and modern meeting houses of The Church of Jesus Christ of Latter-day Saints (Corley 2018).

Not surprisingly, remunerations continue after the Yarovaya Laws. In 2019, the Kremlin announced it would restore at a cost of 43 million USD, the Church's Feodorovsky Gorodok complex which serves as the patriarch's residence while he is in St Petersburg (Moscow Times 2019). In 2020, the Russian Orthodox Church and Russian Armed Forces unveiled the newly constructed 'Cathedral of the Armed Forces' some forty miles outside Moscow. At the same time, church state collusion remains unambiguous. The joint takedown of Bishop Flavian of Cherepovets and Belozersk in 2020 was particularly revealing. In March 2020, agents of the Federal Security Service (FSB) raided an apartment linked to the bishop where they allegedly found illegal drugs. For this he was dismissed from his post by Patriarch Kirill and now resided in London. He claims the FSB was punishing him for refusing to serve as an informant—reminiscent of Soviet times.

Conclusion

Russia is sadly not a particularly novel case study in religious intolerance. The extent of religious oppression occurring around the world, and the corresponding indifference of Western nations is hard to comprehend. As this book goes to print, up to a million Uighurs are imprisoned, a half million children are taken from their parents, untold thousands are in labor camps and others are undergoing forced sterilization, torture and other abuses. On a lesser scale than the Uighurs, Chinese actions against Tibetan Buddhists and Protestant congregations make Russian persecutions look like child's play. Turn the globe and one sees the destruction of millennia-old Christian societies throughout the Middle East since 2010, where atrocities have bordered on genocide and evictions from historic lands have occurred on a biblical scale. Jonathan Fox provides an in-depth analysis of the sharp rise in government discrimination against religious minorities over the past two decades in his excellent 2020 book. Fortunately, the Russia story has been largely devoid of the violence seen in other regions. Even so, the impact of the 2016 measures on individual freedoms and on the larger institutional design of the religious sphere is significant.

A few concluding thoughts are required to provide context to the assertations presented in this book to avoid misinterpretation. This book is not a hit piece on illiberal clergy or on the Russian Orthodox Church as a whole. The number of Russian Orthodox clergy who died courageously for their convictions during Soviet oppression is too great to enumerate. Countless men were faced with unbearable choices, quite literally at gunpoint. Standing in judgement on their motives three-quarters of century later is not only impossible, but deeply unfair. Those, like the Metropolitans that sat with Stalin in 1943, cooperated with authorities for many reasons, some undoubtedly noble. The point is not to condemn, but to understand that as Kristina Steockl argued "the experience of communist totalitarianism represents a watershed for Orthodox thought" (2009, 16). That experience has staying power to our day, and is, at least in part, a contributing factor to the present-day demise of religious pluralism in Russia. The research findings for this book attest to the long and bleak shadow of Sovietism over the church's posture on religious liberties. Put more broadly, by Stoeckl, the totalitarianism of the 20th Century continues to frustrate western individualist-liberalism in the post-Communist space (ibid., 11).

Second, far from condemning Russian Orthodoxy, my research stands as a rebuttal to the oft-repeated generalizations which tie Eastern Orthodoxy with totalitarianism. Such extrapolations are indeed inaccurate. Post-Soviet analysis of Russian Orthodox Church clergy reveals a diversity of opinion on key issues relating to church-state interaction and the treatment of non-traditional churches. This divide suggests that developmental factors, not theology, account for authoritarian tendencies among some Eastern Orthodox traditions. The promising path taken by the new Ukrainian Orthodox Church on both issues further underscores that socio-cultural and historical factors are paramount in understanding the proclivity among many Orthodox churches, particularly in the former Soviet space, to authoritarianism (Flake 2020, 13-17). In short, Orthodox churches are not predestined to support such draconian measures as the Yarovaya Law.

Third, and notwithstanding the first two points, it is hard to be particularly sanguine about the state of freedoms in general in Russia in light of developments in the religious sphere. The attack on religious minorities highlights the structural mechanisms and institutional immaturities so pervasive in Russia today. These impediments prohibit not only the establishment of a free and vibrant religious system, but also a broader liberal-democratic system. The type of unambiguous oppression seen against religious groups in Russia up to 2021 is a poor omen for the rest of society. We probably did not need further evidence that Francis Fukuyama's (1989, 16) optimism for the triumph of individualist-liberal ideas has been unequivocally proven inaccurate in the former Soviet Union. But the drastic roll-back of religious freedoms in Russia is evidence nonetheless.

Another way of looking at the development of collusion is within the context of political culture as explained by Almond and Verba. As quoted in chapter 2, "political cultures may or may not be congruent with structures of the political system" (1963, 21). And indeed, that was the case in the 1990s when Russia was a struggling participant political culture and the church remained oriented to a subject political culture. Since 2000, and especially 2007, rather than the church liberalizing to meet the state at modernity, the two have converged at a political cultural far from the ideal thanks to Putin's penchant for authoritarianism. The ensuant religious oppression bodes poorly for a swift reset to liberalism in Russia. Even after a decade of Putin, a liberal alternative to authoritarianism in Russia was nonetheless plausible in 2010. There were still off-ramps available on the road to totalitarianism. But as institutions gradually changed their design to align with the political culture and operational imperatives of the Kremlin, favorable regime change becomes ever more improbable. With each passing year, possible off-ramps disappear as institutions and civil society entities are folded into the approved structure. That assimilation has been made possible by a deliberate democratization process in Russia whereby civil society entities have been systematically attacked, subjugated, and appropriated. Unfortunately for Russia, civil society has proven a fairly good barometer for the ideological course of a particular country. Inclinations in civil society can often strengthen the political and social direction of a nation (Requena 2019). The more influential the institution, the greater the pull in one direction or the other. This is precisely the concern with the religious sphere following the well-trodden path of journalism, the electoral system, and so many other institutions in Russia. Religion is an extraordinarily strong cultural force in

Russian society. Religious intolerance once ingrained will be difficult to dislodge, no matter the identities of future members of the Kremlin inner circle. The totalitarian appropriation of almost every non-governmental institution in Russia, most recently Russian Orthodoxy, all but ensures that Putinism will outlive Putin.

Bibliography

Alimov G. and G. Charodeyev, 1992: "Patriarch Aleksi II: I Accept Responsibility for all that Happened", *Religion, State and Society,* 20:241-245.

Alisauskiene, Rasa, 2016: "Public Opinion Survey, Residents of Georgia, March—April 2016", International Republican Institute. https://www.iri.org/sites/default/files/wysiwyg/ georgia_2016.pdf.

Allingham, Michael, 1999: *Rational Choice,* St. Martin's, New York. Quote from Hume, *A Treatise of Human Nature,* 1740, 415-416.

Almond, Gabriel and Sidney Verba, 1963: *The Civil Culture: Political Attitudes and Democracy in Five Nation,* Princeton University Press, Princeton.

Almond, Gabriel and Powell Bingham, 1978: *Comparative Politics: System, Process and Policy,* Little & Brown, Boston.

Anderson, John, 2002: "Social, Political, and Institutional Constraints on Religious Pluralism in Central Asia", *Journal of Contemporary Religion,* 17:181-196.

Anderson, John, 2003: *Religious Liberty in Transitional Societies: The Politics of Religion,* Cambridge University Press, Cambridge.

Anderson, John, 2007: "Putin and the Russian Orthodox Church: Asymmetric Symphonia?", *Journal of International Affairs,* 61:185-201.

Andreyev, Ivan, 1950: "The Catacomb Church in the Soviet Union", originally printed in 1950s in *Orthodox Life.* http://www.monasterypress.com/catacomb.html.

Anishchuk, Alexei, 2014: "Russia's Putin Outlaws Denial of Nazi Crimes", *Reuters,* May 5. https://news.yahoo.com/russias-putin-outlaws-denial-nazi-crimes-161 442992--sector.html.

Arel, Maria Salomon, 2016: "Cultural Diversity, Imperial Strategies, and the Issue of Faith: Religious Toleration in Early Modern Russia in Comparative Perspective", in *The Tapestry of Russian Christianity,* edited by Nickolas Lupinin, Ohio Slavic Papers Vol. 10, Eastern Christian Studies vol .2, Columbus.

Arnold, John, 1993: "A Day of Reckoning and a Message of Reconciliation", *Religion, State and Society,* 21:251-256.

Arnold, Victoria, 2019: "Russia: Jehovah's Witness Criminal Cases." *Forum 18 News Service,* May 31. http://forum18.org/archive.php?article_id=2482.

Arnold, Victoria, 2019a: "Russia: 159 'Anti-missionary' Prosecutions in 2018", *Forum 18 News Service,* May 7. http://forum18.org/archive.php?article_id=2475.

Arnold, Victoria, 2019b: "Russia: Obstructions to Protestant Theological Education Systemic, Intentional?", *Forum 18 News Service,* March 25. http://forum18.org/archive.php?article_id=2465.

Arnold, Victoria, 2018: "RUSSIA: Two Years' Jail to Punish Religious Study Meetings", *Forum 18 News Service,* July 2. http://forum18.org/archive.php?article_id=2391.

Arnold, Victoria, 2020: "RUSSIA: 42 known "missionary activity" prosecutions in first half of 2020—list", *Forum 18 News Service*, August 21. https://www.forum18.org/archive.php?article_id=2595.

Arnold, Victoria, 2020a: "RUSSIA: 6.5 years' jail for building "world theocratic state" with 700 roubles", *Forum 18 News Service*, June 16. https://www.forum18.org/archive.php?article_id=2578.

Arrow, Kenneth and Enrico Colomatto, 1996: *The Rational Foundations of Economic Behavior*, proceedings of the IEA Conference held in Turin, Italy, Macmillan, London.

Azzi, Corry and Ronald Ehrenberg, 1975: "Household Allocation of Time and Church Attendance", *Journal of Political Economy*, 83:415-423.

Bainbridge, William, 1995: "Social Influence and Religious Pluralism", in *Advances in Group Processes*, edited by Edward Lawler, JAI Press, Oxford, 1-18.

Balzar, Harley, 2003: "Managed Pluralism: Vladimir Putin's Emerging Regime", *Post-Soviet Affairs,* 19:189-227.

Barber, Lionel, 2019: "Vladimir Putin Says Liberalism has 'Become Obsolete'", *Financial Times*, June 28. https://www.ft.com/content/670039ec-98f3-11e9-9573-ee5cbb98ed36.

Barrett, David and George Kurian and Todd Johnson, 2001: *World Christian Encyclopedia*, Oxford University Press, New York.

Begadze, Mariam, 2017: "Georgian Constitutional Agreement with the Georgian Orthodox Church: A Legal Analysis", Occasional Papers on Religion in Eastern Europe, 37:1-38. https://digitalcommons.georgefox.edu/ree/vol37/iss2/2/.

Blitt, Robert, 2011: "Russia's Orthodox Foreign Policy: The Growing Influence of the Russian Orthodox Church in Shaping Russia's Policies Abroad", *University of Pennsylvania Journal of International Law*, 33:363-460.

Bociurkiw, Bohdan, 1973: "The Shaping of Soviet Religious Policy", *Problems of Communism*, May-June, 37-51.

Bogomilova, Nonka, 2004: "Reflections on the Contemporary Religious "Revival" Religion, Secularization, Globalization", Occasional Papers on Religion in Eastern Europe: vol. 24, 4:1-10. https://digitalcommons.georgefox.edu/ree/vol24/iss4/1.

Borowik, Irena, 1994: "Religion in Post-communist Countries", in *Politics and Religion in Central and Eastern Europe*, edited by W.H. Swatas, Praeger, London.

Bourdeaux, Michael, 2001: "Russia Renewal—Russian Orthodox Eastern Church and State", *Christian Century*, April 4. https://www.christiancentury.org/article//russian-renewal.

Bourdeaux, Michael, 1995: *The Politics of Religion in Russia and the New States of Eurasia*, M.E. Sharpe, London.

Bourdeaux, Michael, 1993: "Patriarch Aleksii: Between the Hammer and the Anvil", *Religion, State and Society*, 20:231-236.

Bourdeaux, Michael, 1979: *Land of Crosses: The Struggle for Religious Freedom in Lithuania: 1939-1978*, Augustine Publishing Company, Devon.

Brik, Tymofil and Stanislav Korolkov, 2020: "Religious Markets in Ukraine: Post-communist Revivals and New Directions", in *Ukraine in Transformation: From Soviet Republic to European Society*, edited by Alberto Veira-Ramos, Tetiana Liubyva, and Ievhenii Golovakha, Palgrave Macmillan.

Bruce, Steve, 1999: *Choice and Religion*, Oxford University Press, Oxford.

Bruce, Steve, 2000: "The Supply-Side Model of Religion: The Nordic and Baltic States", *Journal for the Scientific Study of Religion*, 39:32-46.

Bruce, Steve, 2008: "The Social Limits of Religious Markets", in *Salvation Goods and Religious Markets: Theory and Applications*, edited by Jorg Stolz, Peter Lang, Bern.

Bulmer, Simon, 1997: "New Institutionalism, The Single Market and EU Governance", ARENA Working Papers WP 97/25. https://www.sv.uio.no/arena/e nglish/rese arch/publications/arena-working-papers/1994-2000/1997/wp9 7_25.htm.

Bryanski, Gleb, 2012: "Russian Patriarch Calls Putin Era a Miracle of God", *Reuters*, February 8. https://uk.reuters.com/article/uk-russia-putin-religion/russian-patri arch-calls-putin-era-miracle-of-god-idUKTRE81722Y20120208.

Burgess, John, 2017: *Holy Rus': The Rebirth of Orthodoxy in the New Russia*, New Haven, Yale University Press, New Haven.

Burgess, John, 2014: "Retrieving the Martyrs in order to Rethink the Political Order: The Russian Orthodox Case", *Journal of Soviet of Christian Ethics*, 34:177-197.

Carbonnel, Alissa de, 2012: "Russian Orthodox Church Takes a Gamble on Putin", *Reuters*, April 4. https://www.reuters.com/article/russia-church/russian-orthodo x-church-takes-a-gamble-on-putin-idUSL6E8F40QX20120404.

Ceballos, Lindsay, 2018: "Exhibition Review: 'Russia — My History' at Moscow's VDNKh", NYU Jordan Center for the Advanced Study of Russia, September 19. http://jordanrussiacenter.org/news/exhibition-review-russia-my-history-at-moscows-vdnkh/#.Xt4YHkVKiUl.

Chaplin, Sergey, 2020: "Православный фундаментализм. Приведет ли пандемия к расколу РПЦ", June 29, Carnegie Russia. https://carnegie.ru/commentary/82167.

Champion, Francoise, 1999: "The Diversity of Religious Pluralism", *International Journal of Multicultural Societies*, 1:40-54.

Chronicle of the Catholic Church in Lithuania 1972-1974, vol. 1, 1981, Loyola University Press, Chicago.

Chronicle of the Catholic Church in Lithuania 1979-1981, vol. 6, 1989, Kingsport Press, Kingsport.

Chumachenko Tatian A., 2002: *Church and State in Soviet Russia; Russian Orthodoxy from World War II to the Khrushchev Years*, M.E. Sharpe, New York.

Church History, 2020: "Twentieth Century: The Orthodox Church in Russia", https://www.oca.org/orthodoxy/the-orthodox-faith/church-history/twentieth-century/the-orthodox-church-in-russia.

Clay, J. Eugene, 2018: "Religious Freedom, the Religious Market, and Spiritual Entrepreneurship in Russia after 1997", in *Religious Freedom in Modern Russia*, edited by Randell Poole and Paul Werth, University of Pittsburgh Press, Pittsburgh, 182-213.

Collier, Ruth and David Collier, 1991: *Shaping the Political Arena: Critical Junctures, the Labour Movement, and Regime Dynamics in Latin America*, Princeton University Press, Princeton.

Connell, Michael and Sarah Vogler, 2017: "Russia's Approach to Cyber Warfare," CAN Occasional Paper, March. https://www.cna.org/CNA_files/PDF/DOP-2016-U-014231-1Rev.pdf.

Conquest, Robert, 1968: *Religion in the USSR*, The Bodley Head, London.

Corley, Felix, 2002: "Georgia: Sectarians Have to be Shot Dead", *Keston News Service*, February 13. http://www.starlightsite.co.uk/keston/kns/2002/020213GE.htm.

Corley, Felix, 2003: "Georgia: Should Violent Orthodox Group be Banned?", *Forum 18 News Service*, November 13. http://www.forum18.org/Archive.php?article_id=182.

Corley, Felix, 2003a: "Georgia; Catholics Fail to Break Orthodox Monopoly", *Forum 18 News Service*, December 25. http://www.forum18.org/Archive.php?article_id=144.

Corley, Felix, 2003b: "Georgia: Religious Minorities Concerned by 'Voluntary' Religion and Culture Classes", *Forum 18 News Service*, November 19. http://www.forum18.org/Archive.php?article_id=189.

Corley, Felix, 2003c: "Georgia: Orthodox Permission Needed for Religious Literature Imports", *Forum 18 News Service*, November 20. http://www.forum18.org/Archive.php?article_id=192.

Corley, Felix, 2003d: "Georgia: Why Can't Minority Faiths Build Places of Worship?", *Forum 18 News Service*, November 14. http://www.forum18.org/Archive.php?article_id=184.

Corley, Felix, 2003e: "Georgia: Will Non-Orthodox Faiths Ever Get Legal Status?", *Forum 18 News Service*, September 25. https://www.refworld.org/pdfid/46891843d.pdf.

Corley, Felix, 2003f: "Georgia: Baptist Deny They Burnt Down Own Church", *Forum 18 News Service*, July 3. http://www.forum18.org/Archive.php?article_id=96.

Corley, Felix, 2003g: "Georgia: We'll be back, Mob Warns Pentecostals", *Forum 18 News Service*, June 16. http://www.forum18.org/Archive.php?article_id=81.

Corley, Felix, 2004: "Georgia: Religious Freedom Survey, August 2004", *Forum 18 News Service*, August 23. http://www.forum18.org/Archive.php?articleid=400.

Corley, Felix, 2004a: "Georgia: Will Violent Attackers of Religious Minorities be Punished?", *Forum 18 News Service*, August 16. http://www.forum18.org/Archive.php?article_id=394.

Corley, Felix, 2004b: "Georgia: Violence against Religious Minorities Continues", *Forum 18 News Service*, November 5. http://www.forum18.org/Archive.ph p?article_id=446.

Corley, Felix, 2005: "Eastern Europe: OSCE Conference on Intolerance Regional Survey", *Forum 18 News Service*, June 1. http://www.forum18.org/Archive.php?article_id=574.

Corley, Felix, 2005a: "Georgia: Only 'Very Small Percentage' of Attacks in Trial Charges", *Forum 18 News Service*, January 17. http://www.forum18.org/Archive.php?article_id=490.

Corley, Felix, 2005b: "Georgia: Who incites anti-Baptist Village Mobs?", *Forum 18 News Service*, January 14. http://www.forum18.org/Archive.php?article_id=489.

Corley, Felix, 2005c: "Georgia: Attacks on Religious Minorities Unpunished", *Forum 18 News Service*, January 18. http://www.forum18.org/Archive.php?article_id=492.

Corley, Felix, 2005d: "Eastern Europe: OSCE Conference on Intolerance Regional Survey", *Forum 18 News Service*, June 1, cited from September 2004 OSCE Conference on Tolerance. http://www.forum18.org/Archive.php?article_id=574.

Corley, Felix, 2006: "Georgia: Legal Improvements, But Little Practical Improvements", *Forum 18 News Service*, May 24. http://www.forum18.org/Archive.ph p?article_id=568

Corley, Felix, 2018: "Donetsk: Places of Worship Seized, Sealed", *Forum 18 News Service*, October 12. http://www.forum18.org/archive.php?article_id=2422.

Coyer, Paul, 2015: "(Un)Holy Alliance: Vladimir Putin, The Russian Ortho-dox Church and Russian Exceptionalism," *Forbes*, May 21. https://www.forbes.com/sites/paulcoyer/2015/05/21/unholy-alliance-vladimir-putin-and-the-russian-orthodox-church/#30b84a7427d5.

Credo Press, 2019: "Crudest Interference in Church Affairs by Western States and Our Ukrainian Neighbors" April 12. Translation—https://www2.stetson.edu/~psteeves/relnews/190412b.html.

Credo Press, 2019a: "The State Duma of the Russian Federation Supported the Idea of Replacing the "Gulag Archipelago" in the School Curriculum with the Bible", July 1. https://credo.press/225325/.

Cullen, Patrick J. and Erik Reichborn-Kjennerud, 2017: "Understanding Hybrid Warfare", A Multinational Capability Development Campaign Project, January. https://assets.publishing.service.gov.uk/government/uploads/system/uploads/attachment_data/file/647776/dar_mcdc_hybrid_warfare.pdf.

David, Paul A., 2000: "Path Dependence, its Critics and the Quest for 'Historical Economics'", June. https://econwpa.ub.uni-muenchen.de/econ-wp/eh/papers/0502/0502003.pdf.

Davis, Nathaniel, 2003: *A Long Walk to Church: A Contemporary History of Russian Orthodoxy*, Westview Press, Boulder.

Deeg, Richard, 2001: "Institutional Change and the Uses and Limits of Path Dependency: The Case of German Finance", MPIfG Discussion Paper 01/6, November. http://www.mpi-fg-koeln.mpg.de/pu/mpifg_dp/dp01-6.pdf.

Del Turco, Arielle, 2020: "Russia's Quiet Persecution of Religion", Family Research Council, September 16. https://www.frc.org/updatearticle/20200916/russia-religion.

Della Cava, Ralph, 1997: "Reviving Orthodoxy in Russia: An Overview of the Factions in the Russian Orthodox Church, in the Spring of 1996", *Cahiers du Monde russe*, 38. Cited in Zoe Knox, "Russian Orthodoxy and Religious Pluralism".

Democratic National Committee (DNC), 2019: "Resolution Regarding the Religiously Unaffiliated Demographic", August. https://secular.org/wp-content/uploads/2019/08/DNC-Resolution-on-the-Nonreligious-Demographic.pdf.

Digges, Charles, 2015: "Foreign Agent Law has put 33 Percent of Russia's NGOs out of Business," Bellona Organization, October 20. https://bellona.org/news/russian-human-rights-issues/russian-ngo-law/2015-10-foreign-agent-law-has-put-33-percent-of-russias-ngos-out-of-business.

Dixon, Robyn, 1997: "Why the Orthodox Church has taken to Bible Bashing its Rivals", *Sydney Morning Herald*, July 26. http://www.stetson.edu/~psteeve s/relnews/.

Domanska, Maria, 2019: "The Myth of the Great Patriotic War as a Tool of the Kremlin's Great Power Policy", OSW Commentary, December 31. https://www.osw.waw.pl/en/publikacje/osw-commentary/2019-12-31/myth-great-patriotic-war-a-tool-kremlins-great-power-policy#_ftn25.

Dubroviskiy, Dmitry, 2018: "Academic Freedom in Russia: Between the Scylla of Conservatism and the Charybdis of Neoliberalism", *Baltic Worlds*, 4:1-11.

Dunlop, John, 1995: "The Moscow Patriarchate As An Empire Saving Institution", in *The Politics of Religion in Russia and the New States of Eurasia*, edited by Michael Bourdeaux, M.E. Sharp, Armonk, endnote 2.

Elliot, Mark and Sharyl Corrado, 1997: "The Protestant Missionary Presence in the Former Soviet Union", *Religion, State & Society*, 25:233-251.

Ellis, Jane, 1996: *The Russian Orthodox Church: Triumphalism and Defensiveness*, St. Martin's Press, New York.

Ellis, Jane, 1996a: *The Russian Orthodox Church: A Contemporary History*, Indiana University Press, Bloomington.

Ellis, Jane, 1990: "Hierarchs and Dissidents: Conflict over the Future of the Russian Orthodox Church", *Religion in Communist Lands*, 10:307-318.

Emerson, John, 2015: "Exposing Russian Disinformation", remarks at an Atlantic Council conference, Berlin, June 29. https://www.atlanticcouncil.org/blogs/ukrainealert/exposing-russian-disinformation/.

European Council, Copenhagen, 1993: "Relations with the Countries of Central and Eastern Europe", June 21-22. https://www.europarl.europa.eu/enlargement/ec/cop_en.htm.

European Parliament, 2019: "Resolution on the Importance of European Remembrance for the Future of Europe, (2019/2819(RSP)—RC-9-2019-0097. https://www.europarl.europa.eu/doceo/document/RC-9-2019-0097_EN.html.

Fabiny, Tibor, 2004: "Theologies of Church Government in the Hungarian Lutheran Church during Communism (1945-1900)", *Religion in Eastern Europe*, 4:11-29.

Fagan, Geraldine, 2005: "Russia: Religious Freedom Survey", *Forum 18 News Service*, February 14. http://www.forum18.org/Archive.php?article_id=509.

Fagan, Geraldine, 2005a: "Russia: Orthodox Pressure Railway into Cancelling JWCongress", *Forum 18 News Service*, July 8. http://www.forum18.org/Archive.php?article_id=601.

Fagan, Geraldine, 2005b: "Russia: How Many Missionaries Now Denied Visas", *Forum 18 News Service*, September 7. http://www.forum18.org/Archive.php?article_id=644.

Faustova, Milena, 2019: "Orthodox Church Reacts Defensively to Signs of Secularization", *Nezaveziamya Gazeta*, August 20. Translation https://www2.stetson.edu/~psteeves/relnews/190820b.html.

Fein, Esther B., 1989: "Ukrainian Catholics Move into the Open", *New York Times*, October 29. https://www.nytimes.com/1989/10/29/world/ukrainian-catholics-move-into-the-open.html.

Filatov, Sergei, 1993: "New Religious Movements' and the Socio-Religious Situation in Post-Soviet Russia", *East-West Church & Ministry Report*, 1.

Finke, Roger, 1997: "The Consequences of Religious Competition: Supply-side Explanations for Religious Change", in *Rational Choice Theories and Religion*, edited by Laurence Young, Routledge, New York.

Finley, Julie, 2006: at the time U.S. Ambassador to the Organization for Security and Co-operation in Europe (OSCE), quoted in State Department article "US Says Russian NGO Law Does not Meet Human Rights Commitments", January 27. http://usinfo.state.gov/xarchives/display.html?p=washfile-english&y=2006&m=January&x=200601271541201CJsamohT0.4548456&t=dhr/democracy-latest.html.

Flake, Lincoln and Jeremy Lamoreaux, 2018: "The Russian Orthodox Church, the Kremlin, and Religious (il)liberalism in Russia", *Nature*, Palgrave Communications, 4:115. https://doi.org/10.1057/s41599-018-0169-6.

Flake, Lincoln, 2020: "Charting A Distinctive Course: The Ukrainian Orthodox Church, Religious Pluralism, and Church-State Relations", *Ukrainian Policymaker*, 7:13-19.

Flake, Lincoln, 2021: "Contending with History: World War II in Contemporary Eurasian Politics", *Journal of Slavic Military Studies*, (forthcoming).

Fletcher, William, 1971: *The Russian Orthodox Church Underground, 1917-1970*, Oxford University Press, Oxford.

Fletcher, William, 1997: "Backwards from Reactionism: The De-modernization of the Russian Orthodox Church", *Religion and Modernisation in the Soviet Union*, edited by Dennis Dunn, Westview Press, Boulder.

Fox, Jonathan, 2020: *Thou Shalt Have No Other Gods before Me: Why Governments Discriminate against Religious Minorities*, Cambridge University Press, Cambridge.

Freedom Report, 2003: "Russia: International Religious Freedom Report 2003", US Department of State, Bureau of Democracy, Human Rights, and Labor. http://www.state.gov/g/drl/rls/irf/2004/35455.htm.

Freedom Report, 2004: "Georgia: International Religious Freedom Report 2004", U.S. Department of State, Bureau of Democracy, Human Rights, and Labor. http://www.state.gov/g/drl/rls/irf/2004/3534 4.htm.

Freedom Report, 2004a: "Lithuania: International Religious Freedom Report 2004", US Department of State, Bureau of Democracy, Human Rights, and Labor. http://www.state.gov/g/drl/rls/irf /2004/35468.htm.

Freedom Report, 2017: "Lithuania: International Religious Freedom Report 2017", US Department of State, Bureau of Democracy, Human Rights, and Labor. https://www.state.gov/wp-content/uploads/2019/01/Lithuania-2.pdf.

Freedom Report, 2018: "2018 Report on International Religious Freedom: Georgia", U.S. Department of State, Office of International Religious Freedom. https://www.state.gov/reports/2018-report-on-international-religious-freedom/georgia/.

Freeze, Gregory, 1983: *The Parish Clergy in Nineteenth-Century Russia: Crisis, Reform and Counter-reform*, Princeton University Press, Princeton.

Freeze, Gregory, 1996: "Subversive Piety: Religion and the Political Crisis in Late Imperial Russia", *Journal of Modern History*, 68:308-350.

Freeze, Gregory, 1996a: "Religion and the Political Crisis in Late Imperial Russia", *Journal of Modern History*, 68:308-350.

Freeze, Gregory, 2017: "Russian Orthodoxy and Politics in the Putin Era", Carnegie Endowment for International Peace, Task Force White Paper, February 9. https://carnegieendowment.org/2017/02/09/russian-orthodoxy-and-politics-in-putin-era-pub-67959.

Freud, Sigmund, 1927: *The Future of an Illusion*, Doubleday, New York.

Froese, Paul and Steven Pfaff, 2001: "Replete and Desolate Markets: Poland, East Germany, and the New Religious Paradigm", *Social Forces*, 80:481-507.

Froese, Paul, 2001: "Hungary for Religion: A Supply-Side Interpretation of the Hungarian Religious Revival", *The Journal for the Scientific Study of Religion*, 40:251-268.

Froese, Paul 2004: "Forced Secularisation in Soviet Russia: Why an Atheistic Monopoly Failed", *Journal for the Scientific Study of Religion*, 43:35-50.

Froese, Paul, 2004a: "After Atheism: An Analysis of Religious Monopolies in the Post-Communist World", *Sociology of Religion*, 65:57-75.

Fukyama, Francis, 1989: "The End of History?", *The National Interest*, 16:3-18.

Galeotti, Mark, 2016: "Hybrid, Ambiguous, and Non-linear? How New is Russia's 'new Way of War'?", *Small Wars & Insurgencies*, 27:282-301

Gavtadze, Mariam and Eka Chitanava, 2020: "GEORGIA: Religious freedom survey, October 2020", *Forum 18 News Service*, October 29. https://www.forum 18.org/archive.php?article_id=2613.

Gavtadze, Mariam and Eka Chitanava, 2019: "Georgia: Who needs a Religion Law?", *Forum 18 News Service*, August 15. http://www.forum18.org/ar chive.php?arti cle_id=2501.

Gerasimov, Valery, 2013: "The Value of Science is in the Foresight: New Challenges Demand Rethinking the Forms and Methods of Carrying Out Combat Operations", *Military-Industrial Kurier*, February 27, translated by Robert Coalson, 2016: *Military Review* 96, 23.

Gibson, James and Raymond Duch and Kent Tedin, 1992: "Democratic Values and the Transformation of the Soviet Union", *The Journal of Politics*, 54:329-371.

Gilbert, Leah, 2016: "Crowding Out Civil Society: State Management of Social Organizations in Putin's Russia", *Europe-Asia Studies*, 68:1553-1578.

Gill, Anthony, 1994: "Rendering unto Caesar? Religious Competition and Catholic Political Strategy in Latin America, 1962-79", *American Journal of Political Science*, 38:403-425.

Gill, Anthony, 1998: *Rendering unto Caesar: The Catholic Church and the State in Latin America*, University of Chicago Press, Chicago.

Gill, Anthony, 2005: "The Political Origins of Religious Liberty: A Theoretical Outline", *Interdisciplinary Journal of Research on Religion*, 1:1-33.

Goble, Paul, 2019: "Church of Ukraine Won't be a State Church but it Will Have the Support of the State", *The Ukrainian Weekly*, February 9. http://www.ukrwee kly.com/uwwp/church-of-ukraine-wont-be-a-state-church-but-it-will-have-the-support-of-the-state/.

Goble, Paul, 2020: "Orthodox Fundamentalism Threatens Russian Patriarchate and Kremlin", *Jamestown*, July 14. https://jamestown.org/program/orthodox-funda mentalism-threatens-russian-patriarchate-and-kremlin/

Golovchenko, Yevgeniy and Mareike Hartmann and Rebecca Adler-Nissen, 2018: "State, Media and Civil Society in the Information Warfare over Ukraine: Citizen Curators of Digital Disinformation", *International Affairs*, 94:975–994.

Goodin, Robert, 1996: *The Theory of Institutional Design*, Cambridge University Press, Cambridge.

Hall, Peter and Rosemary Taylor, 1996: "Political Science and the Three New Institutionalisms", paper presented at MPIFG conference, Koln, May 9. http://www.mpi-fg-koeln.mpg.de/pu/mpifg_dp/dp96-6.pdf.

Hansen, Flemming Splidsboel, 2017: "Russian Hybrid War: A Study of Disinformation", Danish Institute for International Studies. https://pure.diis.dk/ws/files/950041/DIIS_RP_2017_6_web.pdf.

Hausner, Jerry and Bob Jessop, 1995: *Strategic Choice and Path-Dependency in Post-Socialism Institutional Dynamics in the Transformation Process,* Edward Elgar Publishing, Aldershot.

Hay, Colin," 1995: "Structure and Agency", in *Theory and Methods in Political Science,* edited by D. Marsh and G. Stoker, Macmillan, London, 189-206.

Haynes, Jeffrey, 1998: *Religion in Global Politics,* Longman, London.

Haynes, Jeffrey, 2001: *Resistance and Rebellion: Lessons from Eastern Europe,* Cambridge University Press, Cambridge.

Hechter, Michael, 1997: "Religion and Rational Choice Theory", in *Rational Choice Theory and Religion: Summary and Assessment,* edited by Lawrence A. Young, Routledge, New York.

Horvat, Vedran, 2004: "Church in Democratic Transition between the State and the Civil Society", *Religion in Eastern Europe,* 2:1-18.

Human Rights Watch, 2002: "'Georgia: 'Vicious' Assault on Rights Leaders", July 12. http://hrw.org/english/docs/2002/07/12/georgi4109.htm.

Husband, William, 1998: "Soviet Atheism and Russian Orthodox Strategies of Resistance: 1917-1932", *The Journal of Modern History,* 70:74-107.

Iannaccone, Laurence, 1990: "Religious Practice: A Human Capital Approach", *Journal of Scientific Study of Religion,* 29:297-314.

Iannaccone, Laurence, 1992: "Sacrifice and Stigma: Reducing Free-Riding in Cults, Communes, and Other Collectives", *Journal of Political Economy,* 100:271-291.

Iannaccone, Laurence, 1995: "Voodoo Economics? Reviewing the Rational Choice Approach to Religion", *The Journal for the Scientific Study of Religion,* 34:76-89.

Iannaccone, Laurence, 1997: "The Framework for the Scientific Study of Religion", in *Rational Choice Theory and Religion: Summary and Assessment,* edited by Lawrence A. Young, Routledge, New York.

Iannaccone, Laurence, 1998: "Introduction to the Economies of Religion", *Journal of Economic Literature,* 36:1465-1496.

Iannaccone, Laurence and Rodney Stark, 1994: "Progress in the Economics of Religion", *Journal of Institutional and Theoretical Economics,* 150:737-744.

Interfax, 2019: "Medvedev created a commission under the President of the Russian Federation to Counter Attempts to Falsify History to the Detriment of Russia's Interests", May 19. https://www.interfax.ru/russia/80400.

Ivanov, Sergey, 2018: "The Three Pillars on Which the Exhibition Rests are Monarchism, Clericalism, and an All-Pervasive Conspiracy Theory", in "Russia: My History: History as an Ideological Tool", PONARS Eurasia, August 5. http://ww w.ponarseurasia.org/point-counter/russia-my-history-as-ideological-tool.

JAM News, 2020: "Coronavirus and the Church of the Last Days—why the Georgian church won't cancel church services", April 17. https://jam-news.net/corona virus-and-the-church-of-the-last-days-why-the-georgian-church-wont-cancel-church-services/.

Jessop, Bob, 1990: *State Theory: Putting the Capitalist State in its Place*, Polity Press, Cambridge.

Jones, Stephen, 1989: "Soviet Religious Policy and the Georgian Orthodox Apostolic Church: From Khrushchev to Gorbachev", *Religion in Communist Lands*, 17:292-312.

Karber, Phillip, 2015: "The Russian Military Forum: Russia's Hybrid War Campaign: Implications for Ukraine and Beyond," The Center for Strategic International Studies and the Potomac Foundation, March 10.

Kinzelbach, Katrin, and Janika Spannagel and Ilyas Saliba, 2020: "Free Universities: Putting the Academic Freedom Index into Action", Global Public Policy Institute, March 26. https://www.gppi.net/2020/03/26/free-universities.

Kishkovsky, Sophia, 2010: "Russia to Return Church Property", *New York Times*, November 23. https://www.nytimes.com/2010/11/24/world/europe/24iht-mos cow.html.

Kiskovsky, Leonid, quoted in Mojzes, Paul, 1996: "Ecumenism, Evangelism and Religious Liberties", *Religion in Eastern Europe*, 2. http://www.georgefox.edu/ac ademics/undergrad/ departments/soc-swk/ree/MOJZES_ECU.html.

Kobahidze, Vassily, 1997: "Interview with the head of the Press Office of the Georgian Patriarchate, Press Secretary of the Catholicos-Patriarch of All Georgia", Moscow Patriarchate's Department for External Church Relations, July 19, Moscow. http://incommunion.org/articles/resource s/ecumenical-movement/kobah idze-interview.

Kodácsy, Tamas, 2004: "The Church and Democracy in Central Europe", *Religion in Eastern Europe*, 24:34-38.

Kolesnikova, Valentine, 1997: "A Biography of Patriarch Tikhon (1865-1925)", *Russian Life*, 32-34.

Köllner, Tobias, 2016: "Patriotism, Orthodox Religion and Education: Empirical Findings from Contemporary Russia", *Religion, State & Society*, 44:366–386.

Kopaliani, Badri, 2000: Minister and Founding Member of the Union of Jehovah's Witnesses in Georgia, statement before the Supreme Court of Georgia during a hearing on December 20. http://www.jw-media.org/region/europe/georgia/en glish/legal_cases/e_001213.htm.

Knox, Zoe, 2003: "Russian Orthodoxy and Religious Pluralism: Post-Soviet Challenges", Contemporary Europe Research Centre—Working paper series—1, April. http://www.cerc.unimelb.edu.au/publication/CERCWP012003.pdf.

Kremlin, 2014: Vladimir Putin addressed State Duma deputies, Federation Council members, heads of Russian regions and civil society representatives in the Kremlin, March 18. http://en.kremlin.ru/events/president/news/20603.

Kremlin, 2017: Meeting of Council for Civil Society and Human Rights, Vladimir Putin chaired a meeting of the Council for Civil Society and Human Rights at the Kremlin, October 30. http://en.kremlin.ru /events/president/news/55947.

Kung, Hans, 1994: *Christianity: The Religious Situation of Our Time*, SCM Press, London.

Kurilla, Ivan, 2018: "History as an Ideological Tool" in "Russia: My History: History as an Ideological Tool", PONARS Eurasia, August 5. http://www.ponarseurasia. org/point-counter/russia-my-history-as-ideological-tool.

Kurilla, Ivan, 2014: "The Implications of Russia's Law against the 'Rehabili-tation of Nazism'", Policy Memo 331 PONARS Eurasia, August. http://www.ponars eur asia.org/memo/201408_Kurilla.

Kuzio, Taras, 2019: "Old Wine in a New Bottle: Russia's Modernization of Traditional Soviet Information Warfare and Active Policies Against Ukraine and Ukrainians", *The Journal of Slavic Military Studies*, 32:485-506.

Johnston, Hank, 1994: "Religion-Nationalist Subcultures under the Communists: Comparisons from the Baltics, Transcaucasia and Ukraine", in *Politics and religion in Central and Eastern Europe: Traditions and Transitions*, edited by W.H. Swatos, Praeger, Westport.

Johnson, Marcia and, Carol Raye, Hugh Foley, and Mary Ann Foley, 1981: "Cognitive Operations and Decision Bias in Reality Monitoring", *The American Journal of Psychology*, 94:37-64.

Lane, Christel, 1978: *Christian Religion in the Soviet Union*, George Allen & Unwin, London.

Law, Russia's Foreign Agent 2012: "On Amendments to Legislative Acts of the Russian Federation regarding the Regulation of the Activities of Non-profit Organizations Performing the Functions of a Foreign Agent", July 20. http://publicati on.pravo.gov.ru/Document/View/0001201207230003.

Law, Russia's Undesirable Organization 2015: "On Amendments of Some Legislative Acts of the Russian Federation", May 23. http://publication.pravo.gov.ru/Docu ment/View/0001201505230001.

Leustean, Lucian, 2017: "Eastern Orthodoxy, Geopolitics and the 2016 Holy and Great Synod of the Orthodox Church", *Geopolitics*, 23:201–216.

Leynes, Andrew and Alyssa Cairns, and Jarret T. Crawford, "Event-Related Potentials Indicate That Reality Monitoring Differs from External Source Monitoring", *The American Journal of Psychology*, 118:497-524.

Liberty Institute, 2003: "Freedom of Religion Report", Tbilisi. http://www.liberty.ge/eng/files/Freedom%20of%20Religion%20Report.pdf.

Lindenberg, Siegwart, 1992: "The Method of Decreasing Abstraction" in *Rational Choice Theory: Advocacy and Critique*, edited by James Coleman and Thomas Fararo, Sage, New York.

Lomjaria, Nino, 2020 Tolerance Center of the Public Defender of Georgia with the support of the Promoting Integration, Tolerance and Awareness Program (PITA) of the UN Association of Georgia, funded by the U.S. Agency for International Development (USAID), Sept. https://civil.ge/wp-content/uploads/2020/09/CR-Recommendations-Geo-2020.pdf.

Luong, Pauline Jones, 2002: *Institutional Change and Political Continuity in Post-Soviet Central Asia: Power, Perceptions, and Pacts*, Cambridge University Press, Cambridge.

Lutsevych, Orysia, 2016: "Agents of the Russian World: Proxy Groups in the Contested Neighborhood", Chatham House Paper, April 14. https://www.chathamhouse.org/publication/agents-russian-world-proxy-groups-contested-neighbourhood?45KJB,LNGSLS,F3T97.

Madeley, John, 2000: "Towards an Inclusive Typology of Church-State Relations in Europe, North and South, East and West: A Rokkanian Approach", paper presented Consortium for Political Research Joint Workshop Session, Copenhagen, Denmark, April 14-19.

Madeley, John, 2016: "A Framework for the Comparative Analysis of Church-State Relations in Europe", In *Law and Religion. An Overview—Volume I*, edited by Silvio Ferrari and Rinaldo Cristofori, 23-50, Routledge, New York.

Mahoney, James, 2001: *The Legacies of Liberalism: Path Dependence and Political Regimes in Central Asia*, John Hopkins University Press, Baltimore.

Mahoney, James, 2001a: "Path-Dependent Explanations of Regime Change: Central America in Comparative Perspective", *Studies in Comparative International Development*, 36:111-141.

Malik, Hafeez, 1991: "Muslim Resurgence in Soviet Central Asia", Occasional Papers on Religion in Eastern Europe, 11:1-11. https://digitalcommons.georgefox.edu/ree/vol11/iss2/1.

Mangeloja, Esa, 2003: "Application of Economic Concepts on Religious behavior", 1-23. https://econwpa.ub.uni-muenchen.de/econ-wp/othr/papers/0310/0310003.pdf.

March, Christopher and Mark Froese, 2004: "The State of Freedom in Russia: A Regional Analysis of Freedom of Religion, Media and Markets", *Religion, State and Society*, 32:137-149.

Mateski, Mark, 2016: "Russia, Reflexive Control, and the Subtle Art of Red Teaming", *Red Team Journal*, October 13. http://redteamjournal.com/2016/10/reflexive-control/.

McFarland, Neill, 1967: *The Rush Hour of the Gods: A Study of New Religious Movements in Japan*, Macmillan, New York.

McFaul, Michael, 1999: "Lessons from Russia's Protracted Transition from Communist Rule", *Political Science Quarterly*, 114:103-130.

McFaul, Michael, 2001: *Russia's Unfinished Revolution: Political Change from Gorbachev to Putin*, Cornell University Press, Ithaca.

Meyendorff, John, 1978: "Russian Bishops and Church Reform in 1905" in *Russian Orthodoxy under the Old Regime*, edited by Robert Nichols and Theofanis Stavrou, University of Minnesota Press, St Paul, 170-82.

Military Doctrine of the Russian Federation, 2010, approved by Russian Federation presidential edict on February 5. Translated http://carnegieendowment.org/files/2010russia_military_doctrine.pdf.

Military Doctrine of the Russian Federation, 2014, approved by Russian Federation presidential edict on December 25. Translated https://www.rusemb.org.uk/press/2029.

Miller, Robert, 2007: "Church-State Relations in Post-Communist Countries: The Idea of Path Dependency May Have Something Useful to Tell Us", in *Civil Society, Religion and Global Governance Paradigms of Power and Persuasion*, edited by Helen James, Taylor & Francis, London.

Mishler, William and Richard Rose, 2001: "What are the Origins of Political Trust? Testing Institutional and Cultural Theories in Post-Communist Societies", *Comparative Political Studies*, 34:30-62.

Misiunas Romuald and Rein Taagepera, 1993: *The Baltic States: Years of Dependence 1940-1990*, University of California Press, Berkeley.

Molchanov, Mikhail, 2002: *Political Culture and National Identity in Russian-Ukrainian Relations*, Texas A&M University Press, Texas.

Moscow Times, 2019: "Kremlin Is Spending $43M to Renovate Imperial Mansion for Orthodox Patriarch, Media Reports", May 21. https://www.themoscowtimes.com/2019/05/21/kremlin-is-spending-43-million-renovate-imperial-mansion-orthodox-patriarch-a65667.

Muizneks, Nils, 1997: "Latvia: Restoring a State, Rebuilding a Nation", in *New States, New Politics: Building the post-Soviet Nations*, edited by Ian Bremner and Ray Taras, Cambridge University Press, Cambridge.

Myers, Steven Lee, 2002: "Attacks on Minority Faiths Rise in Post-Soviet Georgia", *New York Times*, August 17. https://www.nytimes.com/2002/08/17/world/attacks-on-minority-faiths-rise-in-post-soviet-georgia.

Nathaniel, Archbishop, 1985: "The Russian Orthodox Church Outside of Russia", in *Conversations on Holy Scripture and Faith*, vol 5, Russian Orthodox Youth Committee, New York. https://www.synod.com/01newstucture/pagesen/English/pages/legacy/nathnielrocor.html

National Public Radio (NPR), 2015: "In Russia, A High-Ranking Orthodox Priest Is Sacked—And Hits Back", December 26. https://www.npr.org/sections/para llels/2015/12/26/461047919/in-russia-a-high-ranking-orthodox-priest-is-sacke d-and-hits-back?t=1577714245069.

National Security Strategy to 2020, Russian, May 12, 2009. https://www.files.ethz.ch/ isn/154915/Russia's%20National%20Security%20Strategy%20to%202020% 20-%20Rustrans.pdf.

National Security Strategy, Russia, December 2015. http://www.ieee.es/Galerias/fi chero/OtrasPublicaciones/Internacional/2016/Russian-National-Security-Strat egy-31Dec2015.pdf.

Neitz, Mary Jo and Peter Mueser, 1997: "Economic Man and the Sociology of Religion", in *Rational Choice Theory and Religion: Summary and Assessment*, edited by Lawrence A. Young, Routledge, New York.

Newbury John, 1996: "Georgian Orthodox Church Withdraws from the WCC", *WCC News and Information Office*, June 26. http://www.wfn.org/1997/07/msg0 0167.

Newsroom, 2000: "Fate of Religion in Putin's Russia Uncertain", January 7. https://ww w2.stetson.edu/~psteeves/relnews/0001a.html.

Novik, Veniamin, 1999: *Pravoslavie, Khristianstvo, Demokratiia: Sbornik Statei*, Aleteiia, St. Petersburg. Cited by Zoe Know, 2003: "Russian Orthodoxy and Religious Pluralism: Post-Soviet Challenges", 41. http://www.cerc.unimelb.edu.au /pub lication/CERCWP012003.pdf.

Petro, Nicolai, 1995: *The Rebirth of Russian Democracy: An Interpretation of Political Culture*, Harvard University Press, Cambridge.

Pierson, Paul and Theda Skocpol 2002: "Historical Institutionalism in Contemporary Political Science", in *The State of the Discipline*, edited by Ira Katznelson and Helen Milner, Norton, London, 693-721.

Plokhy, Serhii, 1999: "Church, State and Nation in Ukraine", Occasional Papers on Religion in Eastern Europe, 19:1-34. https://digitalcommons.georgefox.edu/re e/vol19/iss5/2.

Pollis, Adamantia, 1993: "Eastern Orthodoxy and Human Rights", in *Human Rights Quarterly*, Johns Hopkins University Press, 15:339-356.

Nielsen, Niels C., 1994: *Christianity after Communism: Social, Political, and Cultural Struggle in Russia*, Westview Press, Boulder.

Offe, Claus, 1996: "Designing Institutions in East European Transitions", in *The Theory of Institutional Design,* edited by Robert Goodin, Cambridge University Press, Cambridge.

Ogden, Karen, 1996: "Religions Compete in Russia", *Associated Press*, December 28. https://www2.stetson.edu/~psteeves/relnews/missionaries2812.html.

Orlov, Boris and Sophia Kotzer, 1998: "The Russian Orthodox Church in a Changing Society" in *Russia at a Crossroads: History, Memory and Political Practice*, edited by Nurit Schleifman, Frank Case, London.

Osa, Maryjane, 1997: "Creating Solidarity: The Religious Foundation of the Polish Social Movement", *East European Politics and Societies*, 11:339-365.

Open Letter to Patriarch Ilia II of Georgia From the Brotherhood of the Monastery of Saint Shio of Mghvime, 1997. https://www2.stetson.edu/~psteeves/relnews/georgia.html.

Papanikolaou, Aristotle, 2012: *The Mystical as Political*, Notre Dame University Press, Notre Dame.

Papkova, Irina, 2011: *The Orthodox Church and Russian Politics*, Oxford University Press, New York.

Pankhurst, Jerry, 2012 "Religious Culture: Faith in Soviet and Post-Soviet Russia", in Dmitri N. Shalin, 32-28. https://digitalscholarship.unlv.edu/russian_culture/7.

Perkins, Douglas, 2001: "Rendering unto the Tsar? Church-State Relations and Confessional Party Formation in Post-Soviet Russia", paper presented at American Political Science Association, San Francisco, August 30—September 2. http://psweb.sbs.ohio-state.edu/grads/dperkin s/portfolio/apsa2001.pdf #search='Perkins%2C%20Douglas%20Rendering%20unto%20the%20Tsar.

Petersen, Roger, 2001: *Resistance and Rebellion: Lessons from Eastern Europe*, Cambridge University Press, Cambridge.

Peuch, Jean-Christophe, 2004: "Georgia: Reformist Priest Blasts Church Leaders Over Intolerance, Corruption", *Radio Free Europe*, December 22. http://www.rferl.org/featuresarticle/2004/12/9969C7 AB-17BC-4443-A6C4-0BBAC 808AC02.html.

Pew Research Center, 2014: "Russians Return to Religion But Not to Church", January 2. https://www.pewforum.org/2014/02/10/russians-return-to-religion-but-not-to-church/.

Pew Research Center, 2018: "Eastern and Western Europeans Differ on Importance of Religion, Views of Minorities, and Key Social", October. https://www.pewforum.org/2019/07/15/a-closer-look-at-how-religious-restrictions-have-risen-around-the-world/.

Pew Research Center, 2019: "A Closer Look at How Religious Restrictions Have Risen Around the World", July 15. https://www.pewforum.org/2019/07/15/a-closer-look-at-how-religious-restrictions-have-risen-around-the-world/.

Phillips, Andrew, 1999: *The Lighted Way: Orthodox Christian Perspectives for the Third Millennium*, English Orthodox Trust, Felixstowe. http://orthodoxengland.org.uk/ruschu.htm.

Pierson, Paul, 2000: "Increasing Returns, Path Dependence, and the Study of Politics'", *American Political Science Review*, 94:251-268.

Pollack, Detlef, 2010: "Modifications in the Religious Field of Central and Eastern Europe", *European Societies*, 3:135-165.

Polyakov, Yevgeny, 1994: "The Activities of the Moscow Patriarchate During 1991", *Religion, State and Society*, 22:145-161.

Pomerantsev, Peter, 2015: "Authoritarianism Goes Global (II): The Kremlin's Information War", *Journal of Democracy*, 26:40–50.

Pospielovsky, Dimitry, 1984: *The Russian Church Under the Soviet Regime, 1917-1982*, St. Vladimir's Seminary Press, New York.

Pospielovsky, Dimitry, 1997: "The Renovationist Movement in the Orthodox Church in Light of Archival Documents", *Journal of Church and State*, 39:85-105.

Pozdnyayev, Mikhail, 1993: "Cooperated with the KGB, but I was not an Informer: An Interview with Archbishop Khrizoskom of Vilnius and Lithuania", *Religion, State and Society*, 21:345-350.

Pugachev, Alexander, 2019: "Russian Security Penalizes Baptist Preacher for Opposing Orthodox Church", *Nostoiashchee Vremia*, December 16. English translation—https://www2.stetson.edu/~psteeves/relnews/191216c.html.

Pushkarev, Sergei, and Vladimir Rusak, Gleb Yakunin, 1989: *Christianity and Government in Russia and the Soviet Union: Reflections on the Millennium*, Westview Press, Boulder.

Ramet, Sabrina, 1989: *Religion and Nationalism in Soviet and East European Politics*, Duke University Press, Raleigh.

Ramet, Sabrina, 1998: *Nihil Obstat: Religion, Politics, and Social Change in East-Central Europe and Russia*, Duke University Press, Durham.

Ramet, Sabrina, 1993: *Religious Policy in the Soviet Union*, Cambridge University Press, Cambridge

Reddaway, Peter, 1975: "The Georgian Orthodox Church: Corruption and Renewal", *Religion in Communist Lands*, 13:14-23.

Religious Information Service of Ukraine (RISU), 2019: "Sign Petition: Ten Theses for the Orthodox Church of Ukraine", February 12. https://risu.org.ua/en/index/monitoring/74683/.

Religious Information Service of Ukraine (RISU), 2019a: "The Militants Closed Two More Evangelical Churches in the Occupied Donetsk Region", November 11. https://risu.org.ua/ru/index/all_news/community/vandalism/77757/.

Remond, Rene, 1999: *Religion and Society in Modern Europe*, Blackwell, Oxford.

Requena, Felix, 2019: "The Catholic Church and Consolidation of Democratic Civil Society in Spain", *Journal of Civil Society*, 15:249-266.

Riis, Ole, 1999: "Modes of Religious Pluralism Under Conditions of Globalization", *International Journal of Multicultural Societies*, 1:21-34.

Rock, Stella, 2002: "Militant Piety': Fundamentalist Tendencies in the Russian Orthodox Brotherhood Movement", *Occasional Papers on Religion in Eastern Europe*: 22:2. https://digitalcommons.georgefox.edu/cgi/viewcontent.cgi?article=1648&context=ree.

Rogaleva, Irina, 2020: "Russian President Vladimir Putin, Secretary of the Russian Security Council", VKontact, November 2. https://vk.com/wall6689514330973.

Roslof, Edward, 2002: *Red Priests: Renovationism, Russian Orthodoxy and Revolution, 1905-1946*, University of Indiana Press, Bloomington.

Rotar, Igor, 2005: "Kazakhstan: Religious Minorities Face Increasing State Pressure", *Forum 18 News Service*, July 20. http://www.forum18.org/Archive.p hp?artic le_id=612.

Rubin, Michail, and Maria Zholobova and Roman Badanin, 2019: "Master of Pup-pets: The Man Behind the Kremlin's Control of the Russian Media", *Proekt*, June 5. https://www.proekt.media/portrait/alexey-gromov-eng/.

Rousselet, Kathy, 2000: "The Challenges of Religious Pluralism in Post-Soviet Russia", *International Journal of Multicultural Societies*, 2:57-77.

'Saint Basil of Kineshma: Russian Orthodox Church', http://www.russianorthodox-r oac.com/SaintBasil.html.

Satter, Raphael, 2018: "Ungodly Espionage: Russian Hackers Targeted Orthodox Clergy", *Associated Press*, August 27. https://apnews.com/26815e0d06d348 f4b85350e96b78f6a8/Ungodly-espionage:-Russian-hackers-targeted-Orthodo x-clergy.

Schleifman, Nurit, 1998: *Russia at a Crossroads: History, Memory and Political Practice*, Frank Cass, London.

Schmidt, Leigh, 1998: *Religion in America: Toward a History of Practice*, Princeton University Press, Princeton.

Scorer, Peter, 1996: "The Russian Orthodox Church 1991-1994", in *The New Russia*, edited by Michael Pursglove, Europa 2, Intellect Books, Oxford.

Sergianism, 1992: "About Sergianism", *Journal of the Diocese of the West*, Autocephalous Orthodox Church in America, summer. https://www.holy-trinity. org/ecclesiology/tikhon.about-sergianism.html.

Shavtvaladze, Mikheil. 2018: "The State and Ethnic Minorities: The Case of Georgia", *Region*, 7:43-68.

Shenfield, Stephen, 2001: *Russian Fascism: Traditions, Tendencies, Movements*, M. E. Sharpe, New York.

Sherkat, Darren, 1997: "Embedding Religious Choices: Integrating Preferences and Social Constraints into Rational Choice Theories of Religious Behavior", in *Rational Choice Theory and Religion: Summary and Assessment*, edited by Lawrence A. Young, Routledge, New York.

Sheymov, Victor, 1993: *Tower of Secrets*, Naval Institute Press, Maryland.

Simon, Gerhard, 1974: *Church, State and Opposition in the USSR*, Hurst & Company, London.

Simons, Greg, 2016: "The Russian Orthodox Church: Toward a New, Global Role?", Cicero Foundation Great Debate Papers 16/06, May. https://www.cicerofounda tion.org/wp-content/uploads/Greg_Simons_The_Russian_Orthodox_Church. pdf.

Smith, Adam, 1776: *The Wealth of Nations*, in *The Essential Adam Smith*, edited by Robert L. Heilbroner, 1986, Norton, New York.

Snegovaya, Maria, 2015: "Putin's Information Warfare in Ukraine: Soviet Origins of Russia's Hybrid Warfare", Institute for the Study of War, September. https://www.files.ethz.ch/isn/193932/Russian%2 0Report%201%20 Putin's%20Inf ormtion%20Warfare%20in%20Ukraine-%20Soviet%20Origins%20of%20Rus sias%20Hybrid%20Warfare.pdf.

Snegovaya, Maria, 2015a: "Stifling the Public Sphere: Media and Civil Society in Russia," *National Endowment for Democracy.* https://www.academia.edu/30525 589/Stifling_the_Public_Sphere_Media_and_Civil_Society_in_Russia

Solodovnik, Svetlana, 2014: "Russia: The Official Church Chooses the State", *Russian Social Science Review*, 6:55-83.

Solzhenitsyn, Alexander, 1983: "Men Have Forgotten God", from his Templeton address, May 10, London. https://pravoslavie.ru/47643.html.

Spickard, James, 1998: "Rethinking Religious Social Action: What is 'Rational' about Rational-Choice Theory?", *Sociology of Religion*, 59:99-115.

Spinka, Matthew, 1956: *The Church in Soviet Russia*, Oxford University Press, New York.

Sputnik News, 2018: "Putin Discusses Orthodox Church Crisis in Ukraine with Russian Security Council", October 10. https://sputniknews.com/russia/20181012 1068843182-russia-ukraine-putin-security-council-orthodox-church-crisis/.

Stark, David, 1996: "Recombinant Property in East European Capitalism", *American Journal of Sociology*, 101:993-1027.

Stark, Rodney and Laurence Iannaccone, 1994: "A Supply-Side Reinterpretation of the 'Secularization' of Europe", *Journal for the Scientific Study of Religion*, 33:230-252.

Stark, Rodney, 1997: "Bringing Theory Back In", in *Rational Choice Theories and Religion*, edited by Laurence A. Young, Routledge, New York.

Stark, Rodney and Laurence Iannaccone, 1997: "Why are the Jehovah Witness' Growing So Fast: A Theoretical Approach", *Journal of Contemporary Religion*, 12:133-158.

Starr, Frederick, 1994: *The Legacy of History in Russia and the New States of Eurasia*, M.E. Sharpe, London.

Stephens, John and Robyn McCallum, 1998: *Retelling Stories, Framing Culture: Traditional Story and Metanarratives in Children's Literature*, Garland, New York.

Stoeckl, Kristina, 2009: *Community after Totalitarianism: The Russian Orthodox Intellectual Tradition and Philosophical Discourse of Political Modernity*, Peter Lang, Frankfurt.

Strassberg, Barbara, 1998: "Changes in Religious Culture in Post War II Poland", *Sociological Analysis*, 48:342-354.

Streikus, Arunas, 2001: "The Resistance of the Church to the Soviet Regime from 1944-1967", in *The Anti-Soviet Resistance in the Bal-tic States*, edited by Arvydas Anusauskas, Genocide and Resistance Research Centre of Lithuania, Vilnius.

Streikus, Arunas, 2006: "Lithuanian Catholic Clergy and the KGB", *Religion, State and Society*, 34:63-70.

Struve, Nikita A., 1967: *Christians in Contemporary Russia*, Scribner, New York.

Sumbadze, Nana and George Tarkhan-Mouravi, 2003: "Political Profiles from the Georgian Electorate", Institute for Policy Studies, June, Tbilisi. http://pdc.ceu.h u/archive/00001417/ 01/Panel_JuneEnglish.pdf.

Suslov, Mikhail, 2016: "The Russian Orthodox Church and the Crisis in Ukraine", in *Churches in the Ukrainian Crisis*, edited by Andrii Krawchuk and Thomas Bremer, Palgrave Macmillan, London, 132-162.

Talantov, Boris, 1982: "The Moscow Patriarchate and Sergianism", in *Russia's Catacomb Saints,* edited by Ivan Andreyev, St. Herman of Alaska, Press.

Thornton, Laura and Koba Turmanidze 2019: "Public Attitudes in Georgia", National Democratic Institute, July. https://www.ndi.org/sites/default/files/NDI%20July% 202019%20poll-Issues_ENG_For%20distribution_VF.pdf.

Tolerance Edict, 1905: Full Collection of Russian Imperial Law, 3rd series, no. 26126, April 30.

Tolstaya, Katya, 2014: "Stained Glasses and Coloured Lenses: The Pussy Riot Case as a Critical Issue for Multidisciplinary Scholarly Investigations", *Religion and Gender*, 4:100-120.

Tolz, Vera and Yuri Teper, 2018: "Broadcasting Agitainment: A New Media Strategy of Putin's Third Presidency", *Post-Soviet Affairs*, 34:213-227.

Towster, Julian, 1948: *Political Power in the USSR 1917-1947*, Oxford University Press, New York.

Uitermark, Justus, 2005: "The Genesis and Evolution of Urban Policy: A Confrontation of Regulationist and Governmentality Approaches", *Political Geography*, 24:137-163.

Uzzell, Lawrence, 2000: former director of the Keston Institute, Oxford, quoted in "Fate of Religion in Putin's Russia Uncertain", January 7. https://www2.stetson. edu/~psteeves/relnews/0001a.html.

Valliere, Paul, 1976: "The Problem of Liberal Orthodoxy in Russia, 1905", *St. Vladimir's Orthodox Theological Quarterly*, 20:115-131.

Van Dijk, Teun A., 2006: "Discourse and Manipulation," *Discourse & Society*, 17:359–383.

Vandiver, John, 2014: "SACEUR: Allies Must Prepare for Russia 'Hybrid War'", *Stars and Stripes*, September 4. https://www.stripes.com/news/saceur-allies-must-prepare-for-russia-hybrid-war-1.301464.

Vardys, Stanley, and Judith B. Sedaitis, 1997: *Lithuania: The Rebel Nation*, Westview Press, Boulder.

Vardys, Stanley, 1981: "Freedom of Religion, Lithuania and the Chronicle: An Introduction", in *The Chronicle of the Catholic Church in Lithuania*, vol. 1, Loyola University Press, Chicago.

Volf, Miroslav, 1996: "Fishing in the Neighbor's Pond: Mission and Proselytism in Eastern Europe", *International Bulletin of Missionary Research*, 20:26-31.

Wallace, Daniel, 1996: "Religion and the Struggle for Russia's Future", *Religion, State and Society*, 24:367-383.

Walters, Philip, 1993: "A Survey of Soviet Religious Policy" in *Religious Policy in the Soviet Union*, edited by Sabrina Ramet, Cambridge University Press, Cambridge.

Warner, Stephen, 1993: "Towards a New Paradigm for the Sociological Study of Religion in the United States", *American Journal of Sociology*, 98:1044-1093.

Welch, Stephen, 1993: *The Concept of Political Culture*, Macmillan, London.

Werth, Paul W., 2014: *The Tsar's Foreign Faiths: Toleration and the Fate of Religious Freedom in Imperial Russia*, Oxford University Press, Oxford.

Stephen White, 1979: *Political Culture and Soviet Politics*, St. Martin's, London.

White, Stephen, 1994: "Pluralism, Civil Society, and Post-Soviet Politics", in *In Search of Pluralism: Soviet and Post-Soviet Politics*, edited by Carol Saivetz and Anthony Jones, Westview Press, Boulder.

Young, Lawrence A., 1997: *Rational Choice Theory and Religion: Summary and Assessment*, Routledge, New York.

Ziegler, Charles, 2016: "Russia as a Nationalizing State: Rejecting the Western Liberal Order", *International Politics*, 53:555–573.

Appendix: Interview/Questionnaire Questions

Soviet Period

1. How would you describe your church's relationship with the Soviet State?
2. What role, if any, did your church play in opposing the Soviet Union?
3. How would you characterize the behavior of your church leadership under communism?
4. What if anything to do you miss about life before the fall of the Soviet Union?
5. How would you describe the effects of communism on your church's infrastructure (ability to operate)?
6. What is your opinion of the behavior of the Orthodox (Catholic) church hierarchy under communism?
7. Do you believe that the residual effects of communism have hindered your church's progress since 1991? If so, in what way?
8. It has been suggested that one consequence of Soviet religious policy on your church was a weakening of ties with society. Do you believe such an assessment is accurate?

Post-Soviet Period

1. Where have you seen the greatest changes in the religious sphere since independence? What is your personal assessment of these changes?
2. Have the duties and responsibilities of your work changed since independence? If so, how?
3. How would you rate your church's current relationship with society?
4. From your point of view, what is the greatest threat to the spiritual health of society?
5. What, in your opinion, is the greatest threat to your nation's future stability?
6. What are your church's most important achievements since independence?
7. What do you view as the primary task of your church in the transition?
8. What in your opinion is the greatest obstacle to further democratization in your country?
9. Do you believe that the plurality of religious organizations in your community is beneficial to the spiritual health of society?
10. Since the fall of communism, the activities of non-traditional religious groups have increased in your nation. What is your personal assessment of their activity?

11. Do you believe that the infusion of such sectarian groups into your community has resulted in an increase in societal tension? If so, why? 12. What do you believe should be the role of the government regarding the activities of sectarian groups?
13. In your opinion should such groups be able to proselytize freely? Own property?

Church-State Relations

1. What role do you see your church playing in the political processes of the future?
2. What do you believe is the proper role of your church in the legislation of religious law in your nation?
3. How would you define religious pluralism?
4. In your opinion, should traditional dominant churches be privileged over other churches due to their historical and cultural significances and contributions?
5. How much confidence do you have in your government's ability to regulate religious activity?
6. Some church leaders have argued that living under communism crippled historically dominant churches, making them non-competitive. Do you agree with such an assessment?
7. The American system provides for complete separation of church and state activities. Do you believe that such a model of church-state relations should be followed in your country?

Standardized Questionnaire

1. Do you believe that religion is more or less important today to the citizens of this country than it was twenty years ago? *more, less, not sure*
2. How would you rate your church's current relationship with society in general? *very good, good, bad, very bad, no opinion*
3. How would you characterize the effects of communism on your church? *very beneficial, somewhat beneficial, no effect, somewhat detrimental, extremely detrimental*
4. What best describes your opinion regarding your church hierarchy's behavior under communism? *Their actions were—consistent with the canonical teachings of the church, appropriate considering the difficult circumstances, sometimes at odds with doctrinal policies, clearly unbecoming of an ecclesiastical body, others*

5. What best describes your church's association with the Soviet state? *close collaboration, mutually assisting relationship, often in disagreement, in clear opposition, not sure*
6. In general, was it more or less difficult to serve in your position under communism? *much more difficult, somewhat more difficult, somewhat less difficult, much less difficult, no difference*
7. Shortly after the fall of the Soviet Union in 1991 how well suited do you feel your church was to compete for the souls of people? *well prepared, somewhat prepared, somewhat not prepared, poorly prepared, not sure*
8. How well prepared is your church now? *well prepared, somewhat prepared, somewhat not prepared, poorly prepared, not sure*
9. What, in your opinion, is the greatest threat to the spiritual health of society?
10. What are your church's most important achievements since independence? *building of church buildings, strengthening ties with society, increasing the spirituality of society, improving relations with the state, expanding humanitarian projects, other*
11. What is your personal opinion of the spread of foreign religious groups in your community? *I am pleased with their expansion, their activities are of no concern to me, I am unhappy with the expansion of such groups, I have no opinion, not sure*
12. Do you think the activities of these groups are a threat to your church's success? *yes, no, not sure*
13. Do you believe that foreign religious groups add to the vitality of the religious community and to the spiritual health of the people? *yes, no, not sure*
14. What policy do you believe the government should take on the activities of sectarian groups? *ban such groups, isolate them from society, provide them with assistance, leave them alone, not sure*
15. Do you believe that a plurality of religious organizations operating in a community is good for society? *very good, good, bad, very bad, not sure*
16. What is the proper role of your church in enacting government legislation on religious activity? *equal partner with the state, the most influential religious voice, one of many religious organizations adding to public dialogue, no role, not sure*
17. During what time period do you feel your church was most connected with its members? *tsarist period, under communism, 1990's, currently, other*
18. During what time period do you feel your church was the least connected with its members? *tsarist period, under communism, 1990's, currently, other*

19. In general, do you have a very positive, somewhat positive, neutral, somewhat negative or very negative opinion of how your church behaved during the Soviet Union? *very positive, somewhat positive, neutral, somewhat negative, very negative*

20. How much influence, if any, do you think your church has on the decisions taken by the government? *a great deal of influence, some influence, very little influence, no influence, not sure*

21. In general, do you favor or oppose the efforts being made to restrict the activities of non-traditional religious organizations? *favor—very much, favor—to some extent, oppose—to some extent, oppose—very much, not sure*

22. From your point of view, what has done the most harm to the spiritual health of your community during the past century?

23. Below is a list of various institutions. On a scale of 1-5, please indicate how strongly you personally trust each of these institutions. Where 1 indicates no trust at all and 5 very strong trust. *USSR Council for Religious Affairs, the parliament in your country, the president of your country, your church's hierarchy, non-traditional religious organizations, media*

24. Please express you views on the following groups and organizations. State how favorably you view them on a scale from 1-5, where 1 represents very unfavorable and 5 very favorable. *Jews, Mormons, Jehovah Witness, Baptists, Catholics, Muslims*

25. Below is a list of ideals that many feel are important to your nation. Please state whether, in your opinion, they are very important, rather important, less important or not important. *a democratically elected government, an efficient and non-corrupt public service, respect for human rights, freedom of media, respect for minorities*

26. Please indicate whether you agree or disagree with the following statements using—*completely agree, mostly agree, mostly disagree, completely disagree*
    a) The Soviet state was successful in its attempt to create an atheistic society.
    b) Soviet religious policy was effective in infiltrating and controlling church leadership.
    c) My church's ties with society were weakened during the Soviet Union
    d) Churches should abstain from directly participating in the political process.
    e) Churches should refrain from endorsing political candidates or political parties.

f) Because of their historical contributions to society, traditional churches should be privileged over non-traditional churches.
g) The church and state should work closely together to ensure the spiritual health of society.
h) The infusion of sectarian groups into the community after 1991 has resulted in societal tension.

SOVIET AND POST-SOVIET POLITICS AND SOCIETY
Edited by Dr. Andreas Umland | ISSN 1614-3515

1 *Андреас Умланд (ред.)* | Воплощение Европейской конвенции по правам человека в России. Философские, юридические и эмпирические исследования | ISBN 3-89821-387-0

2 *Christian Wipperfürth* | Russland – ein vertrauenswürdiger Partner? Grundlagen, Hintergründe und Praxis gegenwärtiger russischer Außenpolitik | Mit einem Vorwort von Heinz Timmermann | ISBN 3-89821-401-X

3 *Manja Hussner* | Die Übernahme internationalen Rechts in die russische und deutsche Rechtsordnung. Eine vergleichende Analyse zur Völkerrechtsfreundlichkeit der Verfassungen der Russländischen Föderation und der Bundesrepublik Deutschland | Mit einem Vorwort von Rainer Arnold | ISBN 3-89821-438-9

4 *Matthew Tejada* | Bulgaria's Democratic Consolidation and the Kozloduy Nuclear Power Plant (KNPP). The Unattainability of Closure | With a foreword by Richard J. Crampton | ISBN 3-89821-439-7

5 *Марк Григорьевич Меерович* | Квадратные метры, определяющие сознание. Государственная жилищная политика в СССР. 1921 – 1941 гг | ISBN 3-89821-474-5

6 *Andrei P. Tsygankov, Pavel A. Tsygankov (Eds.)* | New Directions in Russian International Studies | ISBN 3-89821-422-2

7 *Марк Григорьевич Меерович* | Как власть народ к труду приучала. Жилище в СССР – средство управления людьми. 1917 – 1941 гг. | С предисловием Елены Осокиной | ISBN 3-89821-495-8

8 *David J. Galbreath* | Nation-Building and Minority Politics in Post-Socialist States. Interests, Influence and Identities in Estonia and Latvia | With a foreword by David J. Smith | ISBN 3-89821-467-2

9 *Алексей Юрьевич Безугольный* | Народы Кавказа в Вооруженных силах СССР в годы Великой Отечественной войны 1941-1945 гг. | С предисловием Николая Бугая | ISBN 3-89821-475-3

10 *Вячеслав Лихачев и Владимир Прибыловский (ред.)* | Русское Национальное Единство, 1990-2000. В 2-х томах | ISBN 3-89821-523-7

11 *Николай Бугай (ред.)* | Народы стран Балтии в условиях сталинизма (1940-е – 1950-е годы). Документированная история | ISBN 3-89821-525-3

12 *Ingmar Bredies (Hrsg.)* | Zur Anatomie der Orange Revolution in der Ukraine. Wechsel des Elitenregimes oder Triumph des Parlamentarismus? | ISBN 3-89821-524-5

13 *Anastasia V. Mitrofanova* | The Politicization of Russian Orthodoxy. Actors and Ideas | With a foreword by William C. Gay | ISBN 3-89821-481-8

14 *Nathan D. Larson* | Alexander Solzhenitsyn and the Russo-Jewish Question | ISBN 3-89821-483-4

15 *Guido Houben* | Kulturpolitik und Ethnizität. Staatliche Kunstförderung im Russland der neunziger Jahre | Mit einem Vorwort von Gert Weisskirchen | ISBN 3-89821-542-3

16 *Leonid Luks* | Der russische „Sonderweg"? Aufsätze zur neuesten Geschichte Russlands im europäischen Kontext | ISBN 3-89821-496-6

17 *Евгений Мороз* | История «Мёртвой воды» – от страшной сказки к большой политике. Политическое неоязычество в постсоветской России | ISBN 3-89821-551-2

18 *Александр Верховский и Галина Кожевникова (ред.)* | Этническая и религиозная интолерантность в российских СМИ. Результаты мониторинга 2001-2004 гг. | ISBN 3-89821-569-5

19 *Christian Ganzer* | Sowjetisches Erbe und ukrainische Nation. Das Museum der Geschichte des Zaporoger Kosakentums auf der Insel Chortycja | Mit einem Vorwort von Frank Golczewski | ISBN 3-89821-504-0

20 *Эльза-Баир Гучинова* | Помнить нельзя забыть. Антропология депортационной травмы калмыков | С предисловием Кэролайн Хамфри | ISBN 3-89821-506-7

21 *Юлия Лидерман* | Мотивы «проверки» и «испытания» в постсоветской культуре. Советское прошлое в российском кинематографе 1990-х годов | С предисловием Евгения Марголита | ISBN 3-89821-511-3

22 *Tanya Lokshina, Ray Thomas, Mary Mayer (Eds.)* | The Imposition of a Fake Political Settlement in the Northern Caucasus. The 2003 Chechen Presidential Election | ISBN 3-89821-436-2

23 *Timothy McCajor Hall, Rosie Read (Eds.)* | Changes in the Heart of Europe. Recent Ethnographies of Czechs, Slovaks, Roma, and Sorbs | With an afterword by Zdeněk Salzmann | ISBN 3-89821-606-3

24　*Christian Autengruber* | Die politischen Parteien in Bulgarien und Rumänien. Eine vergleichende Analyse seit Beginn der 90er Jahre | Mit einem Vorwort von Dorothée de Nève | ISBN 3-89821-476-1

25　*Annette Freyberg-Inan with Radu Cristescu* | The Ghosts in Our Classrooms, or: John Dewey Meets Ceauşescu. The Promise and the Failures of Civic Education in Romania | ISBN 3-89821-416-8

26　*John B. Dunlop* | The 2002 Dubrovka and 2004 Beslan Hostage Crises. A Critique of Russian Counter-Terrorism | With a foreword by Donald N. Jensen | ISBN 3-89821-608-X

27　*Peter Koller* | Das touristische Potenzial von Kam"janec'-Podil's'kyj. Eine fremdenverkehrsgeographische Untersuchung der Zukunftsperspektiven und Maßnahmenplanung zur Destinationsentwicklung des „ukrainischen Rothenburg" | Mit einem Vorwort von Kristiane Klemm | ISBN 3-89821-640-3

28　*Françoise Daucé, Elisabeth Sieca-Kozlowski (Eds.)* | Dedovshchina in the Post-Soviet Military. Hazing of Russian Army Conscripts in a Comparative Perspective | With a foreword by Dale Herspring | ISBN 3-89821-616-0

29　*Florian Strasser* | Zivilgesellschaftliche Einflüsse auf die Orange Revolution. Die gewaltlose Massenbewegung und die ukrainische Wahlkrise 2004 | Mit einem Vorwort von Egbert Jahn | ISBN 3-89821-648-9

30　*Rebecca S. Katz* | The Georgian Regime Crisis of 2003-2004. A Case Study in Post-Soviet Media Representation of Politics, Crime and Corruption | ISBN 3-89821-413-3

31　*Vladimir Kantor* | Willkür oder Freiheit. Beiträge zur russischen Geschichtsphilosophie | Ediert von Dagmar Herrmann sowie mit einem Vorwort versehen von Leonid Luks | ISBN 3-89821-589-X

32　*Laura A. Victoir* | The Russian Land Estate Today. A Case Study of Cultural Politics in Post-Soviet Russia | With a foreword by Priscilla Roosevelt | ISBN 3-89821-426-5

33　*Ivan Katchanovski* | Cleft Countries. Regional Political Divisions and Cultures in Post-Soviet Ukraine and Moldova| With a foreword by Francis Fukuyama | ISBN 3-89821-558-X

34　*Florian Mühlfried* | Postsowjetische Feiern. Das Georgische Bankett im Wandel | Mit einem Vorwort von Kevin Tuite | ISBN 3-89821-601-2

35　*Roger Griffin, Werner Loh, Andreas Umland (Eds.)* | Fascism Past and Present, West and East. An International Debate on Concepts and Cases in the Comparative Study of the Extreme Right | With an afterword by Walter Laqueur | ISBN 3-89821-674-8

36　*Sebastian Schlegel* | Der „Weiße Archipel". Sowjetische Atomstädte 1945-1991 | Mit einem Geleitwort von Thomas Bohn | ISBN 3-89821-679-9

37　*Vyacheslav Likhachev* | Political Anti-Semitism in Post-Soviet Russia. Actors and Ideas in 1991-2003 | Edited and translated from Russian by Eugene Veklerov | ISBN 3-89821-529-6

38　*Josette Baer (Ed.)* | Preparing Liberty in Central Europe. Political Texts from the Spring of Nations 1848 to the Spring of Prague 1968 | With a foreword by Zdeněk V. David | ISBN 3-89821-546-6

39　*Михаил Лукьянов* | Российский консерватизм и реформа, 1907-1914 | С предисловием Марка Д. Стейнберга | ISBN 3-89821-503-2

40　*Nicola Melloni* | Market Without Economy. The 1998 Russian Financial Crisis | With a foreword by Eiji Furukawa | ISBN 3-89821-407-9

41　*Dmitrij Chmelnizki* | Die Architektur Stalins | Bd. 1: Studien zu Ideologie und Stil | Bd. 2: Bilddokumentation | Mit einem Vorwort von Bruno Flierl | ISBN 3-89821-515-6

42　*Katja Yafimava* | Post-Soviet Russian-Belarussian Relationships. The Role of Gas Transit Pipelines | With a foreword by Jonathan P. Stern | ISBN 3-89821-655-1

43　*Boris Chavkin* | Verflechtungen der deutschen und russischen Zeitgeschichte. Aufsätze und Archivfunde zu den Beziehungen Deutschlands und der Sowjetunion von 1917 bis 1991 | Ediert von Markus Edlinger sowie mit einem Vorwort versehen von Leonid Luks | ISBN 3-89821-756-6

44　*Anastasija Grynenko in Zusammenarbeit mit Claudia Dathe* | Die Terminologie des Gerichtswesens der Ukraine und Deutschlands im Vergleich. Eine übersetzungswissenschaftliche Analyse juristischer Fachbegriffe im Deutschen, Ukrainischen und Russischen | Mit einem Vorwort von Ulrich Hartmann | ISBN 3-89821-691-8

45　*Anton Burkov* | The Impact of the European Convention on Human Rights on Russian Law. Legislation and Application in 1996-2006 | With a foreword by Françoise Hampson | ISBN 978-3-89821-639-5

46　*Stina Torjesen, Indra Overland (Eds.)* | International Election Observers in Post-Soviet Azerbaijan. Geopolitical Pawns or Agents of Change? | ISBN 978-3-89821-743-9

47　*Taras Kuzio* | Ukraine – Crimea – Russia. Triangle of Conflict | ISBN 978-3-89821-761-3

48　*Claudia Šabić* | „Ich erinnere mich nicht, aber L'viv!" Zur Funktion kultureller Faktoren für die Institutionalisierung und Entwicklung einer ukrainischen Region | Mit einem Vorwort von Melanie Tatur | ISBN 978-3-89821-752-1

49　*Marlies Bilz* | Tatarstan in der Transformation. Nationaler Diskurs und Politische Praxis 1988-1994 | Mit einem Vorwort von Frank Golczewski | ISBN 978-3-89821-722-4

50　*Марлен Ларюэль (ред.)* | Современные интерпретации русского национализма | ISBN 978-3-89821-795-8

51　*Sonja Schüler* | Die ethnische Dimension der Armut. Roma im postsozialistischen Rumänien | Mit einem Vorwort von Anton Sterbling | ISBN 978-3-89821-776-7

52　*Галина Кожевникова* | Радикальный национализм в России и противодействие ему. Сборник докладов Центра «Сова» за 2004-2007 гг. | С предисловием Александра Верховского | ISBN 978-3-89821-721-7

53　*Галина Кожевникова и Владимир Прибыловский* | Российская власть в биографиях I. Высшие должностные лица РФ в 2004 г. | ISBN 978-3-89821-796-5

54　*Галина Кожевникова и Владимир Прибыловский* | Российская власть в биографиях II. Члены Правительства РФ в 2004 г. | ISBN 978-3-89821-797-2

55　*Галина Кожевникова и Владимир Прибыловский* | Российская власть в биографиях III. Руководители федеральных служб и агентств РФ в 2004 г. | ISBN 978-3-89821-798-9

56　*Ileana Petroniu* | Privatisierung in Transformationsökonomien. Determinanten der Restrukturierungs-Bereitschaft am Beispiel Polens, Rumäniens und der Ukraine | Mit einem Vorwort von Rainer W. Schäfer | ISBN 978-3-89821-790-3

57　*Christian Wipperfürth* | Russland und seine GUS-Nachbarn. Hintergründe, aktuelle Entwicklungen und Konflikte in einer ressourcenreichen Region| ISBN 978-3-89821-801-6

58　*Togzhan Kassenova* | From Antagonism to Partnership. The Uneasy Path of the U.S.-Russian Cooperative Threat Reduction | With a foreword by Christoph Bluth | ISBN 978-3-89821-707-1

59　*Alexander Höllwerth* | Das sakrale eurasische Imperium des Aleksandr Dugin. Eine Diskursanalyse zum postsowjetischen russischen Rechtsextremismus | Mit einem Vorwort von Dirk Uffelmann | ISBN 978-3-89821-813-9

60　*Олег Рябов* | «Россия-Матушка». Национализм, гендер и война в России XX века | С предисловием Елены Гощило | ISBN 978-3-89821-487-2

61　*Ivan Maistrenko* | Borot'bism. A Chapter in the History of the Ukrainian Revolution | With a new Introduction by Chris Ford | Translated by George S. N. Luckyj with the assistance of Ivan L. Rudnytsky | Second, Revised and Expanded Edition ISBN 978-3-8382-1107-7

62　*Maryna Romanets* | Anamorphosic Texts and Reconfigured Visions. Improvised Traditions in Contemporary Ukrainian and Irish Literature | ISBN 978-3-89821-576-3

63　*Paul D'Anieri and Taras Kuzio (Eds.)* | Aspects of the Orange Revolution I. Democratization and Elections in Post-Communist Ukraine | ISBN 978-3-89821-698-2

64　*Bohdan Harasymiw in collaboration with Oleh S. Ilnytzkyj (Eds.)* | Aspects of the Orange Revolution II. Information and Manipulation Strategies in the 2004 Ukrainian Presidential Elections | ISBN 978-3-89821-699-9

65　*Ingmar Bredies, Andreas Umland and Valentin Yakushik (Eds.)* | Aspects of the Orange Revolution III. The Context and Dynamics of the 2004 Ukrainian Presidential Elections | ISBN 978-3-89821-803-0

66　*Ingmar Bredies, Andreas Umland and Valentin Yakushik (Eds.)* | Aspects of the Orange Revolution IV. Foreign Assistance and Civic Action in the 2004 Ukrainian Presidential Elections | ISBN 978-3-89821-808-5

67　*Ingmar Bredies, Andreas Umland and Valentin Yakushik (Eds.)* | Aspects of the Orange Revolution V. Institutional Observation Reports on the 2004 Ukrainian Presidential Elections | ISBN 978-3-89821-809-2

68　*Taras Kuzio (Ed.)* | Aspects of the Orange Revolution VI. Post-Communist Democratic Revolutions in Comparative Perspective | ISBN 978-3-89821-820-7

69　*Tim Bohse* | Autoritarismus statt Selbstverwaltung. Die Transformation der kommunalen Politik in der Stadt Kaliningrad 1990-2005 | Mit einem Geleitwort von Stefan Troebst | ISBN 978-3-89821-782-8

70　*David Rupp* | Die Rußländische Föderation und die russischsprachige Minderheit in Lettland. Eine Fallstudie zur Anwaltspolitik Moskaus gegenüber den russophonen Minderheiten im „Nahen Ausland" von 1991 bis 2002 | Mit einem Vorwort von Helmut Wagner | ISBN 978-3-89821-778-1

71　*Taras Kuzio* | Theoretical and Comparative Perspectives on Nationalism. New Directions in Cross-Cultural and Post-Communist Studies | With a foreword by Paul Robert Magocsi | ISBN 978-3-89821-815-3

72　*Christine Teichmann* | Die Hochschultransformation im heutigen Osteuropa. Kontinuität und Wandel bei der Entwicklung des postkommunistischen Universitätswesens | Mit einem Vorwort von Oskar Anweiler | ISBN 978-3-89821-842-9

73　*Julia Kusznir* | Der politische Einfluss von Wirtschaftseliten in russischen Regionen. Eine Analyse am Beispiel der Erdöl- und Erdgasindustrie, 1992-2005 | Mit einem Vorwort von Wolfgang Eichwede | ISBN 978-3-89821-821-4

74 *Alena Vysotskaya* | Russland, Belarus und die EU-Osterweiterung. Zur Minderheitenfrage und zum Problem der Freizügigkeit des Personenverkehrs | Mit einem Vorwort von Katlijn Malfliet | ISBN 978-3-89821-822-1

75 *Heiko Pleines (Hrsg.)* | Corporate Governance in post-sozialistischen Volkswirtschaften | ISBN 978-3-89821-766-8

76 *Stefan Ihrig* | Wer sind die Moldawier? Rumänismus versus Moldowanismus in Historiographie und Schulbüchern der Republik Moldova, 1991-2006 | Mit einem Vorwort von Holm Sundhaussen | ISBN 978-3-89821-466-7

77 *Galina Kozhevnikova in collaboration with Alexander Verkhovsky and Eugene Veklerov* | Ultra-Nationalism and Hate Crimes in Contemporary Russia. The 2004-2006 Annual Reports of Moscow's SOVA Center | With a foreword by Stephen D. Shenfield | ISBN 978-3-89821-868-9

78 *Florian Küchler* | The Role of the European Union in Moldova's Transnistria Conflict | With a foreword by Christopher Hill | ISBN 978-3-89821-850-4

79 *Bernd Rechel* | The Long Way Back to Europe. Minority Protection in Bulgaria | With a foreword by Richard Crampton | ISBN 978-3-89821-863-4

80 *Peter W. Rodgers* | Nation, Region and History in Post-Communist Transitions. Identity Politics in Ukraine, 1991-2006 | With a foreword by Vera Tolz | ISBN 978-3-89821-903-7

81 *Stephanie Solywoda* | The Life and Work of Semen L. Frank. A Study of Russian Religious Philosophy | With a foreword by Philip Walters | ISBN 978-3-89821-457-5

82 *Vera Sokolova* | Cultural Politics of Ethnicity. Discourses on Roma in Communist Czechoslovakia | ISBN 978-3-89821-864-1

83 *Natalya Shevchik Ketenci* | Kazakhstani Enterprises in Transition. The Role of Historical Regional Development in Kazakhstan's Post-Soviet Economic Transformation | ISBN 978-3-89821-831-3

84 *Martin Malek, Anna Schor-Tschudnowskaja (Hgg.)* | Europa im Tschetschenienkrieg. Zwischen politischer Ohnmacht und Gleichgültigkeit | Mit einem Vorwort von Lipchan Basajewa | ISBN 978-3-89821-676-0

85 *Stefan Meister* | Das postsowjetische Universitätswesen zwischen nationalem und internationalem Wandel. Die Entwicklung der regionalen Hochschule in Russland als Gradmesser der Systemtransformation | Mit einem Vorwort von Joan DeBardeleben | ISBN 978-3-89821-891-7

86 *Konstantin Sheiko in collaboration with Stephen Brown* | Nationalist Imaginings of the Russian Past. Anatolii Fomenko and the Rise of Alternative History in Post Communist Russia | With a foreword by Donald Ostrowski | ISBN 978-3-89821-915-0

87 *Sabine Jenni* | Wie stark ist das „Einige Russland"? Zur Parteibindung der Eliten und zum Wahlerfolg der Machtpartei im Dezember 2007 | Mit einem Vorwort von Klaus Armingeon | ISBN 978-3-89821-961-7

88 *Thomas Borén* | Meeting-Places of Transformation. Urban Identity, Spatial Representations and Local Politics in Post-Soviet St Petersburg | ISBN 978-3-89821-739-2

89 *Aygul Ashirova* | Stalinismus und Stalin-Kult in Zentralasien. Turkmenistan 1924-1953 | Mit einem Vorwort von Leonid Luks | ISBN 978-3-89821-987-7

90 *Leonid Luks* | Freiheit oder imperiale Größe? Essays zu einem russischen Dilemma | ISBN 978-3-8382-0011-8

91 *Christopher Gilley* | The 'Change of Signposts' in the Ukrainian Emigration. A Contribution to the History of Sovietophilism in the 1920s | With a foreword by Frank Golczewski | ISBN 978-3-89821-965-5

92 *Philipp Casula, Jeronim Perovic (Eds.)* | Identities and Politics During the Putin Presidency. The Discursive Foundations of Russia's Stability | With a foreword by Heiko Haumann | ISBN 978-3-8382-0015-6

93 *Marcel Viëtor* | Europa und die Frage nach seinen Grenzen im Osten. Zur Konstruktion ‚europäischer Identität' in Geschichte und Gegenwart | Mit einem Vorwort von Albrecht Lehmann | ISBN 978-3-8382-0045-3

94 *Ben Hellman, Andrei Rogachevskii* | Filming the Unfilmable. Casper Wrede's 'One Day in the Life of Ivan Denisovich' | Second, Revised and Expanded Edition | ISBN 978-3-8382-0044-6

95 *Eva Fuchslocher* | Vaterland, Sprache, Glaube. Orthodoxie und Nationenbildung am Beispiel Georgiens | Mit einem Vorwort von Christina von Braun | ISBN 978-3-89821-884-9

96 *Vladimir Kantor* | Das Westlertum und der Weg Russlands. Zur Entwicklung der russischen Literatur und Philosophie | Ediert von Dagmar Herrmann | Mit einem Beitrag von Nikolaus Lobkowicz | ISBN 978-3-8382-0102-3

97 *Kamran Musayev* | Die postsowjetische Transformation im Baltikum und Südkaukasus. Eine vergleichende Untersuchung der politischen Entwicklung Lettlands und Aserbaidschans 1985-2009 | Mit einem Vorwort von Leonid Luks | Ediert von Sandro Henschel | ISBN 978-3-8382-0103-0

98 *Tatiana Zhurzhenko* | Borderlands into Bordered Lands. Geopolitics of Identity in Post-Soviet Ukraine | With a foreword by Dieter Segert | ISBN 978-3-8382-0042-2

99 Кирилл Галушко, Лидия Смола (ред.) | Пределы падения – варианты украинского будущего. Аналитико-прогностические исследования | ISBN 978-3-8382-0148-1

100 Michael Minkenberg (Ed.) | Historical Legacies and the Radical Right in Post-Cold War Central and Eastern Europe | With an afterword by Sabrina P. Ramet | ISBN 978-3-8382-0124-5

101 David-Emil Wickström | Rocking St. Petersburg. Transcultural Flows and Identity Politics in the St. Petersburg Popular Music Scene | With a foreword by Yngvar B. Steinholt | Second, Revised and Expanded Edition | ISBN 978-3-8382-0100-9

102 Eva Zabka | Eine neue „Zeit der Wirren"? Der spät- und postsowjetische Systemwandel 1985-2000 im Spiegel russischer gesellschaftspolitischer Diskurse | Mit einem Vorwort von Margareta Mommsen | ISBN 978-3-8382-0161-0

103 Ulrike Ziemer | Ethnic Belonging, Gender and Cultural Practices. Youth Identitites in Contemporary Russia | With a foreword by Anoop Nayak | ISBN 978-3-8382-0152-8

104 Ksenia Chepikova | ‚Einiges Russland' - eine zweite KPdSU? Aspekte der Identitätskonstruktion einer postsowjetischen „Partei der Macht" | Mit einem Vorwort von Torsten Oppelland | ISBN 978-3-8382-0311-9

105 Леонид Люкс | Западничество или евразийство? Демократия или идеократия? Сборник статей об исторических дилеммах России | С предисловием Владимира Кантора | ISBN 978-3-8382-0211-2

106 Anna Dost | Das russische Verfassungsrecht auf dem Weg zum Föderalismus und zurück. Zum Konflikt von Rechtsnormen und -wirklichkeit in der Russländischen Föderation von 1991 bis 2009 | Mit einem Vorwort von Alexander Blankenagel | ISBN 978-3-8382-0292-1

107 Philipp Herzog | Sozialistische Völkerfreundschaft, nationaler Widerstand oder harmloser Zeitvertreib? Zur politischen Funktion der Volkskunst im sowjetischen Estland | Mit einem Vorwort von Andreas Kappeler | ISBN 978-3-8382-0216-7

108 Marlène Laruelle (Ed.) | Russian Nationalism, Foreign Policy, and Identity Debates in Putin's Russia. New Ideological Patterns after the Orange Revolution | ISBN 978-3-8382-0325-6

109 Michail Logvinov | Russlands Kampf gegen den internationalen Terrorismus. Eine kritische Bestandsaufnahme des Bekämpfungsansatzes | Mit einem Geleitwort von Hans-Henning Schröder und einem Vorwort von Eckhard Jesse | ISBN 978-3-8382-0329-4

110 John B. Dunlop | The Moscow Bombings of September 1999. Examinations of Russian Terrorist Attacks at the Onset of Vladimir Putin's Rule | Second, Revised and Expanded Edition | ISBN 978-3-8382-0388-1

111 Андрей А. Ковалёв | Свидетельство из-за кулис российской политики I. Можно ли делать добро из зла? (Воспоминания и размышления о последних советских и первых послесоветских годах) | With a foreword by Peter Reddaway | ISBN 978-3-8382-0302-7

112 Андрей А. Ковалёв | Свидетельство из-за кулис российской политики II. Угроза для себя и окружающих (Наблюдения и предостережения относительно происходящего после 2000 г.) | ISBN 978-3-8382-0303-4

113 Bernd Kappenberg | Zeichen setzen für Europa. Der Gebrauch europäischer lateinischer Sonderzeichen in der deutschen Öffentlichkeit | Mit einem Vorwort von Peter Schlobinski | ISBN 978-3-89821-749-1

114 Ivo Mijnssen | The Quest for an Ideal Youth in Putin's Russia I. Back to Our Future! History, Modernity, and Patriotism according to Nashi, 2005-2013 | With a foreword by Jeronim Perović | Second, Revised and Expanded Edition | ISBN 978-3-8382-0368-3

115 Jussi Lassila | The Quest for an Ideal Youth in Putin's Russia II. The Search for Distinctive Conformism in the Political Communication of Nashi, 2005-2009 | With a foreword by Kirill Postoutenko | Second, Revised and Expanded Edition | ISBN 978-3-8382-0415-4

116 Valerio Trabandt | Neue Nachbarn, gute Nachbarschaft? Die EU als internationaler Akteur am Beispiel ihrer Demokratieförderung in Belarus und der Ukraine 2004-2009 | Mit einem Vorwort von Jutta Joachim | ISBN 978-3-8382-0437-6

117 Fabian Pfeiffer | Estlands Außen- und Sicherheitspolitik I. Der estnische Atlantizismus nach der wiedererlangten Unabhängigkeit 1991-2004 | Mit einem Vorwort von Helmut Hubel | ISBN 978-3-8382-0127-6

118 Jana Podßuweit | Estlands Außen- und Sicherheitspolitik II. Handlungsoptionen eines Kleinstaates im Rahmen seiner EU-Mitgliedschaft (2004-2008) | Mit einem Vorwort von Helmut Hubel | ISBN 978-3-8382-0440-6

119 Karin Pointner | Estlands Außen- und Sicherheitspolitik III. Eine gedächtnispolitische Analyse estnischer Entwicklungskooperation 2006-2010 | Mit einem Vorwort von Karin Liebhart | ISBN 978-3-8382-0435-2

120 Ruslana Vovk | Die Offenheit der ukrainischen Verfassung für das Völkerrecht und die europäische Integration | Mit einem Vorwort von Alexander Blankenagel | ISBN 978-3-8382-0481-9

121 *Mykhaylo Banakh* | Die Relevanz der Zivilgesellschaft bei den postkommunistischen Transformationsprozessen in mittel- und osteuropäischen Ländern. Das Beispiel der spät- und postsowjetischen Ukraine 1986-2009 | Mit einem Vorwort von Gerhard Simon | ISBN 978-3-8382-0499-4

122 *Michael Moser* | Language Policy and the Discourse on Languages in Ukraine under President Viktor Yanukovych (25 February 2010–28 October 2012) | ISBN 978-3-8382-0497-0 (Paperback edition) | ISBN 978-3-8382-0507-6 (Hardcover edition)

123 *Nicole Krome* | Russischer Netzwerkkapitalismus Restrukturierungsprozesse in der Russischen Föderation am Beispiel des Luftfahrtunternehmens „Aviastar" | Mit einem Vorwort von Petra Stykow | ISBN 978-3-8382-0534-2

124 *David R. Marples* | 'Our Glorious Past'. Lukashenka's Belarus and the Great Patriotic War | ISBN 978-3-8382-0574-8 (Paperback edition) | ISBN 978-3-8382-0675-2 (Hardcover edition)

125 *Ulf Walther* | Russlands „neuer Adel". Die Macht des Geheimdienstes von Gorbatschow bis Putin | Mit einem Vorwort von Hans-Georg Wieck | ISBN 978-3-8382-0584-7

126 *Simon Geissbühler (Hrsg.)* | Kiew – Revolution 3.0. Der Euromaidan 2013/14 und die Zukunftsperspektiven der Ukraine | ISBN 978-3-8382-0581-6 (Paperback edition) | ISBN 978-3-8382-0681-3 (Hardcover edition)

127 *Andrey Makarychev* | Russia and the EU in a Multipolar World. Discourses, Identities, Norms | With a foreword by Klaus Segbers | ISBN 978-3-8382-0629-5

128 *Roland Scharff* | Kasachstan als postsowjetischer Wohlfahrtsstaat. Die Transformation des sozialen Schutzsystems | Mit einem Vorwort von Joachim Ahrens | ISBN 978-3-8382-0622-6

129 *Katja Grupp* | Bild Lücke Deutschland. Kaliningrader Studierende sprechen über Deutschland | Mit einem Vorwort von Martin Schulz | ISBN 978-3-8382-0552-6

130 *Konstantin Sheiko, Stephen Brown* | History as Therapy. Alternative History and Nationalist Imaginings in Russia, 1991-2014 | ISBN 978-3-8382-0665-3

131 *Elisa Kriza* | Alexander Solzhenitsyn: Cold War Icon, Gulag Author, Russian Nationalist? A Study of the Western Reception of his Literary Writings, Historical Interpretations, and Political Ideas | With a foreword by Andrei Rogatchevski | ISBN 978-3-8382-0589-2 (Paperback edition) | ISBN 978-3-8382-0690-5 (Hardcover edition)

132 *Serghei Golunov* | The Elephant in the Room. Corruption and Cheating in Russian Universities | ISBN 978-3-8382-0670-0

133 *Manja Hussner, Rainer Arnold (Hgg.)* | Verfassungsgerichtsbarkeit in Zentralasien I. Sammlung von Verfassungstexten | ISBN 978-3-8382-0595-3

134 *Nikolay Mitrokhin* | Die „Russische Partei". Die Bewegung der russischen Nationalisten in der UdSSR 1953-1985 | Aus dem Russischen übertragen von einem Übersetzerteam unter der Leitung von Larisa Schippel | ISBN 978-3-8382-0024-8

135 *Manja Hussner, Rainer Arnold (Hgg.)* | Verfassungsgerichtsbarkeit in Zentralasien II. Sammlung von Verfassungstexten | ISBN 978-3-8382-0597-7

136 *Manfred Zeller* | Das sowjetische Fieber. Fußballfans im poststalinistischen Vielvölkerreich | Mit einem Vorwort von Nikolaus Katzer | ISBN 978-3-8382-0757-5

137 *Kristin Schreiter* | Stellung und Entwicklungspotential zivilgesellschaftlicher Gruppen in Russland. Menschenrechtsorganisationen im Vergleich | ISBN 978-3-8382-0673-8

138 *David R. Marples, Frederick V. Mills (Eds.)* | Ukraine's Euromaidan. Analyses of a Civil Revolution | ISBN 978-3-8382-0660-8

139 *Bernd Kappenberg* | Setting Signs for Europe. Why Diacritics Matter for European Integration | With a foreword by Peter Schlobinski | ISBN 978-3-8382-0663-9

140 *René Lenz* | Internationalisierung, Kooperation und Transfer. Externe bildungspolitische Akteure in der Russischen Föderation | Mit einem Vorwort von Frank Ettrich | ISBN 978-3-8382-0751-3

141 *Juri Plusnin, Yana Zausaeva, Natalia Zhidkevich, Artemy Pozanenko* | Wandering Workers. Mores, Behavior, Way of Life, and Political Status of Domestic Russian Labor Migrants | Translated by Julia Kazantseva | ISBN 978-3-8382-0653-0

142 *David J. Smith (Eds.)* | Latvia – A Work in Progress? 100 Years of State- and Nation-Building | ISBN 978-3-8382-0648-6

143 *Инна Чувычкина (ред.)* | Экспортные нефте- и газопроводы на постсоветском пространстве. Анализ трубопроводной политики в свете теории международных отношений | ISBN 978-3-8382-0822-0

144 Johann Zajaczkowski | Russland – eine pragmatische Großmacht? Eine rollentheoretische Untersuchung russischer Außenpolitik am Beispiel der Zusammenarbeit mit den USA nach 9/11 und des Georgienkrieges von 2008 | Mit einem Vorwort von Siegfried Schieder | ISBN 978-3-8382-0837-4

145 Boris Popivanov | Changing Images of the Left in Bulgaria. The Challenge of Post-Communism in the Early 21st Century | ISBN 978-3-8382-0667-7

146 Lenka Krátká | A History of the Czechoslovak Ocean Shipping Company 1948-1989. How a Small, Landlocked Country Ran Maritime Business During the Cold War | ISBN 978-3-8382-0666-0

147 Alexander Sergunin | Explaining Russian Foreign Policy Behavior. Theory and Practice | ISBN 978-3-8382-0752-0

148 Darya Malyutina | Migrant Friendships in a Super-Diverse City. Russian-Speakers and their Social Relationships in London in the 21st Century | With a foreword by Claire Dwyer | ISBN 978-3-8382-0652-3

149 Alexander Sergunin, Valery Konyshev | Russia in the Arctic. Hard or Soft Power? | ISBN 978-3-8382-0753-7

150 John J. Maresca | Helsinki Revisited. A Key U.S. Negotiator's Memoirs on the Development of the CSCE into the OSCE | With a foreword by Hafiz Pashayev | ISBN 978-3-8382-0852-7

151 Jardar Østbø | The New Third Rome. Readings of a Russian Nationalist Myth | With a foreword by Pål Kolstø | ISBN 978-3-8382-0870-1

152 Simon Kordonsky | Socio-Economic Foundations of the Russian Post-Soviet Regime. The Resource-Based Economy and Estate-Based Social Structure of Contemporary Russia | With a foreword by Svetlana Barsukova | ISBN 978-3-8382-0775-9

153 Duncan Leitch | Assisting Reform in Post-Communist Ukraine 2000–2012. The Illusions of Donors and the Disillusion of Beneficiaries | With a foreword by Kataryna Wolczuk | ISBN 978-3-8382-0844-2

154 Abel Polese | Limits of a Post-Soviet State. How Informality Replaces, Renegotiates, and Reshapes Governance in Contemporary Ukraine | With a foreword by Colin Williams | ISBN 978-3-8382-0845-9

155 Mikhail Suslov (Ed.) | Digital Orthodoxy in the Post-Soviet World. The Russian Orthodox Church and Web 2.0 | With a foreword by Father Cyril Hovorun | ISBN 978-3-8382-0871-8

156 Leonid Luks | Zwei „Sonderwege"? Russisch-deutsche Parallelen und Kontraste (1917-2014). Vergleichende Essays | ISBN 978-3-8382-0823-7

157 Vladimir V. Karacharovskiy, Ovsey I. Shkaratan, Gordey A. Yastrebov | Towards a New Russian Work Culture. Can Western Companies and Expatriates Change Russian Society? | With a foreword by Elena N. Danilova | Translated by Julia Kazantseva | ISBN 978-3-8382-0902-9

158 Edmund Griffiths | Aleksandr Prokhanov and Post-Soviet Esotericism | ISBN 978-3-8382-0903-6

159 Timm Beichelt, Susann Worschech (Eds.) | Transnational Ukraine? Networks and Ties that Influence(d) Contemporary Ukraine | ISBN 978-3-8382-0944-9

160 Mieste Hotopp-Riecke | Die Tataren der Krim zwischen Assimilation und Selbstbehauptung. Der Aufbau des krimtatarischen Bildungswesens nach Deportation und Heimkehr (1990-2005) | Mit einem Vorwort von Swetlana Czerwonnaja | ISBN 978-3-89821-940-2

161 Olga Bertelsen (Ed.) | Revolution and War in Contemporary Ukraine. The Challenge of Change | ISBN 978-3-8382-1016-2

162 Natalya Ryabinska | Ukraine's Post-Communist Mass Media. Between Capture and Commercialization | With a foreword by Marta Dyczok | ISBN 978-3-8382-1011-7

163 Alexandra Cotofana, James M. Nyce (Eds.) | Religion and Magic in Socialist and Post-Socialist Contexts. Historic and Ethnographic Case Studies of Orthodoxy, Heterodoxy, and Alternative Spirituality | With a foreword by Patrick L. Michelson | ISBN 978-3-8382-0989-0

164 Nozima Akhrarkhodjaeva | The Instrumentalisation of Mass Media in Electoral Authoritarian Regimes. Evidence from Russia's Presidential Election Campaigns of 2000 and 2008 | ISBN 978-3-8382-1013-1

165 Yulia Krasheninnikova | Informal Healthcare in Contemporary Russia. Sociographic Essays on the Post-Soviet Infrastructure for Alternative Healing Practices | ISBN 978-3-8382-0970-8

166 Peter Kaiser | Das Schachbrett der Macht. Die Handlungsspielräume eines sowjetischen Funktionärs unter Stalin am Beispiel des Generalsekretärs des Komsomol Aleksandr Kosarev (1929-1938) | Mit einem Vorwort von Dietmar Neutatz | ISBN 978-3-8382-1052-0

167 Oksana Kim | The Effects and Implications of Kazakhstan's Adoption of International Financial Reporting Standards. A Resource Dependence Perspective | With a foreword by Svetlana Vlady | ISBN 978-3-8382-0987-6

168 *Anna Sanina* | Patriotic Education in Contemporary Russia. Sociological Studies in the Making of the Post-Soviet Citizen | With a foreword by Anna Oldfield | ISBN 978-3-8382-0993-7

169 *Rudolf Wolters* | Spezialist in Sibirien Faksimile der 1933 erschienenen ersten Ausgabe | Mit einem Vorwort von Dmitrij Chmelnizki | ISBN 978-3-8382-0515-1

170 *Michal Vít, Magdalena M. Baran (Eds.)* | Transregional versus National Perspectives on Contemporary Central European History. Studies on the Building of Nation-States and Their Cooperation in the 20th and 21st Century | With a foreword by Petr Vágner | ISBN 978-3-8382-1015-5

171 *Philip Gamaghelyan* | Conflict Resolution Beyond the International Relations Paradigm. Evolving Designs as a Transformative Practice in Nagorno-Karabakh and Syria | With a foreword by Susan Allen | ISBN 978-3-8382-1057-5

172 *Maria Shagina* | Joining a Prestigious Club. Cooperation with Europarties and Its Impact on Party Development in Georgia, Moldova, and Ukraine 2004–2015 | With a foreword by Kataryna Wolczuk | ISBN 978-3-8382-1084-1

173 *Alexandra Cotofana, James M. Nyce (Eds.)* | Religion and Magic in Socialist and Post-Socialist Contexts II. Baltic, Eastern European, and Post-USSR Case Studies | With a foreword by Anita Stasulane | ISBN 978-3-8382-0990-6

174 *Barbara Kunz* | Kind Words, Cruise Missiles, and Everything in Between. The Use of Power Resources in U.S. Policies towards Poland, Ukraine, and Belarus 1989–2008 | With a foreword by William Hill | ISBN 978-3-8382-1065-0

175 *Eduard Klein* | Bildungskorruption in Russland und der Ukraine. Eine komparative Analyse der Performanz staatlicher Antikorruptionsmaßnahmen im Hochschulsektor am Beispiel universitärer Aufnahmeprüfungen | Mit einem Vorwort von Heiko Pleines | ISBN 978-3-8382-0995-1

176 *Markus Soldner* | Politischer Kapitalismus im postsowjetischen Russland. Die politische, wirtschaftliche und mediale Transformation in den 1990er Jahren | Mit einem Vorwort von Wolfgang Ismayr | ISBN 978-3-8382-1222-7

177 *Anton Oleinik* | Building Ukraine from Within. A Sociological, Institutional, and Economic Analysis of a Nation-State in the Making | ISBN 978-3-8382-1150-3

178 *Peter Rollberg, Marlene Laruelle (Eds.)* | Mass Media in the Post-Soviet World. Market Forces, State Actors, and Political Manipulation in the Informational Environment after Communism | ISBN 978-3-8382-1116-9

179 *Mikhail Minakov* | Development and Dystopia. Studies in Post-Soviet Ukraine and Eastern Europe | With a foreword by Alexander Etkind | ISBN 978-3-8382-1112-1

180 *Aijan Sharshenova* | The European Union's Democracy Promotion in Central Asia. A Study of Political Interests, Influence, and Development in Kazakhstan and Kyrgyzstan in 2007–2013 | With a foreword by Gordon Crawford | ISBN 978-3-8382-1151-0

181 *Andrey Makarychev, Alexandra Yatsyk (Eds.)* | Boris Nemtsov and Russian Politics. Power and Resistance | With a foreword by Zhanna Nemtsova | ISBN 978-3-8382-1122-0

182 *Sophie Falsini* | The Euromaidan's Effect on Civil Society. Why and How Ukrainian Social Capital Increased after the Revolution of Dignity | With a foreword by Susann Worschech | ISBN 978-3-8382-1131-2

183 *Valentyna Romanova, Andreas Umland (Eds.)* | Ukraine's Decentralization. Challenges and Implications of the Local Governance Reform after the Euromaidan Revolution | ISBN 978-3-8382-1162-6

184 *Leonid Luks* | A Fateful Triangle. Essays on Contemporary Russian, German and Polish History | ISBN 978-3-8382-1143-5

185 *John B. Dunlop* | The February 2015 Assassination of Boris Nemtsov and the Flawed Trial of his Alleged Killers. An Exploration of Russia's "Crime of the 21st Century" | ISBN 978-3-8382-1188-6

186 *Vasile Rotaru* | Russia, the EU, and the Eastern Partnership. Building Bridges or Digging Trenches? | ISBN 978-3-8382-1134-3

187 *Marina Lebedeva* | Russian Studies of International Relations. From the Soviet Past to the Post-Cold-War Present | With a foreword by Andrei P. Tsygankov | ISBN 978-3-8382-0851-0

188 *Tomasz Stępniewski, George Soroka (Eds.)* | Ukraine after Maidan. Revisiting Domestic and Regional Security | ISBN 978-3-8382-1075-9

189 *Petar Cholakov* | Ethnic Entrepreneurs Unmasked. Political Institutions and Ethnic Conflicts in Contemporary Bulgaria | ISBN 978-3-8382-1189-3

190 *A. Salem, G. Hazeldine, D. Morgan (Eds.)* | Higher Education in Post-Communist States. Comparative and Sociological Perspectives | ISBN 978-3-8382-1183-1

191 *Igor Torbakov* | After Empire. Nationalist Imagination and Symbolic Politics in Russia and Eurasia in the Twentieth and Twenty-First Century | With a foreword by Serhii Plokhy | ISBN 978-3-8382-1217-3

192 *Aleksandr Burakovskiy* | Jewish-Ukrainian Relations in Late and Post-Soviet Ukraine. Articles, Lectures and Essays from 1986 to 2016 | ISBN 978-3-8382-1210-4

193 *Natalia Shapovalova, Olga Burlyuk (Eds.)* | Civil Society in Post-Euromaidan Ukraine. From Revolution to Consolidation | With a foreword by Richard Youngs | ISBN 978-3-8382-1216-6

194 *Franz Preissler* | Positionsverteidigung, Imperialismus oder Irredentismus? Russland und die „Russischsprachigen", 1991–2015 | ISBN 978-3-8382-1262-3

195 *Marian Madeła* | Der Reformprozess in der Ukraine 2014-2017. Eine Fallstudie zur Reform der öffentlichen Verwaltung | Mit einem Vorwort von Martin Malek | ISBN 978-3-8382-1266-1

196 *Anke Giesen* | „Wie kann denn der Sieger ein Verbrecher sein?" Eine diskursanalytische Untersuchung der russlandweiten Debatte über Konzept und Verstaatlichungsprozess der Lagergedenkstätte „Perm'-36" im Ural | ISBN 978-3-8382-1284-5

197 *Alla Leukavets* | The Integration Policies of Belarus and Ukraine vis-à-vis the EU and Russia. A Comparative Case Study Through the Prism of a Two-Level Game Approach | ISBN 978-3-8382-1247-0

198 *Oksana Kim* | The Development and Challenges of Russian Corporate Governance I. The Roles and Functions of Boards of Directors | With a foreword by Sheila M. Puffer | ISBN 978-3-8382-1287-6

199 *Thomas D. Grant* | International Law and the Post-Soviet Space I. Essays on Chechnya and the Baltic States | With a foreword by Stephen M. Schwebel | ISBN 978-3-8382-1279-1

200 *Thomas D. Grant* | International Law and the Post-Soviet Space II. Essays on Ukraine, Intervention, and Non-Proliferation | ISBN 978-3-8382-1280-7

201 *Slavomír Michálek, Michal Štefansky* | The Age of Fear. The Cold War and Its Influence on Czechoslovakia 1945–1968 | ISBN 978-3-8382-1285-2

202 *Iulia-Sabina Joja* | Romania's Strategic Culture 1990–2014. Continuity and Change in a Post-Communist Country's Evolution of National Interests and Security Policies | With a foreword by Heiko Biehl | ISBN 978-3-8382-1286-9

203 *Andrei Rogatchevski, Yngvar B. Steinholt, Arve Hansen, David-Emil Wickström* | War of Songs. Popular Music and Recent Russia-Ukraine Relations | With a foreword by Artemy Troitsky | ISBN 978-3-8382-1173-2

204 *Maria Lipman (Ed.)* | Russian Voices on Post-Crimea Russia. An Almanac of Counterpoint Essays from 2015–2018 | ISBN 978-3-8382-1251-7

205 *Ksenia Maksimovtsova* | Language Conflicts in Contemporary Estonia, Latvia, and Ukraine. A Comparative Exploration of Discourses in Post-Soviet Russian-Language Digital Media | With a foreword by Ammon Cheskin | ISBN 978-3-8382-1282-1

206 *Michal Vít* | The EU's Impact on Identity Formation in East-Central Europe between 2004 and 2013. Perceptions of the Nation and Europe in Political Parties of the Czech Republic, Poland, and Slovakia | With a foreword by Andrea Petö | ISBN 978-3-8382-1275-3

207 *Per A. Rudling* | Tarnished Heroes. The Organization of Ukrainian Nationalists in the Memory Politics of Post-Soviet Ukraine | ISBN 978-3-8382-0999-9

208 *Kaja Gadowska, Peter Solomon (Eds.)* | Legal Change in Post-Communist States. Progress, Reversions, Explanations | ISBN 978-3-8382-1312-5

209 *Paweł Kowal, Georges Mink, Iwona Reichardt (Eds.)* | Three Revolutions: Mobilization and Change in Contemporary Ukraine I. Theoretical Aspects and Analyses on Religion, Memory, and Identity | ISBN 978-3-8382-1321-7

210 *Paweł Kowal, Georges Mink, Adam Reichardt, Iwona Reichardt (Eds.)* | Three Revolutions: Mobilization and Change in Contemporary Ukraine II. An Oral History of the Revolution on Granite, Orange Revolution, and Revolution of Dignity | ISBN 978-3-8382-1323-1

211 *Li Bennich-Björkman, Sergiy Kurbatov (Eds.)* | When the Future Came. The Collapse of the USSR and the Emergence of National Memory in Post-Soviet History Textbooks | ISBN 978-3-8382-1335-4

212 *Olga R. Gulina* | Migration as a (Geo-)Political Challenge in the Post-Soviet Space. Border Regimes, Policy Choices, Visa Agendas | With a foreword by Nils Muižnieks | ISBN 978-3-8382-1338-5

213 *Sanna Turoma, Kaarina Aitamurto, Slobodanka Vladiv-Glover (Eds.)* | Religion, Expression, and Patriotism in Russia. Essays on Post-Soviet Society and the State. ISBN 978-3-8382-1346-0

214 *Vasif Huseynov* | Geopolitical Rivalries in the "Common Neighborhood". Russia's Conflict with the West, Soft Power, and Neoclassical Realism | With a foreword by Nicholas Ross Smith | ISBN 978-3-8382-1277-7

215 *Mikhail Suslov* | Geopolitical Imagination. Ideology and Utopia in Post-Soviet Russia | With a foreword by Mark Bassin | ISBN 978-3-8382-1361-3

216 *Alexander Etkind, Mikhail Minakov (Eds.)* | Ideology after Union. Political Doctrines, Discourses, and Debates in Post-Soviet Societies | ISBN 978-3-8382-1388-0

217 *Jakob Mischke, Oleksandr Zabirko (Hgg.)* | Protestbewegungen im langen Schatten des Kreml. Aufbruch und Resignation in Russland und der Ukraine | ISBN 978-3-8382-0926-5

218 *Oksana Huss* | How Corruption and Anti-Corruption Policies Sustain Hybrid Regimes. Strategies of Political Domination under Ukraine's Presidents in 1994-2014. With a foreword by Tobias Debiel and Andrea Gawrich | ISBN 978-3-8382-1430-6

219 *Dmitry Travin, Vladimir Gel'man, Otar Marganiya* | The Russian Path. Ideas, Interests, Institutions, Illusions. With a foreword by Vladimir Ryzhkov | ISBN 978-3-8382-1421-4

220 *Gergana Dimova* | Political Uncertainty. A Comparative Exploration. With a foreword by Todor Yalamov and Rumena Filipova | ISBN 978-3-8382-1385-9

221 *Torben Waschke* | Russland in Transition. Geopolitik zwischen Raum, Identität und Machtinteressen. Mit einem Vorwort von Andreas Dittmann | ISBN 978-3-8382-1480-1

222 *Steven Jobbitt, Zsolt Bottlik, Marton Berki (Eds.)* | Power and Identity in the Post-Soviet Realm. Geographies of Ethnicity and Nationality after 1991 | ISBN 978-3-8382-1399-6

223 *Daria Buteiko* | Erinnerungsort. Ort des Gedenkens, der Erholung oder der Einkehr? Kommunismus-Erinnerung am Beispiel der Gedenkstätte Berliner Mauer sowie des Soloveckij-Klosters und -Museumsparks | ISBN 978-3-8382-1367-5

224 *Olga Bertelsen (Eds.)* | Russian Active Measures. Yesterday, Today, Tomorrow. With a foreword by Jan Goldman | ISBN 978-3-8382-1529-7

225 *David Mandel* | "Optimizing" Higher Education in Russia. University Teachers and their Union "Universitetskaya solidarnost'" | ISBN 978-3-8382-1519-8

226 *Mykhailo Minakov, Gwendolyn Sasse, Daria Isachenko (Eds.)* | Post-Soviet Secessionism | Nation-Building and State-Failure after Communism | ISBN 978-3-8382-1538-9

227 *Jakob Hauter (Ed.)* | Civil War? Interstate War? Hybrid War? | Dimensions and Interpretations of the Donbas Conflict in 2014–2020. With a foreword by Andrew Wilson | ISBN 978-3-8382-1383-5

228 *Tima T. Moldogaziev, Gene A. Brewer, J. Edward Kellough (Eds.)* | Public Policy and Politics in Georgia | Lessons from Post-Soviet Transition. With a foreword by Dan Durning | ISBN 978-3-8382-1535-8

229 *Oxana Schmies (Eds.)* | NATO's Enlargement and Russia | A Strategic Challenge in the Past and Future With a foreword by Vladimir Kara-Murza | ISBN 978-3-8382-1478-8

230 *Christopher Ford* | A Lost Left: Essays on Ukrainian Socialism | ISBN 978-3-8382-0899-2

231 *Anna Kutkina* | Between Lenin and Bandera | Decommunization and Multivocality in Post-Euromaidan Ukraine. With a foreword by Juri Mykkänen | ISBN 978-3-8382-1506-8

232 *Lincoln E. Flake* | Defending the Faith | The Russian Orthodox Church and the Demise of Religious Pluralism. With a foreword by Peter Martland | ISBN 978-3-8382-1378-1

233 *Nikoloz Samkharadze* | Russia's Recognition of the Independence of Abkhazia and South Ossetia | Analysis of a Deviant Case in Moscow's Foreign Policy Behavior. With a foreword by Neil MacFarlane | ISBN 978-3-8382-1414-6

ibidem.eu